The Bible

The Living Word of God

TEACHER GUIDE

Living in Christ

Lauren M. Lefrancois and Vanessa Sibley Mudd

saint mary's press

The publishing team included Gloria Shahin, editorial director; Christine Schmertz Navarro, development editor; prepress and manufacturing coordinated by the production departments of Saint Mary's Press.

Thank you to the ninth- and tenth-grade students and the religion faculty at Cathedral Catholic High School in Del Mar, California, who piloted unit 6 prior to publication, with special appreciation to Mr. Keith Warrick, who made this piloting possible. We thank the religion faculty at Calvert Hall, Baltimore; Saint Patrick's, Chicago; and St. Agnes, Houston, who reviewed the same unit. In addition, thank you to our original June 2006 teacher focus group of Anne Herrick, Gary Meegan, Holly Hoey-Germann, Georgia Skopal, Sr. Katherine Feely, and Michael Greene as well as two early reviewers, Patrick Tiernan and Sr. Ann Marie Lustig, OP.

Printed in the United States of America

1244

ISBN 978-1-59982-001-9

To access the ancillary teaching resources for this course (item 1244), go to www.smp.org/livinginchrist/theBible

Contents

To Rory, Kate, Mary, and Liam, for all you have taught me
and for all those you continue to teach.

Lauren

Thank you to my family and colleagues for your support
as well as to all of my students for teaching me what is
most important in education.

Vanessa

To access the ancillary teaching resources
for this course (item 1244), go to
www.smp.org/livinginchrist/theBible

Introducing the Living in Christ Series

The Bible: The Living Word of God is the first-semester ninth-grade course in the Living in Christ series.

Saint Mary's Press developed the Living in Christ series in response to the needs of important stakeholders in the catechesis process. The courses in the series follow the sequence and contain the material from the United States Conference of Catholic Bishops' "Doctrinal Elements of a Curriculum Framework for the Development of Catechetical Materials for Young People of High School Age" (2008). Each course also contains other material in the student book and teacher guide that students should know, understand, and be able to do. Each course responds to the varied needs that you express, especially about limited time and the range of catechized youth you encounter in your classes, offering wisdom from "secular" educational methods that can address both time limits and diversity in the classroom.

After three years of study, Catholic high school students will understand foundational concepts about the Bible, Jesus Christ as a member of the Trinity, the Paschal Mystery, the Church, the Sacraments, and morality. They will also have skills to learn more about their faith by studying the Scriptures, reading primary theological sources, consulting the Catholic faith community, doing self-reflection, and having conversations with their peers. With your guidance your graduates will possess a lived faith as they move into their future.

The Living in Christ Series

The Living in Christ series has a different look and feel from traditional high school theology textbooks and teaching manuals.

- **The teacher guide, rather than the student book, provides the scope and sequence for the course.** Teaching with the student book is more like teaching with *The Catholic Faith Handbook for Youth* (Saint Mary's Press, 2008) than with a textbook. The sequence of a textbook is important because the content builds on what has come before. A handbook provides material in a sensible order, but because the content does not rely on what has come before in quite the same way, the material can be presented in several different sequences.

- **The teacher guide provides you with ideas about how to teach not only with the student book but also with the Bible, resources on the Saint Mary's Press Web site *(smp.org/LivinginChrist)*, and other resources found on the Internet.** The teacher guide works as a command center for the course, providing ways for you to teach key concepts to the students by bringing in a wide variety of resources.

- **The Living in Christ series invites you as teacher to develop your abilities to facilitate learning.** This series asks you to become an expert about your own students, discern how they learn best, and then lead them to understand main concepts in a way that speaks to their lived experience and the issues of the day.
- **The Living in Christ series invites the students to be more engaged in their own learning.** This series asks the students to take charge of their learning process and to practice what it will mean to be adult Catholics who must translate scriptural and Church teaching into their real world.

These changes will enable the students to consider the most important concepts in the course at a deeper level.

Introducing *The Bible: The Living Word of God*

The eight units of *The Bible: The Living Word of God* lead the students toward a deeper understanding of the Bible and the history of our salvation presented within it. The students learn to navigate the Bible and use basic exegetical skills. They examine the relationship among Revelation, Inspiration, and vocation. They learn why salvation history is necessary. They then come to know the people of salvation history: the early leaders of Israel, the judges and kings, and the prophets. They come to understand that Jesus Christ is the fulfillment of salvation history and the Israelites' covenant relationship with God. They learn about the early Christian Church with a focus on Saint Paul and other key figures of the time.

The majority of the course focuses on the Bible itself and the Old Testament, with the last two units bringing in Christianity. Because the second course, *Jesus Christ: God's Love Made Visible,* is a Christology course with a strong scriptural foundation, it would have been redundant to spend an equal amount of time on both the Old and the New Testaments in *The Bible* course. The authors of this teacher guide had to prioritize which knowledge, skills, and understanding would be most important for the students to understand.

The course has eight units centered on eight important questions and concepts, or understandings, about the Bible and salvation history. Each unit builds on the knowledge, skills, and understanding of the previous unit. Within each unit the knowledge, skills, and understanding also build as the unit progresses. The eight units are as follows:

- Unit 1: What Is the Bible?
- Unit 2: How Can We Know God? Revelation, Inspiration, and Vocation
- Unit 3: What Is Salvation History?
- Unit 4: God Calls the Early Leaders of Israel

- Unit 5: Israel's Response to the Covenant under the Judges and Kings
- Unit 6: The Prophets: Bearers of Challenge and Hope
- Unit 7: Jesus Fulfills the Covenant
- Unit 8: The First Christians: Witnesses to the New Covenant

The Structure of Each Unit in This Teacher Guide

This teacher guide offers the teacher one path through each unit, referring the students to the student book, the Bible, resources on the Saint Mary's Press Web site *(smp.org/LivinginChrist)*, and other Internet resources.

The path for each unit has the goal of leading all the students to comprehend four "understandings" with the related knowledge and skills. This curriculum model assumes that you will adjust your teaching according to the needs and capabilities of the students in your class. You do not have to complete every learning experience provided, and we hope you substitute your own ideas for those in the teacher guide when needed.

Each unit has three basic parts: the Overview, the Learning Experiences, and handouts.

The Overview

The Overview is a snapshot of the whole unit. This section should help you make connections between the Scripture courses you currently teach and *The Bible* course. The Overview provides the following information:

- the concepts or understandings the students should understand by the end of the unit
- the questions the students should be able to answer by the end of the unit
- a brief description of the summary assessments (final performance tasks) offered, which will show that the students understand the most important concepts
- a summary of the steps in the Learning Experiences section (Each step in the unit builds on the one before but must be adjusted to fit your schedule and the needs of the students. The use of *steps* is more flexible than is a structure based on 60-minute periods, for example.)
- a list of background material on content and methods that can be found on the Saint Mary's Press Web site *(smp.org/LivinginChrist)*
- a list of articles from the student book covered in the unit
- a list of Scripture passages used
- a list of vocabulary that comes from the student book and from the learning experiences in the teacher guide

Learning Experiences

The instruction and learning occur in this section. Each unit contains a similar process for instruction.

Preassess Student Knowledge of the Concepts

Each unit opens with one or more options for preassessing what the students already know about a topic. It is useful to know this information as you prepare to present new material.

Preassessing the students' knowledge can help you determine how to use your time effectively throughout the unit. It is not worth your time to teach the students what they already know or to teach above their heads. Students learn most effectively when new concepts build on what they already know. More often, you have a mixed group knowledge-wise, which is good, because the students can help one another.

Present the Final Performance Tasks to the Students

A final performance task is a type of summary assessment, a means of determining what the students understand, know, and can do after a period of instruction such as a unit. (The unit test is also a summary assessment.)

In addition to providing a unit test, we encourage you to assess (determine) student understanding of the four most important concepts in each unit by assigning one of the short projects called final performance tasks. Through these projects the students can demonstrate their understanding of the main concepts. This assignment allows you to have another snapshot of what the students understand.

For example, the four understandings for unit 1 are:

- The Bible is the story of our salvation and tells us of God's enduring love for humanity.
- *Bible* is a word that means "books" and is a collection of sacred books containing the truth of God's Revelation.
- Biblical exegesis, or the critical interpretation and explanation of a biblical text, can lead to a deeper understanding of the Bible's meaning for the people it was written to and a more accurate interpretation of what it means for us today.
- Catholics both read the Bible and believe in the Church's Tradition. Through the inspiration of the Holy Spirit, Catholic Church leaders and scholars help to explain and interpret the Sacred Scriptures.

The handout "Final Performance Task Options for Unit 1" (Document #: TX001084) in the teacher guide outlines the assignment options. Note that for all the options, the students must show their understanding of these four concepts. The first final performance task option on this handout has the students research and write about a Genesis story. The second asks the student to create a narrative that imitates biblical storytelling. Though a test might directly ask what the concepts mean, the performance tasks provide another way to get a picture of what the students do and do not understand.

We suggest that you explain the performance task options early in the unit so the students can focus on the knowledge and skills they can use for the final performance task they choose. This also helps to decrease the number of "Are we learning anything today?" or "Why do we have to learn this?" questions by giving the students the big picture of where they are headed and how they will get there.

Provide Learning Experiences for the Students to Deepen Their Understanding of the Main Concepts

This teacher guide uses the term *learning experiences* rather than *activities* to emphasize that much of what goes on in the classroom should contribute to student learning, such as explaining assignments; presenting new material; asking the students to work individually, in pairs, or in groups; testing the students; and asking them to present material to their peers.

Each step in the teacher guide leads the students toward deeper understanding of the four key understandings of a unit. At times learning experiences are grouped into a single step because they work toward the same goal. At other times a step includes only one learning experience. If you have a better way of achieving a step's goal, by all means use it. However, if new vocabulary or content is introduced in a step you have chosen to skip, you may want to go over that material in some way or remove that material from the unit test.

Throughout the steps, references are made to student book articles, resources at *smp.org/LivinginChrist*, and other Internet resources. Often the teacher guide addresses the content in the student book early in the unit and then asks the students to uncover a deeper meaning with various learning experiences throughout. When applicable the book refers to *smp.org/LivinginChrist* for resources at your fingertips.

The goal of this course is for the students to gain a deeper understanding of the material. But what is understanding? The understanding we want the students to gain is multifaceted. Understanding encompasses several of the "facets of understanding," used by Jay McTighe and Grant Wiggins in their book *Understanding by Design:*

> We have developed a multifaceted view of what makes up a mature understanding, a six-sided view of the concept. When we truly understand we

Can explain—via generalizations or principles, providing justified and systematic accounts of phenomena, facts, and data; make insightful connections and provide illuminating examples or illustrations.

Can interpret—tell meaningful stories; offer apt translations; provide a revealing or personal historical dimension to ideas and events; make the object of understanding personal or accessible through images, anecdotes, analogies, and models.

Can apply—effectively use and adapt what we know in diverse and real contexts—we can "do" the subject.

Have perspective—see and hear points of view through critical eyes and ears; see the big picture.

Can empathize—find value in what others might find odd, alien, or implausible; perceive sensitively on the basis of prior direct experience.

Have self-knowledge—show metacognitive awareness; perceive the personal style, prejudices, projections, and habits of mind that both shape and impede our own understanding; are aware of what we do not understand; reflect on the meaning of learning and experience.

(P. 84)

Note that Saint Mary's Press has created icons for each facet of understanding. When a majority of facets are present, there will be an "understanding icon." When relevant, all facets of understanding should be addressed in each unit. If you are used to Bloom's Taxonomy, see *smp.org/LivinginChrist* for a comparison of both models of understanding and learning.

Provide a Day or Partial Day for the Students to Work on the Final Performance Tasks

This guide encourages you to give the students time in class to work on their final performance tasks if you have assigned them. You do not, however, have to wait until the end of the unit. Not only does this day give the students time to work in groups if needed or to do some research, but it also gives you the opportunity to identify any students who may be having trouble with the assignment and allows you to work with them during class time.

Give the Students a Tool to Help Them Reflect on Their Learning

The handout "Learning about Learning" (Document #: TX001159; see Appendix) is a generic way to help the students think about what they have learned during the entire unit. This process, whether done this way or in another fashion, is valuable for several reasons:

- The students do not get much time to reflect while they are moving through each unit. Looking over the unit helps them to make connections, revisit any "aha!" moments, and identify which concepts remain difficult for them to understand.
- We give students a gift when we help them learn how they learn best. Insights such as "I didn't get it until we saw the video" or "Putting together the presentation required that I really knew my stuff" can be applied to all the disciplines they are studying.

Feel free to have the students discuss the handout questions in pairs at times for variety.

Handouts

All the handouts in the teacher guide, as well as the unit tests, are available on the Saint Mary's Press Web site at *smp.org/LivinginChrist*, as both PDFs and Word documents, for downloading, customizing, and printing. The handouts found at the end of each unit in this guide are simply for teacher reference.

Appendix

The teacher guide has one appendix, which consists of handouts that are used in each unit. The handouts are also available at *smp.org/LivinginChrist* for downloading, customizing, and printing.

Thank You

We thank you for putting your confidence in us by adopting the Living in Christ series. Our goal is to graduate students who are in a relationship with Jesus Christ, are religiously literate, and understand their faith in terms of their real lives.

Please contact us and let us know how we are doing. We are eager to improve this curriculum, and we value your knowledge and expertise. E-mail us at *LivinginChrist@smp.org* to offer your feedback.

Unit 1   What Is the Bible?

Overview

This first unit of the teacher guide of *The Bible: The Living Word of God* provides a wide and deep foundation for the rest of the course. Because of the amount of material presented in the student book and in this guide, you may want to allot more time for your students to move through it at a comfortable pace.

Key Understandings and Questions

At the end of this unit, the students will possess a deeper understanding of the following important concepts:

- The Bible is the story of our salvation and tells us of God's enduring love for humanity.
- *Bible* is a word that means "books" and is a collection of sacred books containing the truth of God's Revelation.
- Biblical exegesis, or the critical interpretation and explanation of a biblical text, can lead to a deeper understanding of the Bible's meaning for the people it was written to and a more accurate interpretation of what it means for us today.
- Catholics both read the Bible and believe in the Church's Tradition. Through the inspiration of the Holy Spirit, Catholic Church leaders and scholars help to explain and interpret the Sacred Scriptures.

At the end of this unit, the students will have answered these questions:

- What is the Bible?
- What is in the Bible?
- How can I make sense of the Bible if it was written so long ago and to different people?
- How do Catholics read the Bible?

How Will You Know the Students Understand?

These tools will help you to assess the students' understanding of the main concepts:

- handout "Final Performance Task Options for Unit 1" (Document #: TX001084)
- handout "Rubric for Final Performance Tasks for Unit 1" (Document #: TX001085)
- handout "Unit 1 Test" (Document #: TX001294)

The Suggested Path to Understanding

This teacher guide provides you with one path to take with the students, enabling them to begin their study of the Bible, what it contains, and how to read it. It is not necessary to use all the learning experiences, but if you substitute other material from this course or your own material for some of the material offered here, check to see that you have covered all relevant facets of understanding and that you have not missed knowledge or skills required in later units.

Explain   *Step 1:* Preassess what the students already know about the Bible.

Empathize   *Step 2:* Follow this assessment by presenting to the students the handouts "Final Performance Task Options for Unit 1" (Document #: TX001084) and "Rubric for Final Performance Tasks for Unit 1" (Document #: TX001085).

Explain   *Step 3:* Introduce the Bible.

Explain   *Step 4:* Teach the students how to navigate the Bible.

Explain   *Step 5:* Teach how the Bible came to be in its present form.

Apply   *Step 6:* Teach source criticism, using four side-by-side biblical translations.

Apply   *Step 7:* Give a quiz to assess student understanding.

Explain   *Step 8:* Introduce the Catholic Church's role in interpreting the Scriptures with a focus on Revelation, Inspiration, and the relationship between Scripture and Tradition.

Explain   *Step 9:* Introduce the Catholic Church's role in interpreting the Scriptures with a focus on the Church's approach to history, science, and the Bible, and Aquinas's senses of Scripture.

Perceive   *Step 10:* Introduce biblical exegesis.

Apply   *Step 11:* Provide insight into the writing of the Pentateuch.

Interpret   *Step 12:* Evaluate the students' progress with a Socratic seminar.

Step 13: Ask the students to use exegetical skills with the story of Noah's ark and the film *Evan Almighty.*

 Step 14: Send the students on an information quest to discover exegetical tools online.

 Step 15: Now that the students are closer to the end of the unit, make sure they are all on track with their final performance tasks, if you have assigned them.

Step 16: Provide the students with a tool to use for reflecting about what they learned in the unit and how they learned.

Background for Teaching This Content with These Methods

In addition to finding information about the pedagogical approach used in this guide, you will also find background information on these and other topics at *smp.org/LivinginChrist*:

- "Canons and Their Development" (Document #: TX001001)
- "The Story of Noah and Other Flood Narratives" (Document #: TX001003)

The Web site also has background information on the following teaching methods:

- "Introducing Biblical Navigation" (Document # TX001007)
- "Building Scaffolds for Learning" (Document #: TX001004)

Student Book Articles

The articles covered in unit 1 are from "Section 1: Revelation" and "Section 2: Interpretation and Overview of the Bible" of the student book.

- "Sacred Scripture and Sacred Tradition" (article 13)
- "Divine Inspiration and Biblical Inerrancy" (article 14)
- "From the Spoken to the Written Word" (article 15)
- "When Was It Written?" (article 16)
- "Setting the Canon of Scripture" (article 17)
- "Different Translations: The Same Revelation" (article 18)
- "A Vocation to Interpret and Teach" (article 19)
- "Biblical Exegesis" (article 20)
- "Literary Forms in the Bible" (article 21)
- "Senses of the Scriptures" (article 22)
- "Relation to Science and History" (article 23)
- "Other Avenues to Understanding the Scriptures" (article 24)

- "The Old Testament: *Old* Does Not Mean 'Out of Date'" (article 25)
- "The Old Testament: General Overview" (article 26)
- "The Canon of the Old Testament" (article 27)
- "The New Testament: Why Is It Called 'New'?"(article 28)
- "The New Testament: General Overview" (article 29)
- "The Canon of the New Testament" (article 30)

Scripture Passages

- Genesis 1:1—2:4; 2:5–25 (Creation)
- Genesis 3:1–24 (the fall of humanity)
- Genesis 4:1–16 (Cain and Abel)
- Genesis 6:5—9:29 (Noah and the Flood)
- Genesis 11:1–9 (the Tower of Babel)
- Matthew 5:13–16 (the similes of salt and light)
- Luke 1:26–38 (the announcement of the birth of Christ)

Vocabulary

If you choose to provide a vocabulary list for material covered in both the student book and the teacher guide, download and print the handout "Vocabulary for Unit 1" (Document #: TX001086), one for each student.

analogy of faith	Gnostic
apostolic origin	Nag Hammadi manuscripts
Bible	New Testament
biblical exegesis	Old Testament
biblical inerrancy	oral tradition
canon	Pentateuch
contextualist approach	redact
covenant	redemption
deuterocanonical	salvation history
Divine Inspiration	testament
dogma	Torah
Essenes	universal acceptance
the Eucharist	Vulgate
fundamentalist approach	written tradition

Learning Experiences

 Step 1

Preassess what the students already know about the Bible.

There are two preassessment options to choose from: mind map and ungraded association quiz. These exercises will help you and the students to recognize their current understanding of the Bible and identify the skills they will learn in the subsequent coursework. For background on the purpose and value of preassessment, see "Preassessment Informs Teaching" (Document #: TX001008) at *smp.org/LivinginChrist*.

Option 1: Mind Map

This learning experience will allow the students to put on paper all their ideas and thoughts about the Bible to provide a foundation for beginning their study of the Scriptures. It will also provide you with a preassessment of what the students know about and associate with the Scriptures. From this you can determine how much you need to present about the Bible. To learn about how to use a mind map effectively, see the article "Using a Mind Map" (Document #: TX001009) at *smp.org/LivinginChrist*.

1. Prepare by downloading and printing the handout "Mind Map" (Document #: TX001160; see Appendix), one for each student. (*Optional:* Have the students create a large circle in their notebooks with a series of smaller circles connected to it.)

2. Distribute copies of the handout and pens or pencils. Write the prompt word *Bible* on the board in a large circle. Ask the students to do the same on their copies of the handout. In the smaller connecting circles, have them write words or phrases they immediately think of when they hear *Bible*. Allow 5 to 10 minutes for the students to work independently.

3. When the time is up, invite the students to share with the large group what they have written down. Write their suggestions on the board.

4. Once a list is created, ask the students what the suggestions have in common. Common perceptions of the Bible will naturally surface through their suggestions.

5. After writing their suggestions on the board, use colored markers to circle words that can be categorized, for example, the definition of *Bible*, use of the Bible, and so on. These categories will help to address the many aspects of the Bible and answer the question "What is the Bible?"

Option 2: Ungraded Association Quiz

This learning experience will allow you to test the students' prior knowledge about the Bible and how to navigate it. From this you can determine how much you need to present about the Bible.

1. Prepare by downloading and printing the handout "Unit 1 Quiz" (Document #: TX001087), one for each student.

2. Ask the students to clear their desks and distribute pens or pencils.

3. Explain that they will take an ungraded quiz to find out what they know about the Bible and to provide a starting point for this unit. Ask the students to respond honestly and not to worry about material they may be unfamiliar with.

4. Distribute copies of the handout. Allow at least 10 minutes for the students to complete the quiz.

5. When the time is up, collect and review the quizzes with the students by reading the responses anonymously.

> **Teacher Note**
>
> This quiz can be used as a midunit assessment at step 5. See "Using an Ungraded Association Quiz" (Document #: TX001010) at *smp.org/LivinginChrist* for more information.

Empathize

Step 2

Follow this assessment by presenting to the students the handouts "Final Performance Task Options for Unit 1" (Document #: TX001084) and "Rubric for Final Performance Tasks for Unit 1" (Document #: TX001085).

This unit provides you with two options to assess that the students have a deep understanding of the most important concepts in the unit: researching and writing about a Genesis story and creatively imitating biblical storytelling. Refer to "Using Final Performance Tasks to Assess Understanding" (Document #: TX001011) and "Using Rubrics to Assess Work" (Document #: TX001012) at *smp.org/LivinginChrist*.

1. Prepare by downloading and printing the handouts "Final Performance Task Options for Unit 1" (Document #: TX001084) and "Rubric for Final Performance Tasks for Unit 1" (Document #: TX001085), one for each student.

2. Distribute the handouts. Give the students a choice as to which performance task they choose and add more options if you so choose.

Teacher Note

You will want to assign due dates for the performance tasks.

If you have done these performance tasks, or very similar ones, with students before, place examples of this work in the classroom. During this introduction explain how each is a good example of what you are looking for, for different reasons. This allows the students to concretely understand what you are looking for and to understand that there is not only one way to succeed.

Review the directions, expectations, and rubric in class, allowing the students to ask questions.

3. Explain the types of tools and knowledge the students will gain throughout the unit so they can successfully complete the final performance task.

4. Answer questions to clarify the end point toward which the unit is headed. Remind the students as the unit progresses that each learning experience builds the knowledge and skills they will need in order to show you that they understand how to use the Bible.

Step 3

Introduce the Bible.

Ask the students to look in their Bibles to understand what the Bible is and to identify different sections in the Bible.

- To best prepare for the students' levels of need, consider what you have learned from the preassessments. You will want to build new concepts onto the ones they already understand. See "Building Scaffolds for Learning" (Document #: TX001004) at *smp.org/LivinginChrist*.
- This step utilizes the following articles from the student book:
  - "The Old Testament: *Old* Does Not Mean 'Out of Date'" (article 25)
  - "The Old Testament: General Overview" (article 26)
  - "The Canon of the Old Testament" (article 27)
  - "The New Testament: Why Is It Called 'New'?" (article 28)
  - "The New Testament: General Overview" (article 29) ·
  - "The Canon of the New Testament" (article 30)

You may choose to assign the students to read these articles either before the step as preparation or following the step as review.

- Before the class period, review the background article "Bible 101" (Document #: TX001000) at *smp.org/LivinginChrist* for content review and teaching method ideas.
- If you think your students would take notes more successfully with built-in structure, see the handout "Student Notes for Unit 1" (Document #: TX001162) at *smp.org/LivinginChrist*.
- The PowerPoint "What Is the Bible?" (Document #: TX001066) follows the points you will present in this step and provides a visual to accompany your presentation. See *smp.org/LivinginChrist*.

Have the Students Examine Their Bibles and Ask Questions About Them

This quick exercise will invite the students to make their own discoveries so they will be more invested in learning about the Bible.

1. Ask the students to take notes individually on the organization of their Bibles. Allow 5 minutes for the work.

2. When time is up, place the students into small groups of two or three and invite them to share the information they have compiled.

3. Ask volunteers from the small groups to share one or two observations or questions with the large group and to take turns writing them on the board. Note major vocabulary terms, major themes, and so on.

4. Ask the students to keep these observations and questions in mind as they explore the Bible further.

Present Information about the Content of the Bible

1. Prepare by making sure the students have their Bibles and their student books with them. Decide whether you would like to use the PowerPoint "What Is the Bible?" (Document #: TX001066) at *smp.org/LivinginChrist*.

2. Begin by emphasizing that the Bible is about the relationship between God and his People, as shown by the choice of the word *testaments* to describe the two sections. Use the following or similar words:

> **Teacher Note**
>
> In some cases the students may generate questions that require some research on your part. The article "Bible 101" (Document #: TX001000) at *smp.org/LivinginChrist* can be a place to begin this research.

➤ The Bible presents two covenants between God and his People.

➤ *Bible* is a word that means "books" and is a collection of sacred books containing the truth of God's Revelation. From your observation, why is the plural *books* a more appropriate description of the Bible than the singular *book*?

➤ The Bible is divided into two sections. What are they?

➤ The Bible is divided into two testaments. A **testament** is a solemn vow and contract to which God is a witness. It is a synonym of *covenant*.

➤ A **covenant** is a solemn agreement between human beings or between God and a human being in which mutual commitments are made.

➤ Each of the testaments, the Old Testament and the New Testament, describe humans' relating to God in a covenant.

➤ Because of these covenants, it is possible to describe the Bible as an account of God's relationship with his People.

➤ Why is the Bible the story of our salvation?

> ➤ Unfortunately, because the people in the Old and New Testament accounts did not understand, or chose to forget, their relationship with God and sinned, they suffered the natural consequences of their sins by becoming distant from God and by making destructive choices.

> ➤ Since the time of the Genesis story of Adam and Eve's eating the fruit, people have been in the grip of Original Sin and have needed salvation.

> ➤ The covenant relationships God has had with his People include offers of salvation, but the people of the first (Old) Covenant did not respond.

> ➤ In the second (New) Covenant, God sent Jesus to save us from the sins that have existed since Genesis. Because of this the Bible can be called "the story of our salvation."

The Old Testament

This material comes from student book articles 25–27, "The Old Testament: *Old* Does Not Mean 'Out of Date,'" "The Old Testament: General Overview," and "The Canon of the Old Testament."

> ➤ The Old Testament is the account of a loving and communicative relationship between God and the Hebrew people (also called the Israelites and, later, the Jews).

> ➤ The Old Testament can be divided into four categories: books of law, historical books, wisdom books, and prophetic books.

> ➤ The Old Testament is not out of date or insignificant. It is rather the foundation of our identity as a people, a family of faith, profoundly touched by the Incarnation of God. The Old Testament contains the Revelation of God, which lays the framework for our Christian faith.

> ➤ There is a unity between the Old and New Testaments, two pieces that are necessary to see the big picture of God's gift of grace and redemption. The Old and New Testaments have a reciprocal relationship. They have to be read in light of each other.

The New Testament

This material comes from the student book articles 28–30, "The New Testament: Why Is It Called 'New'?," "The New Testament: General Overview," and "The Canon of the New Testament."

> ➤ The New Testament is the twenty-seven books of the Bible written during the early years of the Church in response to the life, mission, death, and Resurrection of Jesus.

> ➤ The twenty-seven books in the New Testament, each unique, can be broken down into the following five categories: the Gospels, the Acts of the Apostles, the Pauline letters, the non-Pauline letters, and the Book of Revelation.

Step 4

Teach the students how to navigate the Bible.

Help the students to learn how to find a biblical verse or passage from simple and more complex citations. Teach the students how to use the table of contents and index to find passages, as well as the format used for citing biblical passages.

1. Prepare by downloading and printing the double-sided copies of the handout "How to Find a Scriptural Reference" (Document #: TX001088), one for each student. You may want to use the background article "Introducing Biblical Navigation" (Document #: TX001007) at *smp.org/LivinginChrist* to give you further ideas about completing this learning experience.

2. On the day of the learning experience, discuss with the students the Bible's table of contents and index. Assign the following two tasks using the table of contents and the index or provide your own search:

> ➤ Locate the Book of Job and find out which book comes before Job and which book comes after. (The students might use the table of contents or simply search through the Bible.)

> ➤ Where could you find the story of Joseph and his brothers? (In *The Catholic Youth Bible®*, third edition [NAB], there is an "Events, People, and Teachings" index on page 1744 that leads the reader to start at Genesis, chapter 37.)

> Note that the students will find these tools helpful when reading scriptural citations.

3. Distribute copies of the handout. Review the handout with the students, teaching them how to find biblical passages and how to understand the way we refer to passages. Assign the matching section of the handout as classwork or homework.

4. Consider assigning the handout "Biblical Scavenger Hunt" (Document #: TX001089) as classwork or homework. It provides the opportunity for the students to practice their new navigation skills. (The answer key for the handout can be found at *smp.org/LivinginChrist*.)

Teacher Note

Handout "How to Find a Scriptural Reference" (Document #: TX001088) answers: (1) b, (2) n, (3) j, (4) h, (5) m, (6) i, (7) g, (8) c, (9) d, (10) l, (11) e, (12) k, (13) f, (14) a

Step 5

Teach how the Bible came to be in its present form.

Give an overview of the Bible's formation and then go into more depth with each section of the learning experience.

- This step utilizes the following articles from the student book:
  - "From the Spoken to the Written Word" (article 15)
  - "When Was It Written?" (article 16)
  - "Setting the Canon of Scripture" (article 17)

  You may choose to assign the students to read these articles either before the step as preparation or following the step as review.

1. Summarize the steps that resulted in the written form of the Bible we have today.

   ➤ **A. People experienced God.** People experienced God's Revelation—over a long period of time as in the Old Testament or through the person of Jesus in the New Testament.

   ➤ **B. People shared the stories verbally.** People told the stories of the experiences they and others had had with God. These people told others, and the Word spread throughout the community and down through time.

   ➤ **C. People wrote down the stories.** Because of their desire to capture the stories for future generations or to record the "true" version, believers put the stories in writing.

   ➤ **D. Religious leaders selected the central writings to be part of the Scriptures.** When writing became the more practical way of keeping these stories in their proper form, religious leaders asked for God's guidance in selecting the most important writings to include in the Scriptures.

   ➤ **E. People speaking different languages translated the Bible into their own languages from the original languages and from other translations.** The variations we see among different translations of the Bible come from the different ways translators converted one language into another. Because words can be read in different ways, there are varied translations.

2. Expand your explanation of biblical formation as follows.

A. People Experienced God

Stories in the Bible were based on human experiences of God's Revelation. Say the following or similar words:

➤ Give three examples of stories in which people experienced God's Revelation in the Old Testament.

➤ Give three examples of stories in which people experienced God's Revelation in the New Testament.

B. People Shared the Stories Verbally

The following material is from student book article 15, "From the Spoken to the Written Word":

➤ **Oral tradition** is the handing on of the message of God's saving plan through words and deeds.

➤ Narratives of God's wonderful work on behalf of humanity were told in groups, families, and other gatherings. During Old Testament times, few people could read and write. Consequently the people relied heavily on the spoken words of their ancestors.

➤ The original material now found in the Bible was first transmitted orally and later written down at various times to ensure that these important stories, morals, and events would not be lost.

Direct the students to look at the chart in student book article 16, "When Was It Written?" to see the gaps in time between when the events happened and when they were recorded.

➤ For example, the sacred wisdom of Genesis was not written down until about 900–500 BC. This was close to one thousand years after Abraham's call, which occurred sometime in the period from the Creation to 1500 BC.

C. People Wrote Down the Stories

The following material is from student book article 15, "From the Spoken to the Written Word":

➤ The people, in both Old and New Testament times, wanted to preserve God's message of salvation.

➤ The New Testament was completed by AD 100. Following the Crucifixion and Resurrection of Jesus Christ (about AD 30–33), Saint Paul traveled and spread the teachings of Jesus Christ and wrote about them through letters. Other disciples wrote down the life of Jesus in the Gospels.

➤ The early Christians were especially concerned about protecting and safeguarding the message of Jesus Christ. They were concerned because many of the people who knew Jesus personally were being persecuted and put to death for their faith. The people did not want to lose the perspective and testimonies of these eyewitnesses to the life, teachings, death, and Resurrection of our Lord and Savior, Jesus Christ.

> **Written tradition,** under the inspiration of the Holy Spirit, is the synthesis in written form of the message of salvation that has been passed down in the oral tradition.

> It is important to know that the Bible was not written by one person but rather that the writing was spread over a considerable period and is traceable to different authors of varying literary excellence.

3. Introduce the students to the notion of canon, helping them to understand how the Christian canon came to be and distinguishing between the Catholic and Protestant canons.

D. Religious Leaders Selected the Central Writings to Be Part of the Scriptures

Some material in this section comes from student book article 17, "Setting the Canon of Scripture."

> The term *canon* comes from a Greek word meaning "rule" or "standard."

> In the Bible, what is the canon a rule or standard of?

Allow time for the students to brainstorm their own definitions. After they have offered suggestions, provide the following definition.

> The **canon** is the collection of books the Church recognizes as the inspired Word of God. These books contain God's Revelation to human beings.

> The canon of the Catholic Bible is composed of forty-six Old Testament books and twenty-seven New Testament books.

> The bishops looked at several criteria as they discerned with the help of the Holy Spirit which books to include in the New Testament.

> **Apostolic origin.** Early bishops investigated whether a book was based on the preaching and teaching of the Apostles and their closest companions and thus had apostolic origin.

> **Universal acceptance.** The early bishops asked, "Was the book accepted and received by all major Christian communities in the Mediterranean world?" If Christians accepted it universally, then it passed this standard.

> **The use of the writings in liturgical celebrations.** If early Christians were weaving the books into their entire worship, the bishops could conclude the texts enhanced the prayer lives of the people.

> **The consistency of a book's message with other Christian and Jewish writings.** If a book's content contradicted the essence of Christian and Jewish teachings, the book would not have been accepted as part of the canon.

Unit 1

➤ Knowing the standards the bishops used in determining the canon of the Bible helps us understand why some books were not selected. For instance, the **Gnostic** gospels were rejected because they placed little importance on the suffering and death of Jesus. The suffering and death of Jesus are essential in understanding God's full plan of salvation. They must be emphasized for us to comprehend the amazing and redemptive work of our God. The canon of the Sacred Scriptures is the true, authoritative record of God's saving plan.

4. Conclude this presentation by talking about the original languages and translations of the Bible that contributed to the difference between the Catholic and some Protestant canons.

   ➤ The Bible was written in more than one language.

   ➤ The three biblical languages are Hebrew, Aramaic, and Greek.

   ➤ The Vulgate, which is the basis of the Catholic Bible, was compiled from Saint Jerome's translation of the Greek and Hebrew Scriptures into the common language, Latin, in AD 405. The Council of Trent (1546) recognized the Vulgate as authoritative, and it became the official Bible of the Roman Catholic Church.

Teacher Note
If you have any written examples of these languages, you may want to show the students.

   ➤ Many Protestant Bibles have only thirty-nine books in the Old Testament. Other Protestant Bibles contain an additional seven. At the time of the Protestant Reformation (1517–1570), Protestant leaders decided to use only the books of the Old Testament that were in Hebrew, thus eliminating the seven books Protestants call the Apocrypha, meaning "noncanonical" or "of doubtful authority." These books came from the Greek-language collection of the Jewish Scriptures called the Septuagint.

   ➤ *Deuterocanonical* is a term used by Catholics to refer to the additional seven Old Testament books in the Catholic canon.

   ➤ These seven books are Tobit, Judith, First and Second Maccabees, Wisdom, Sirach, and Baruch.

Apply

Step 6

Teach source criticism, using four side-by-side biblical translations.

Student book article 18, "Different Translations: The Same Revelation," provides the students with an example of source criticism.

1. Ask several students to read aloud the first four paragraphs in student book article 18, "Different Translations: The Same Revelation." Note that biblical

scholars use many tools to try to discern what the meaning of a text was at the time it was written. They then try to translate that meaning into language readers can understand today.

2. Write the following on the board and ask your students to translate it into English.

   BBLCLSCHLRSNDTKNWSVRLLNGGSTTRNSLTRLYTXTS.

   Note how hard it is to tell what this could say, much less what the author wanted to say. Biblical Hebrew is especially difficult because it contains only consonants and runs together without spaces between words, in a way similar to the line on the board. The "translated" line on the board means "Biblical scholars need to know several languages to translate early texts."

   Emphasize that scholars must not only know what texts meant but also express them in modern languages, all of which differ significantly. Even various translations within a single language are meant for different audiences.

3. Place the students in pairs. Have the pairs compare how various combinations of the four translated passages in the student book resemble and differ from one another. Allow about 5 to 10 minutes for the work. When time is up, invite the students back into the large group.

4. On the board create a chart with four columns. List the translations of Matthew 5:13 at the top of each column in the order they appear in the student book: NAB first, then NRSV, NJB, and GNT. Write words that recur, such as *salt*, and indicate whether there is variation within the various translations. Ask the following questions to help the students explore the words. You may even want to have the students look up the terms in a biblical dictionary.

   ➤ What differences in meaning do the following translations suggest?

   - "You are the salt of the earth." (NAB and NRSV)
   - "You are salt *for* the earth." (NJB, italics added)
   - "You are *like* salt for the *whole human race*." (GNT, italics added)

5. Conclude by noting that looking at several translations for one passage can often expand our interpretation of the passage by challenging our assumptions and widening our sense of what God may be revealing to us.

Step 7

Give a quiz to assess student understanding.

1. Prepare by downloading and printing the handout "Unit 1 Quiz" (Document #: TX001087) one for each student. Note that the quiz is fairly comprehensive, in part because both you and the students want to learn what they do not now know in preparation for a test or the final performance tasks.

2. On the day of the quiz, provide 5 to 10 minutes for the students to review their books and notes. Distribute the quiz and provide sufficient time for the students to work on it. If time remains when the students are done, collect the quizzes and then redistribute them so everyone has someone else's. Go through the quiz, allowing the students to correct one another's work and also giving them an opportunity to affirm or change their understanding of concepts. Collect the quizzes and further your analysis about topics that may need more coverage.

Teacher Note

To save paper, use the electronic copy of the quiz from *smp.org/LivinginChrist* and put it up in a visual place via projector, overhead, monitor, and so on. If these options are unavailable, read the quiz to the students slowly. In both cases, have the students record their answers on loose-leaf paper.

To save time, ask the students to choose two out of the nine short-answer questions to complete.

Step 8

Introduce the Catholic Church's role in interpreting the Scriptures with a focus on Revelation, Inspiration, and the relationship between Scripture and Tradition.

Provide background about the Catholic Church's role in interpreting the Scriptures.

- In preparation for this step, have the students read the student book articles 13 and 14, "The Scriptures and Sacred Tradition" and "Divine Inspiration and Biblical Inerrancy."

1. Ask half the students to write an answer in a notebook or on a sheet of paper to the following question: "Is it true Catholics do not use or read the Bible?" Have the second half write an answer to the following question: "Isn't the Bible just another piece of literature?" Have them share their responses in the large group.

Teacher Note

Student book article 19, "A Vocation to Interpret and Teach," is not covered in the following material. It provides a short overview of the Church's role in interpreting the Scriptures. You may want to have the students read article 19 individually, read it together as a class, or simply highlight the main points.

2. Present information about the Catholic Church and the Bible, using the PowerPoint "The Catholic Church and the Bible" (Document #: TX001068) at *smp.org/LivinginChrist*. Introduce the topic by talking about how God is the author of the Bible. The following material is from the student book article 14, "Divine Inspiration and Biblical Inerrancy."

   - ➤ The Bible is not just another piece of literature—it is God's Revelation.
   - ➤ People often ask, "If human authors were involved in writing the Bible, how is God the author?"
   - ➤ Although human beings can inspire one another (*ask the students for examples*), God is the source of all inspiration.
   - ➤ The word *inspiration* means "to breathe into." God inspires human beings directly and indirectly through the natural world and other people.
   - ➤ The Holy Spirit inspired the human authors of the Bible as they compiled, recorded, or wrote the different books of the Bible.
   - ➤ **Divine Inspiration** is the divine assistance the Holy Spirit gave the authors of the books of the Bible so the authors could write in human words the salvation message God wanted to communicate.
   - ➤ God is the Bible's sole and supreme author, and all that is taught and proclaimed in the Sacred Scriptures is inerrant in matters of faith, Revelation, and salvation.
   - ➤ Did God dictate the Bible to these authors?

      We can't say for sure how God chose to act on the individual prophets and evangelists. Maybe God prompted one way here and a different way there. But in looking at the Bible itself, it seems clear that God doesn't take over people's minds and use them like robots.

      (Mark R. Pierce, *I'm Glad You Asked*, p. 26)

3. Share the following material from student book article 13, "Sacred Scripture and Sacred Tradition," to clarify Catholic teaching about the Bible and Sacred Tradition:

   - ➤ Some people ask, "Is it true Catholics do not use or read the Bible?" or "Why do Catholics have beliefs and practices that are not in the Bible?"
   - ➤ An important difference between Roman Catholics and non-Catholic Christians is that Catholics believe God reveals himself through both Sacred Scripture and Sacred Tradition.
   - ➤ Sacred Tradition teaches the fullness of Divine Revelation. It began with the preaching of the Gospel by the Apostles, was written in the Scriptures, continues to be handed down and lived out in the life of the Church, and is interpreted by the Magisterium under the guidance of the Holy Spirit.

Unit 1

➤ All that is part of Sacred Tradition is a manifestation of what was disclosed through Jesus' teachings and actions during his earthly ministry and the events of the Paschal Mystery—his Passion, death, Resurrection, and Ascension.

➤ The Magisterium of the Church interprets both the Scriptures and Tradition under the guidance of the Holy Spirit.

➤ Nothing taught or proclaimed by the Church ever contradicts the truth of Jesus Christ.

Step 9

Explain

Introduce the Catholic Church's role in interpreting the Scriptures with a focus on the Church's approach to history, science, and the Bible, and Aquinas's senses of Scripture.

Provide further background about the Catholic Church's role in interpreting the Scriptures. This section explains the senses of the Scriptures, the Church's understanding of how Scripture relates to science and history, and other avenues for understanding the Scriptures. In sum, history and science can help us to learn the spiritual truth from the Bible, but the Bible is not where we look for scientific or historical truth. The Bible contains religious truth.

- This step utilizes the following articles from the student book:
  - "Senses of the Scriptures" (article 22)
  - "Relation to Science and History" (article 23)
  - "Other Avenues to Understanding the Scriptures (article 24)

You may choose to assign the students to read these articles either before the step as preparation or following the step as review.

1. You may want to review some terms before presenting the following material.

What Is the Literal Sense?

➤ *Literal sense* comes from the Latin *litera*, meaning "letter," referring to a form of biblical interpretation that emphasizes the obvious meaning of words according to the literary genre of the text.

2. Read a few of the following statements and help the students to see that the literal interpretation of the phrases is far from the meaning most people give them:

> ➤ "She had a cow." (She became very upset.)
>
> ➤ "He is a sitting duck." (He has no protection from some harmful situation.)
>
> ➤ "We killed (or stomped on or ran over) the other team." (We won the game easily.)

3. Having helped the students to understand what a literal interpretation is, move on to a more in-depth explanation:

> ➤ The Catholic Church teaches that faith, science, and history can coexist. She also teaches that they can help inform one another. (For example, the account of the Creation in Genesis can coexist with scientific theories of evolution.)
>
> ➤ Scientists and historians working with the teaching authority of the Church can help biblical scholars and Bible readers to go beyond a **fundamentalist approach** to the Scriptures or a literalist interpretation.
>
> ➤ The Church supports a **contextualist approach.** This interpretation of the Bible takes into account the various contexts for understanding. These contexts include the senses of Scripture, literary forms, historical situations, cultural backgrounds, the unity of the whole of the Scriptures, Tradition, and the analogy of faith.
>
> ➤ However, the Church does not propose that the Bible's purpose is to present historical and scientific facts. Some of the biblical accounts may not be supported by historical experiences or accurate historical references. But this does not mean that the Scriptures are in error or that our scientific explorations are wrong.

Biblical Archaeology

> ➤ The last fifty years have seen a dramatic increase in the number of archaeological digs in Israel. The result has been the discovery of many ancient texts, artifacts, and buildings. Archaeologists have even found entire cities that date back to the time of Christ and earlier. These discoveries have helped us to understand more clearly what life was like in biblical times.
>
> ➤ A particularly important archaeological find is the discovery of ancient texts, both biblical and nonbiblical. We do not have the original version of any biblical book. This is why scholars are always searching for the earliest copies.
>
> ➤ The Dead Sea Scrolls are believed to have been written and preserved by a Jewish religious community, possibly called the **Essenes.** They lived sometime between the first century BC and the first century AD.
>
> ➤ These documents are important to biblical study because they contain pieces of writing from nearly every book in the Old Testament. The

scrolls are perhaps the only surviving copies of biblical documents made before AD 100. They also recount information about the beliefs and customs of the Jewish people of the time.

➤ The Dead Sea Scrolls have helped biblical scholars who look carefully at the origin of biblical texts.

➤ To better understand the meaning the Bible's human authors intended to convey, biblical scholars analyze the Bible as a literary document.

➤ They work to understand how the authors **redacted,** or edited, other writings to create the books we have in the Bible.

4. Present material from student book article 22, "Senses of the Scriptures":

➤ A fine piece of literature can be analyzed from many angles. In the same way, the Bible can be read in a literary sense, but additionally it can be read in a spiritual sense. As we will see, even the allegorical sense differs from the type of allegory we find in other literature.

➤ In the *Summa Theologica*, Saint Thomas Aquinas laid the foundation for modern biblical interpretation.

➤ Aquinas maintained that "one can distinguish between two senses of Scripture: the literal and the spiritual" (*Catechism of the Catholic Church [CCC]*, 115). Aquinas uses the word *senses* to refer to different levels of meaning that can be found in the Sacred Scriptures.

➤ The literal sense lays the framework for all other senses of the Sacred Scriptures.

➤ The interpreter examines the actual events being spoken about. The interpreter also examines key characters and various things described in the text.

➤ The spiritual sense goes beyond the literal sense of the words to consider what the realities and events of Scripture signify.

➤ The allegorical sense looks at how the people, events, and things in the literal sense point to the mystery of Christ. In other words, it examines their **Christological** significance.

> **allegory; allegorical sense.** This word *allegory* or *allegorical sense* came from the Greek allēgoreō, meaning "to imply something beyond what is said." The term refers to a type of biblical interpretation that finds symbolic or prophetic meanings beyond the literal text of the

> **Teacher Note**
>
> Review the meaning of *allegory* with the students. You might want to use some of the Advent readings about the Messiah to illustrate this.

> **Teacher Note**
>
> At this point you may want to introduce the students to another tool for biblical study, the biblical dictionary. It will help the students to pursue the literal meaning of Scripture passages. *Saint Mary's Press® Essential Bible Dictionary* (Winona, MN: Saint Mary's Press, 2005) is appropriate for high school–aged students and can be ordered in print or found free online at *smp.org/LivinginChrist*. See *smp.org/LivinginChrist* for other recommended biblical dictionaries also.

Scriptures; for example, the wandering of the Chosen People in the desert in search of the Promised Land is symbolically understood as the pilgrimage of Christians toward heaven.

(*I'm Glad You Asked,* p. 26)

➤ Fundamental to the moral sense of the Sacred Scriptures is the search for what it means to live a just and ethical life. How does a particular passage instruct us to live in right relationship with God, neighbor, self, and the earth?

➤ The anagogical sense investigates "realities and events in terms of their eternal significance" (*CCC,* 117). In what way does the story lead and direct us toward our future heavenly home?

➤ It is important to study the Sacred Scriptures from every angle: the meaning of words and events, the lessons regarding the role of Christ in salvation, the teachings about moral and just living, and our vocation to be with God always.

5. You may want to practice looking at a passage from the Bible using the different senses. Student book article 22, "Senses of the Scriptures," looks at the various senses found in the Exodus story. Because the students have not yet covered the Exodus in this course, the five senses can also be applied to the familiar story of the Annunciation. See the handout "Senses of Scripture and the Annunciation" (Document #: TX001163) at *smp.org/LivinginChrist.*

Step 10

Perceive

Introduce biblical exegesis.

Expose the students to biblical exegesis methods by providing them with skills to explore Saint Thomas Aquinas's literary sense of the Scriptures.

• In preparation for this step, have the students read the student book articles 20 and 21, "Biblical Exegesis" and "Literary Forms in the Bible."

1. Prepare by downloading and printing the handouts "Biblical Exegesis Chart" (Document #: TX001090) and "Practicing Biblical Exegesis" (Document #: TX001091), one for each student. As background see "Introducing Students to Biblical Exegesis" (Document #: TX001005) and other material at *smp.org/LivinginChrist.*

2. During the next class period, share the following with the students. Use the PowerPoint "Biblical Exegesis" (Document #: TX001069) at *smp.org/LivinginChrist.* Some of the following material comes from student book article 20, "Biblical Exegesis":

➤ When scholars or ordinary men and women study the Bible closely, they use a process called exegesis.

➤ **Biblical exegesis** is the critical interpretation and explanation of a biblical text. Another term for *biblical exegesis* is *biblical criticism*. In this case critical does not mean "looking for fault." Instead it means being thoughtful and rigorous in our interpretations. Exegesis is the analysis of the Scriptures to draw out and explain the meaning of the writing. It looks to understand the language, symbols, culture, history, and meanings intended by the authors of the Bible.

➤ We must, however, take into account that culture and time affect the Bible's words. The human authors used the languages and thinking of their times, so we need to study "the conditions of their time and culture, the literary genres in use at that time, and the modes of feeling, speaking, and narrating then current" (*CCC*, 110) to understand what the authors intended to communicate.

➤ Those who engage in biblical exegesis dispel the myth that the people and lessons of the Bible are outdated. Instead they affirm that the inspired Word of God continues to speak to and guide us.

➤ Can anyone engage in biblical exegesis? Yes and no.

➤ Church leaders and Scripture scholars (known as theologians) are much better equipped to do serious Scripture study than are ordinary people. We rely on them for our biblical criticism.

➤ Everyday Catholics can benefit from studying the Bible with available Scripture tools to better understand the literal sense of the Scriptures.

➤ True biblical criticism cannot be done apart from the larger Catholic Church.

➤ We are blessed with Church leaders and scholars who help to explain and interpret the Sacred Scriptures.

➤ A particular biblical text or passage can be fully understood only within the complete picture of both the Old and New Testaments. This is especially true in relationship to the life, teachings, death, and Resurrection of Jesus Christ.

➤ The **analogy of faith** is the coherence of individual doctrines with the whole of Revelation. In other words, as each doctrine is connected with Revelation, each doctrine is also connected with all other doctrines.

➤ Enlightened by the Holy Spirit, biblical scholars must be aware of the author's intention. They also must be conscious of Church Tradition. They need to be attentive to the whole of Revelation written in the Sacred Scriptures. They also need to be mindful of the unity existing in all Church teachings.

➤ An authentic interpretation of the Sacred Scriptures is carried out "in the light of the same Spirit by whom it was written"[1] (*CCC*, 111).

> ➤ Someone who does not believe in God, for example, and is not open to the Revelation in the Scriptures does not read and interpret the Bible in the same Spirit of faith.

3. Distribute copies of the handout "Biblical Exegesis Chart" (Document #: TX001090) before reviewing the following material with the students:

> ➤ As a result of the many cultures, languages, and time periods over which the Bible was written, people cannot expect to read every book, sometimes even passages, in the same way as other readers because readers bring their own knowledge and experiences to the reading.

> ➤ Different forms of exegesis or biblical criticism are found on the handout: textual, historical, literary, and source.

4. Review the types of biblical criticism on the handout. As you review the chart, you may also want to ask the students to read through student book article 21, "Literary Forms in the Bible." You can refer back to Matthew 5:13–16 to help to illustrate these types of exegeses, but also ask the students for their ideas.

> ➤ **Textual criticism** You used this method when you looked at the passages about salt and light, because you compared different translations of the same book.

> ➤ **Historical criticism** If you looked up the understanding or importance of salt and light at the time of the New Testament writing, you might gain a deeper appreciation for the passage.

> ➤ **Literary criticism** In the same passage, three translations used the literary device of the metaphor "You are the light . . ." while the GNT used a simile, "You are like a light . . ." What might be the significance of using one literary device rather than another?

> ➤ **Source criticism** This would involve researching what materials the scholars used when they made each translation or finding out whether salt and light were commonly used to describe people.

5. Place the students in pairs. Distribute copies of the handout "Practicing Biblical Exegesis" (Document #: TX001091). Allow about 5 minutes for the pairs to complete the handout in class. When time is up, review the students' answers with the large group.

Step 11

Apply

Provide insight into the writing of the Pentateuch.

The students can practice source criticism in two ways: do a close comparison between *The Epic of Gilgamesh* and the Flood narrative or study the JEDP hypothesis in the Pentateuch.

Option 1: Compare *The Epic of Gilgamesh* to the Noah's Ark Story in Genesis

This learning experience provides an example of the way flood myths may have influenced the Genesis Flood account.

1. Prepare by downloading and printing *The Epic of Gilgamesh*, Tablet 11, from *smp.org/LivinginChrist*, one copy for each student. As homework, assign the students to read the Genesis Flood story (see Genesis 6:5—9:29).

2. On the day of the learning experience, distribute copies of *The Epic of Gilgamesh*, Tablet 11. Tell the students that *The Epic of Gilgamesh* is a Mesopotamian flood narrative. If the students are studying ancient history, ask them to supply background about Mesopotamia. Ask the students to read it individually. Allow about 15 minutes for the reading. When time is up, answer students' questions about the reading and make sure everyone understands the story line.

3. Place the students in pairs. Ask them to compare and contrast the two stories for literary style and content. Allow 10 minutes for the students to review the passages and make notes.

4. When the time is up, discuss the following questions as a large group. Write the students' observations on the board.

   ➤ What is similar about these stories?
   ➤ What questions are these stories trying to answer?

5. Present the following background information on the flood narratives of ancient cultures:

   ➤ Most ancient cultures told of a period of flooding.
   ➤ Ancient cultures saw floods as a method of removing previous sins and as movements toward renewal.
   ➤ In a flood, water symbolizes a purifying force.
   ➤ Often in such narratives, one or more deities have been offended by certain behaviors.
   ➤ Following the flood, relationships are renewed or lessons are learned.

6. Have the students discuss in their pairs how this new information supports or challenges their own observations.

7. Discuss the following questions as a large group:

   ➤ Why is it important to examine similar stories from cultures that existed about the same time as the biblical authors?

   ➤ How does such an examination help us to understand the Bible better?

   ➤ What wisdom is contained in the Genesis account of the Flood?

   ➤ What lessons do we learn from these narratives?

8. Conclude by saying that what we find in the Genesis account is religious truth rather than scientific or historical truth. Religious truth teaches us about God.

Option 2: Introduce the JEPD Theory of the Pentateuch

If you think the students would benefit from work in the area of source criticism, see the article "The JEPD Theory" (Document #: TX001002) and a chart illustrating the theory at *smp.org/LivinginChrist*. In this learning experience, the students will learn about four different authors who scholars believe contributed to the **Pentateuch.** You may want to do this in place of the Gilgamesh learning experience or skip this one in favor of the Gilgamesh learning experience.

Interpret

Step 12

Evaluate the students' progress with a Socratic seminar.

This class seminar gives the students the opportunity to test their analytical skills through oral debate. They will support the thematic connection they have identified with direct support or evidence from the Scriptures.

Teacher Note

See "How to Lead a Socratic Seminar" (Document #: TX001006) at *smp.org/LivinginChrist* for background information about how to use this particular form of Socratic seminar.

1. During the class period before the seminar, divide the large group into two smaller groups. Assign one of the following questions to each group:

   • What is the Bible and what role does it play in our lives?

   • What are the literal and spiritual senses of the biblical text?

As homework, assign the students to read one of the following biblical stories. You may assign the same story to the whole class or, based on class size and preference, use more than one story so you can have more seminars. The students should prepare a two-paragraph response to their question based on the assigned passage. Ask them to bring the written response to the seminar.

- Genesis 1:1—2:4; 2:5–25 (Creation)
- Genesis 3:1–24 (the fall of humanity)
- Genesis 4:1–16 (Cain and Abel)
- Genesis 11:1–9 (the Tower of Babel)

Download and print the handouts "The Socratic Seminar" (Document #: TX001015; see Appendix) and "Student Evaluation for the Socratic Seminar" (Document #: TX001013; see Appendix), one for each student. You will need just one copy of the handout "Socratic Seminar Symbol Codes" (Document #: TX001014; see Appendix).

2. Further prepare by arranging the classroom desks into an inner circle and an outer circle, placing one seat inside the inner circle. The inner circle should therefore have one more seat than the outer circle because of the hot seat. The seats in both circles should face inward, toward the center of the circles.

3. On the day of the seminar, review the rules on the handout "The Socratic Seminar" (Document #: TX001015; see Appendix). Ask the students to have available their written homework responses and their Bibles. Both are necessary to participate in the seminar. One group will sit in the inner circle of arranged chairs. The other will sit in the outer circle. The students in the outer circle will observe the inner-circle students during the conversation. Distribute copies of the handout "Student Evaluation for the Socratic Seminar" (Document #: TX001013; see Appendix) to the students in the outer circle so they can take notes.

4. Explain the role of the seat in the middle, the "hot seat":

> ➤ The hot seat is the empty desk in the inner circle. During the seminar only those in the outer circle may choose to sit in the desk and wait to be invited to speak by a classmate in the inner circle. When called on, the outer-circle visitor may speak to one of the following or similar issues:

- Ask an inner-circle student to clarify a statement.
- Ask an inner-circle student to support a statement.
- Respectfully correct an incorrect statement.

Teacher Note

During the Socratic seminar, sit to the side of the class so you don't distract the discussion. The handout "Socratic Seminar Symbol Codes" (Document #: TX001014; see Appendix) contains codes for both positive and negative contributions. Review them with the students. This review will remind the students of the expectations for the learning experience. Use the codes to note the students' participation. Write the appropriate symbols next to the students' names on a class roster or on a chart of the students participating in each discussion group.

- Draw attention to a point that has not yet been addressed.
- Help to redirect the seminar back to the original topic.

➤ Remarks from the hot seat should be brief and respectful. Your participation (positive or negative) contributes toward the inner-circle students' seminar grade.

5. Ask an inner-circle student to state the topic and begin the discussion. Allow 20 minutes for the first round of discussion. With 2 minutes left, announce "final remarks" so the students can make their final points. When the time is up, ask the students in the outer circle to complete their observation handouts. Ask the outer-circle students to share with the large group general observations (without naming names), both positive areas and areas that need improvement.

6. Invite the teams to now switch circles. Distribute a copy of the handout "Student Evaluation for the Socratic Seminar" (Document #: TX001013) to each student now in the outer circle. Ask one of the new inner-circle students to state the question or topic. Then repeat the exercise with the new inner-circle students.

7. After the seminar ask the students to write a short reflection paper to review the major topics presented. Use the written material the students hand in, the seminar itself, and this reflection to assess whether you should present some of the concepts again or whether only a few students need individual assistance.

Apply

Step 13

Ask the students to use exegetical skills with the story of Noah's ark and the film Evan Almighty.

This learning experience illustrates the Flood narrative in a modern scenario. The students compare the scriptural and film presentations of Genesis 6:5—9:29, building on the skills they previously learned.

1. Prepare by previewing the movie *Evan Almighty* (2007, 96 minutes, rated PG and A-II. If the students will not be able to watch the whole film, choose two or three clips from the movie that illustrate an interpretation of the Scriptures, such as the call of Evan (Noah) by God (see Genesis 6:14—7:5), the delivery of ark-building materials by Gopher Wood (see Genesis 6:14), and the Flood scene (see Genesis 7:6–11). In addition to these scenes that directly relate the scriptural story, choose a scene or two that interpret Evan's (Noah's) reaction to the call.

Teacher Note

You can also use the animated film *Joseph, King of Dreams* (2000, 75 minutes, unrated by MPAA and USCCB) if you do not want to show *Evan Almighty.*

2. As homework, ask the students to read and take notes on Genesis 6:5—9:29 or to review their notes if they studied these chapters in step 11. Tell the students they will have 5 to 10 minutes during the next class period to read or review their notes.

3. Introduce the clips you have previewed. Highlight important details or points you want the students to notice. The students should pay special attention to the way *Evan Almighty* interprets various elements from Genesis. View a clip once and then show it again, asking the students to take notes.

4. After you have shown the clips, ask the students to individually reread Genesis 6:5—9:29.

5. Ask the students to write answers to the following questions:

   • What was similar about the biblical story and the movie? What was different?

   • Which parts of the biblical story were included in or excluded from the movie? Identify one major part that was included or excluded and explain why you think the director made that choice.

   • Which types of biblical criticism have we used in this exercise? What questions could we still research?

6. Ask the students to present their observations out loud or in writing.

Explain

Step 14

Send the students on an information quest to discover exegetical tools online.

This search introduces the students to the tools available on the Internet for responsible research, as well as materials they should use with a critical eye only.

1. Prepare by reserving a computer lab so the students have access to the Internet. If a computer lab is not available, give this assignment as homework to be reviewed during the next class period. Download and print the handout "Exegesis Online Information Quest" (Document #: TX001092), one for each student if used as homework. Because you have access to the online version of the handout at *smp.org/LivinginChrist*, you can give the students the option of completing the

Teacher Note

This is an excellent opportunity to review your school's guidelines for safe and reliable Internet research. If certain guidelines are particularly relevant to this search, emphasize them.

Because many Catholic schools use the New American Bible (NAB) or the New Revised Standard Version (NRSV), Catholic edition, the students should use tools most closely connected to those Bibles. See *smp.org/LivinginChrist* for recommended online Bible resource sites.

handout online. Send the handout to the students by e-mail or put it on a secure site where the students can access it.

2. If a computer lab is available, explain the learning experience before arriving at the lab. This will eliminate distraction and misunderstanding of directions. The focus of this learning experience is to identify reliable online biblical navigation and literacy tools for further examination and understanding of the Scriptures.

3. Allow 5 to 10 minutes near the end of class for discussion. If time does not allow, ask the following questions at the beginning of the next class period:

> ➤ What does this exercise illustrate?
> ➤ What are these tools?
> ➤ How might they be helpful?
> ➤ What do we need to be wary of when using resources from the Internet?

Step 15

Now that the students are closer to the end of the unit, make sure they are all on track with their final performance tasks, if you have assigned them.

If possible, devote 50 to 60 minutes for the students to ask questions about the tasks and to work individually.

1. Remind the students to bring to class any work they have already prepared so that they can work on it during the class period. If necessary, reserve the library or media center so the students can do any book or online research. Download and print extra copies of the handouts "Final Performance Task Options for Unit 1" (Document #: TX001084) and "Rubric for Final Performance Tasks for Unit 1" (Document #: TX001085). Review the final performance task options, answer questions, and ask the students to choose one if they have not already done so.

2. Provide some class time for the students to work on their performance tasks. This then allows you to work with the students who need additional guidance with the project.

Step 16

Provide the students with a tool to use for reflecting about what they learned in the unit and how they learned.

This learning experience provides the students with an excellent opportunity to reflect on how their understandings of the Bible have developed throughout the unit.

1. To prepare for this learning experience, download and print the handout "Learning about Learning" (Document #: TX001159; see Appendix), one for each student.

2. Distribute the handout and give the students about 15 minutes to answer the questions quietly. Invite them to share any reflections they have about the content they learned as well as their insights into the way they learned.

Final Performance Task Options for Unit 1

The following are the main ideas you are to understand from this unit. They should appear in this final performance task so your teacher can assess whether you learned the most essential content:

- The Bible is the story of our salvation and tells us of God's enduring love for humanity.
- *Bible* is a word that means "books" and is a collection of sacred books containing the truth of God's Revelation.
- Biblical exegesis, or the critical interpretation and explanation of a biblical text, can lead to a deeper understanding of the Bible's meaning for the people it was written to and a more accurate interpretation of what it means for us today.
- Catholics both read the Bible and believe in the Church's Tradition. Through the inspiration of the Holy Spirit, Catholic Church leaders and scholars help to explain and interpret the Sacred Scriptures.

Option 1: Research and Write about a Genesis Story

In this assignment you will display your ability to use the skills of biblical navigation and biblical literacy. You will explain how a biblical passage contains wisdom for the time it was written and for people today.

- Choose one of the following stories:
  - Genesis 1:1—2:4 and 2:5–25 (Creation)
  - Genesis 3:1–24 (the fall of humanity)
  - Genesis 4:1–16 (Cain and Abel)
  - Genesis 11:1–9 (the Tower of Babel)

- Read your passage and use your skills of biblical criticism to more deeply understand the biblical story you have chosen.
  - First, indicate how God reveals himself through this story.
  - Second, explain how this story fits into the story of our salvation, whether its characters move further from God or closer to God, and how God shows his love for humanity in the story.
  - Third, using what you have learned, explain the meaning this story had for ancient peoples and what questions it answered. Answer the questions below, which are related to the first four rows of handout "Biblical Exegesis Chart" (Document #: TX001090).

- Look at two translations of this story. What terms are translated differently? Do the two translations broaden the reader's understanding of the story? If so, how?
- What was the historical situation during the life of the author? How did the historical setting influence the author's writing?
- What form does the story take? What does the form tell us? Does the passage use literary devices and what do they mean?
- Is there another source for the story? What are the similarities and differences between the two stories?
  - Fourth, using the same passage, explain how the lessons of this story can be applied in our lives today. (If you know how this story relates to Church teaching, include that explanation.)

  Your analysis of this biblical story should be one to one-and-a-half pages typed.

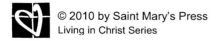

Option 2: Creatively Imitate Biblical Storytelling

- Choose one of the following stories from the **Torah:**
  - Genesis 1:1—2:4; 2:5–25 (Creation)
  - Genesis 3:1–24 (the fall of humanity)
  - Genesis 4:1–16 (Cain and Abel)
  - Genesis 11:1–9 (the Tower of Babel)
  - Genesis 12:1–9 (Abram's call and migration)
  - Genesis 15:1–21 (the Covenant with Abram)
  - Genesis 19:1–29 (the destruction of Sodom and Gomorrah)

- Read the story carefully and answer the following questions in writing:
  - How does God reveal himself in this story?
  - How does the story illustrate or explain whether the people in it are coming closer to God or moving further away? How does the story communicate God's love?
  - What does the story say to the people of its day? (Look at the form of the story, look up any cultural or historical references, and note the source of the story if known. Make a note of these.)
  - What does this story tell us about today? Does it relate to a Church teaching you know? If so, which?

- Write a narrative that could be from an ancient culture. Your invented narrative should be similar in length and style to the biblical narrative. You must be able to defend how your narrative displays the necessary elements for it to be considered a part of ancient oral tradition.

Document #: TX001084

Rubric for Final Performance Tasks for Unit 1

Criteria	4	3	2	1
Assignment includes all items requested in the instructions.	Assignment includes all items requested, and they are completed above expectations.	Assignment includes all items requested.	Assignment includes more than half of the items requested.	Assignment includes less than half of the items requested.
Assignment shows understanding of the concept *the Bible is the story of our salvation and tells us of God's enduring love for humanity.*	Assignment shows unusually insightful understanding of this concept.	Assignment shows good understanding of this concept.	Assignment shows adequate understanding of this concept.	Assignment shows little understanding of this concept.
Assignment shows understanding of the concept Bible *is a word that means "books" and is a collection of sacred books containing the truth of God's Revelation.*	Assignment shows unusually insightful understanding of this concept.	Assignment shows good understanding of this concept.	Assignment shows adequate understanding of this concept.	Assignment shows little understanding of this concept.
Assignment shows understanding of the concept *biblical exegesis, or the critical interpretation and explanation of a biblical text, can lead to a deeper understanding of the Bible's meaning for the people it was written to and a more accurate interpretation of what it means for us today.*	Assignment shows unusually insightful understanding of this concept.	Assignment shows good understanding of this concept.	Assignment shows adequate understanding of this concept.	Assignment shows little understanding of this concept.

Document #: TX001085

Assignment shows understanding of the concept *Catholics both read the Bible and believe in the Church's Tradition. Through the inspiration of the Holy Spirit, Catholic Church leaders and scholars help to explain and interpret the Sacred Scriptures.*	Assignment shows unusually insightful understanding of this concept.	Assignment shows good understanding of this concept.	Assignment shows adequate understanding of this concept.	Assignment shows little understanding of this concept.
Assignment uses proper grammar and spelling.	Assignment has no grammar or spelling errors.	Assignment has one grammar or spelling error.	Assignment has two grammar or spelling errors.	Assignment has more than two grammar or spelling errors.
Assignment uses its assigned or chosen media effectively.	Assignment uses its assigned or chosen media in a way that greatly enhances it.	Assignment uses its assigned or chosen media effectively.	Assignment uses its assigned or chosen media somewhat effectively.	Assignment uses its assigned or chosen media ineffectively.
Assignment is neatly done.	Assignment is not only neat but is exceptionally creative.	Assignment is neatly done.	Assignment is neat for the most part.	Assignment is not neat.

Document #: TX001085

Vocabulary for Unit 1

analogy of faith: The coherence of individual doctrines with the whole of Revelation. In other words, as each doctrine is connected with Revelation, each doctrine is also connected with all other doctrines.

apostolic origin: Being based on the preaching and teaching of the Apostles and their closest companions. One of four criteria the bishops used to determine the canon.

Bible: A word that means "books," a collection of sacred books containing the truth of God's Revelation.

biblical exegesis: The critical interpretation and explanation of a biblical text.

biblical inerrancy: The doctrine that the books of the Scriptures are free from error regarding the truth God wishes to reveal through the Scriptures for the sake of our salvation.

canon: The collection of books the Church recognizes as the inspired Word of God.

contextualist approach: The interpretation of the Bible that takes into account the various contexts for understanding. These contexts include the senses of Scripture, literary forms, historical situations, cultural backgrounds, the unity of the whole of the Scriptures, Tradition, and the analogy of faith.

covenant: A solemn agreement between human beings or between God and a human being in which mutual commitments are made.

deuterocanonical: A term used by Catholics to refer to the additional seven Old Testament books in the Catholic canon.

Divine Inspiration: The divine assistance the Holy Spirit gave the authors of the books of the Bible so the authors could write in human words the salvation message God wanted to communicate.

dogma: Teachings recognized as central to Church teaching, defined by the Magisterium and accorded the fullest weight and authority.

Essenes: A group of pious, ultraconservative Jews who left the Temple of Jerusalem and began a community by the Dead Sea, known as Qumran.

Eucharist, the: The celebration of the entire Mass. The term sometimes refers specifically to the consecrated bread and wine that have become the Body and Blood of Christ.

fundamentalist approach: Interpretation of the Bible and Christian doctrine based on the literal meaning of the Bible's words. The interpretation is made without regard to the historical setting in which the writings or teachings were first developed.

Gnostic: Referring to the belief that salvation comes from secret knowledge available to only a select few.

Nag Hammadi manuscripts: Fourth-century writings discovered in 1945 near the village of Nag Hammadi in Upper Egypt, that are invaluable sources of information regarding Gnostic beliefs, practices, and lifestyle. Gnosticism was an early Church heresy claiming that Christ's humanity was an illusion and the human body is evil.

Document #: TX001086

New Testament: The twenty-seven books of the Bible written in apostolic times, which have the life, teachings, Passion, death, Resurrection, and Ascension of Jesus Christ and the beginnings of the Church as their central theme.

Old Testament: The forty-six books that make up the first part of the Bible and record salvation history before the coming of the Savior, Jesus Christ.

oral tradition: The handing on of the message of God's saving plan through words and deeds.

Pentateuch: A Greek word meaning "five books," referring to the first five books of the Old Testament.

redact: To select and adapt written material to serve an author's purpose.

redemption: From the Latin *redemptio,* meaning "a buying back," referring, in the Old Testament, to Yahweh's deliverance of Israel and, in the New Testament, to Christ's deliverance of all Christians from the forces of sin.

salvation history: The pattern of specific events in human history in which God clearly reveals his presence and saving actions. Salvation was accomplished once and for all through Jesus Christ, a truth foreshadowed and revealed throughout the Old Testament.

testament: A solemn vow and contract to which God is a witness. It is a synonym of *covenant.*

Torah: A Hebrew word meaning "law," referring to the first five books of the Old Testament.

universal acceptance: Acknowledgment among Christians that a book was useful for worship. This criterion helped the early bishops to conclude whether a book was divinely inspired. One of four criteria the bishops used to determine the canon.

Vulgate: Saint Jerome's Latin translation of the Bible completed in the early fifth century AD.

written tradition: Under the inspiration of the Holy Spirit, the synthesis in written form of the message of salvation that has been passed down in the oral tradition.

Document #: TX001086

Unit 1 Quiz

Name: _____

Answer the following questions:

1. Define *Bible*.

2. What is the canon?

3. In a biblical citation, which comes first, chapter or verse?

4. Explain the difference between the Old and New Testaments.

5. List the ten sections of the Bible.

6. Define *Gospel*.

7. How many Gospels are there? List them.

8. What is an epistle?

9. True or false? The Bible was written in one sitting. Explain.

Document #: TX001087

How to Find a Scriptural Reference

Name: _____

Read the following information and follow the instructions:
- The Bible is composed of books.
- Each book is composed of chapters.
- Each chapter is composed of verses.

A scriptural reference provides all the information you need to find a particular passage. Take, for example, the reference **Genesis 1:31.**
- The name of the book comes first. Here the name is Genesis (often abbreviated Gen.).
- The chapter number appears directly after the name of the book. The example gives the number 1, meaning chapter 1.
- The last number, separated from the chapter number by a colon, indicates the verse. The example refers to verse 31. (In some versions of the Bible, a comma, rather than a colon, separates the verse number from the chapter number.)

Look up **Gen. 1:31.** What does it say? Write it down on a separate piece of paper.

Scriptural references generally contain more detailed information than just one chapter and one verse. Here are some examples:
- **Gen. 1:1–8** means Genesis, chapter 1, verses 1 through 8.
- **Gen. 1:3,6,9** means Genesis, chapter 1, verses 3, 6, and 9. (Notice the comma between separate verses from the same chapter.)
- **Gen. 2:8–10,18–25** means Genesis, chapter 2, verses 8 through 10 and verses 18 through 25.
- **Gen. 1–3** means Genesis, chapters 1 through 3.
- **Gen. 1:31—2:3** means Genesis, chapter 1, verse 31, through chapter 2, verse 3.
- Distinct references to different chapters are separated by a semicolon. **Gen. 1; 3** means Genesis, chapters 1 and 3 (but not chapter 2). Similarly, **Gen. 2:4–7,14; 3:1–3,8** means Genesis, chapter 2, verses 4 through 7 and verse 14, then chapter 3, verses 1 through 3 and verse 8.
- A long verse may be broken up into parts. To designate the first part of a verse, the letter *a* is used; for the second part of the verse, *b* is used. **Gen. 1:9a** means Genesis, chapter 1, the first part of verse 9.
- Some books of the Bible share the same name. For instance, *1 Samuel* and *2 Samuel* mean "the First Book of Samuel" and "the Second Book of Samuel." (Sometimes these are written I Samuel and II Samuel.) Notice that the number of the book comes before the name of the book. **2 Sam. 1:11–12** means the Second Book of Samuel, chapter 1, verses 11 through 12.

Look up **Exod. 5:22—6:1,11; 7:6.** What does it say? Write it down on a separate piece of paper.

© 2010 by Saint Mary's Press
Living in Christ Series

Document #: TX001088

Matching

In your Bible look up each scriptural reference from the left-hand column. Then match the reference with its summary on the right, writing the letter of the summary in the blank next to the reference.

_____ 1. Ruth 1:16–18

_____ 2. Dan. 3:13–24

_____ 3. Josh. 3:14–17

_____ 4. Prov. 28:15

_____ 5. Gen. 12:1–3

_____ 6. Ps. 51:3–4

_____ 7. Exod. 11:4–7

_____ 8. 1 Sam. 9:26b—10:1a

_____ 9. Deut. 30:15,19b

_____ 10. Eccles. 3:1–8

_____ 11. Gen. 6:14–16

_____ 12. Ps. 63:2–4

_____ 13. Exod. 20:1–17

_____ 14. Jer. 52:12–14

a. Jerusalem's destruction

b. a pledge to stay with Naomi

c. the anointing of Saul, Israel's first king

d. choosing life

e. instructions for building an ark

f. the Ten Commandments

g. the fate of Egypt's firstborn

h. a wicked ruler

i. the prayer of a guilty person

j. crossing the Jordan River

k. thirst for God

l. a time for everything

m. Abram's call to a new land

n. faithfulness in a fiery furnace

(This handout is adapted from *Teaching Manual for Written on Our Hearts: The Old Testament Story of God's Love,* Third Edition, by Mary Reed Newland [Winona, MN: Saint Mary's Press, 2009], pages 43–44. Copyright © 2009 by Saint Mary's Press. All rights reserved.)

The Bible: The Living Word of God

Biblical Scavenger Hunt

Name: _____

On the chart below, identify the book, chapter, and verses where the following biblical stories can be found. Write how you found the stories. Use the table of contents in the front of your Bible, as well as the appendix at the back. Some stories may be found in more than one place.

Story	**Book, Chapter, Verse**	**How?**

- Creation: Adam and Eve _____
- Cain and Abel _____
- Noah and the Flood _____
- The Tower of Babel _____
- Abram's Call and Migration _____
- The Testing of Abraham _____
- Isaac Blesses Jacob _____
- The Birth and Adoption of Moses _____
- The Burning Bush _____
- The Ten Commandments _____
- The Golden Calf _____
- Joshua Crosses the Jordan _____
- Gideon and the Fleece _____
- Samson _____
- David Fights Goliath _____
- Solomon's Judgment _____
- Elijah and the Prophets of Baal _____
- In the Lions' Den _____
- Jonah in the Whale _____
- The Call of Jeremiah _____

Biblical Exegesis Chart

Type of Method	Description	Questions This Method Asks
Textual Criticism	Scholars attempt to recover the most original version of biblical books, because no originals exist, only copies. These scholars compare different translations of the Scriptures to understand more clearly the meaning of a given passage.	• Of the many ancient copies and fragments of Bible books, which ones are the oldest? • Can we identify why there are differences between different copies of the same book? • Can we identify why different translations use different words in passages?
Historical Criticism	Scholars work to uncover the historical situation, or *Sitz im Leben*, of the writer at the time a particular book or story was written.	• What was the historical situation during the life of the author / editor or of the author / editor's community? • How did the historical situation influence the author's writing?
Literary Criticism	Scholars look at the Scriptures and seek to understand them as a work of literature.	• Did the writer use a particular literary form or device such as a poem, a historical story, a prophecy, a letter, or a gospel? • Did the passage use metaphors, puns, parables, exaggeration, a midrash, or other literary devices? • How did these particular literary forms or devices function in an ancient society?
Source Criticism	Scholars attempt to identify if the biblical authors used an existing story, myth, or other literature as the basis for their work.	• Are other writings from ancient cultures outside the Scriptures similar to a biblical passage? • What is the meaning of the differences between the way a story is told in the Bible and the way it is told in other sources?

(This chart is adapted from the *Saint Mary's Press ® Essential Bible Dictionary*, by Sheila O'Connell-Rousell [Winona, MN: Saint Mary's Press, 2005], page 57. Copyright © 2005 by Saint Mary's Press. All rights reserved.)

Practicing Biblical Exegesis

Name: _____

You will demonstrate your understanding of each type of criticism by completing your own exegesis. For each Bible passage, choose one or two types of biblical criticism from the list below and in a few brief sentences, explain how your choice would help you to understand the passage. Choose each type of criticism at least once.

Textual   **Historical**   **Literary**   **Source**

The Letter to the Romans

Luke 9:18–22, Mark 8:27–33, and Matthew 16:13–23

The Parable of the Mustard Seed, Luke 13:18–19

Mark 1:1–6, Matthew 3:1–6, Luke 3:1–6

See Matthew 16:18: "You are the rock upon which I build my church" (*ekklesia*, Greek, "the church, those called together").

Document #: TX001091

Exegesis Online Information Quest

Name: _____

Fill in the blanks and answer the questions based on the information you find online. You must identify the source of your information where indicated, using traditional citation methods for books and Web sites.

- Locate a concordance.
    - What is a concordance? Explain.
    - Look up *covenant* and list three places it appears in the Old Testament.

    _____   _____   _____

    - List four places *covenant* appears in the New Testament.

    _____   _____

    _____   _____

    - Which Web site did you use?
    - When would this tool be useful in studying the Bible?

- Locate a commentary.
    - What is a commentary?
    - How many results did your internet search provide?
    - Which did you choose?
    - Who wrote it?
    - How did you find out who wrote it?
    - Look up a commentary on Genesis 1:1—2:4. Cut and paste the first paragraph of the commentary into a word document and print it out. Underline key vocabulary and any scriptural references the paragraph makes.
- When would this commentary be useful in studying the Bible?

- Locate a Bible search engine.
    - What is a Bible search engine?
    - Which search options does it present?
    - Look up *prayer.* Which search option did you use?
    - How many results did it return?
    - When would this Bible search engine be useful in navigating the Bible?

Document #: TX001092

Unit 1 Test

Part 1: Multiple Choice

Write your answers in the blank spaces at the left.

1. _____ The New Testament in the Catholic Bible consists of _____ books.
   - **A.** thirty-six
   - **B.** forty-two
   - **C.** twenty-seven
   - **D.** nineteen

2. _____ _____ was a Doctor of the Church, powerful preacher, and writer who tried to make the Sacred Scriptures relevant and accessible to everyday people of faith.
   - **A.** Saint Ambrose
   - **B.** Saint Augustine
   - **C.** Saint Thomas Aquinas
   - **D.** Saint Paul

3. _____ All of the following statements about the books of the Bible are true except _____.
   - **A.** Most do not appear in the order in which they were written.
   - **B.** Many were written shortly after the events they describe had happened.
   - **C.** The Bible's human authors were true authors.
   - **D.** Mark probably wrote the first Gospel.

4. _____ An authentic interpretation of the Sacred Scriptures is grounded in _____.
   - **A.** the faith of the interpreter
   - **B.** the words of Jesus in explaining the text
   - **C.** the parables and examples in Jesus' ministry
   - **D.** the Tradition and teachings of the Church

5. _____ The goals of biblical study are to discover all of the following except _____.
   - **A.** biographical detail
   - **B.** meaning
   - **C.** depth
   - **D.** truth

© 2010 by Saint Mary's Press
Living in Christ Series

Document #: TX001294

6. _____ The infallible definition regarding the books included in the canon was declared at the _____.

 A. Council of Carthage
 B. Ecumenical Council of Trent
 C. Council of Hippo
 D. Vatican Council I

7. _____ At most Sunday Masses, the first reading of the Liturgy of the Word is from _____.

 A. one of the Gospels
 B. the New Testament
 C. one of Paul's letters
 D. the Old Testament

8. _____ The New Testament is called new for all of the following reasons except that _____.

 A. God revealed himself in a new way by his taking on human nature.
 B. God called his People to a new repentance.
 C. God sent his only Son to initiate a New Covenant.
 D. God opened the door to a new freedom.

9. _____ The original languages of the Bible were _____.

 A. Latin, Greek, and Hebrew
 B. Greek, Aramaic, and Latin
 C. Hebrew, Aramaic, and Greek
 D. Hebrew, Latin, and Spanish

10. _____ _____ translated the Bible into Latin, and this version was used by the Church for over one thousand years.

 A. Saint Luke
 B. Saint Athanasius
 C. Saint Jerome
 D. Saint John of the Cross

11. _____ The Catholic Church teaches that faith can coexist with _____.

 A. charity and love
 B. doubt and fear
 C. history and science
 D. geography and algebra

Document #: TX001294

12. _____ Among the list of characteristics of Catholic interpretation are all of the following **except** _____.

    A. challenges of non-believers
    B. the role of Tradition
    C. the task of the interpreter
    D. the relevance of other theological disciplines

13. _____ The Catholic Bible differs from the Protestant Bible in that it contains _____.
    A. the Scriptures of the Jewish People
    B. fewer Pauline letters
    C. the account of the Last Supper
    D. seven additional Old Testament books

14. _____ The principal witnesses to the life and teaching of Jesus are _____.
    A. the Apostles
    B. the Pauline letters
    C. the Gospels
    D. the four Evangelists

15. _____ Part of every Christian's vocation is _____.
    A. to heal the sick
    B. to teach a religious education class
    C. to spread the Good News
    D. to have children

Document #: TX001294

Part 2: Matching

Match each statement in column 1 with a term from column 2. Write the letter that corresponds to your choice in the space provided. (*Note:* There are two extra items in column 2)

Column 1

1. _____ The account of God's saving hand at work in human history and experience.

2. _____ The collection of books the Church recognizes as the inspired Word of God.

3. _____ Sacred text for both Christian and Jewish people.

4. _____ A religious group that strictly adhered to the Torah and preserved the sanctity of the Temple.

5. _____ A book of the Bible containing many kinds of prayer, including prayers of lament, thanksgiving, and praise.

6. _____ A Hebrew word meaning "law," referring to the first five books of the Old Testament.

7. _____ Where Jesus lived and carried out his mission.

8. _____ The handing on of the message of God's saving plan through words and deeds.

9. _____ A Greek word meaning "five books," referring to the first five books of the Old Testament.

10. _____ The eyewitness accounts of Jesus' life.

Column 2

A. Divine Revelation

B. oral tradition

C. the Sacred Scriptures

D. Pentateuch

E. written tradition

F. The Gospels

G. Sadducees

H. the Book of Psalms

I. Old Testament

J. Palestine

K. the canon

L. Torah

Document #: TX001294

Part 3: Fill-in-the-Blank

Use the word bank to fill in the blanks in the following sentences. (*Note:* There are two extra terms in the word bank.)

WORD BANK

absolute mystery	Christological	Parousia
parables	analogy of faith	Pharisees
Essenes	fundamentalist	Pope John Paul II
Pope John XXIII	Protestants	God

1. Unity in doctrine is known as the _____.

2. The Dead Sea Scrolls are believed to have been written and preserved by a Jewish religious community, possibly called the _____.

3. The second coming of Christ at the end of time, fully realizing God's plan and the glorification of humanity is known as the _____.

4. _____ are brief stories that exemplify moral or religious lessons.

5. _____ was known for launching World Youth Day and for being a model of reconciliation.

6. A truth that is so deep and broad that our limited minds cannot fully comprehend is called a(n) _____.

7. Anything having to do with the study of the person and life of Jesus Christ is called _____.

8. The ultimate author of the Sacred Scriptures is _____.

9. The wisdom of academic endeavors such as science and history can free us from an overly literalist or _____ approach to the Scriptures.

10. In the time of Jesus, the _____ were the educated interpreters of the Law.

Document #: TX001294

Part 4: Short Answer

Answer each of the following questions in paragraph form on a separate sheet of paper.

1. In reading the Bible, we learn about the truths of God's Revelation and his never-ending love for his People. Explain the differences between the fundamentalist approach to reading the Scripture and the contextual approach to reading the Scriptures.

2. List the four categories of books found in the Old Testament and the five categories of books found in the New Testament. What is the "big picture" painted by both the Old and New Testaments?

3. What elements are considered in determining the meaning of a text in the Bible in the process of biblical exegesis?

4. What is Sacred Tradition and how is it connected to our knowledge of the Bible?

Document #: TX001294

Unit 1 Test Answer Key

Part 1: Multiple Choice

1.	C	**9.**	C
2.	C	**10.**	C
3.	B	**11.**	C
4.	D	**12.**	A
5.	A	**13.**	D
6.	B	**14.**	C
7.	D	**15.**	C
8.	B		

Part 2: Matching

1.	C	**6.**	L
2.	K	**7.**	J
3.	I	**8.**	B
4.	G	**9.**	D
5.	H	**10.**	F

Part 3: Fill-in-the-Blank

1. analogy of faith
2. Essenes
3. Parousia
4. parables
5. Pope John Paul II
6. absolute mystery
7. Christological
8. God
9. fundamentalist
10. Pharisees

Part 4: Short Answer

1. The fundamentalist approach takes the literalist meaning of the Bible's words, interpreting them without regard to the historical setting in which the writings or teachings were first developed. The contextualist approach takes into account various contexts for understanding the Bible, including senses of Scripture, literary forms, historical situations, cultural backgrounds, the unity of the whole of the Scriptures, Tradition, and the analogy of faith.

2. In the Old Testament, there are the books of law, historical books, wisdom books, and prophetic books. In the New Testament there are the Gospels, the Acts of the Apostles, the Pauline letters, the non-Pauline letters, and the Book of Revelation. The "big picture" is that both the Old and New Testaments show God's gift of grace and redemption.

3. The Church considers its literal and spiritual sense, the sacred spirit in which it was written, and the cultures and conditions in which a passage was written.

4. Sacred Tradition is passing on the Gospel message. It began with the oral communication of the Gospel by the Apostles, was written down in the Scriptures, and is interpreted by the Magisterium under the guidance of the Holy Spirit.

© 2010 by Saint Mary's Press
Living in Christ Series

Document #: TX001295

Unit 2   How Can We Know God? Revelation, Inspiration, and Vocation

Overview

This second unit examines Divine Revelation, the Inspiration God gave the authors of the Bible, and the connection between God's Revelation to people and his call to them. Biblical figures provide examples of the relationship between Revelation and call. The unit then leads the students to reflect on this reality in their lives today.

Key Understandings and Questions

At the end of this unit, the students will possess a deeper understanding of the following important concepts:

- Divine Revelation refers to God's self-communication through which he makes known the mystery of his divine plan.
- God revealed himself in many different ways in the Bible and continues to do so today.
- Divine Inspiration is the divine assistance the Holy Spirit gave the authors of the books of the Bible so the authors could write in human words the salvation message God wanted to communicate.
- Revelation, Inspiration, and vocation are closely connected in scriptural accounts, as well as in our lives today.

At the end of this unit, the students will have answered these questions:

- How can I know God?
- How has God communicated with humanity in the Scriptures?
- What is the relationship between Revelation, Inspiration, and vocation?
- How does God call us in our everyday lives?

How Will You Know the Students Understand?

These tools will help you to assess the students' understanding of the main concepts:

- handout "Final Performance Task Options for Unit 2" (Document #: TX001093)
- handout "Rubric for Final Performance Tasks for Unit 2" (Document #: TX001094)
- handout "Unit 2 Test" (Document #: TX001296)

The Suggested Path to Understanding

This teacher guide provides you with one path to take with the students, enabling them to begin their study of God by deepening their understanding of Divine Revelation, Inspiration, and vocation. It is not necessary to use all the learning experiences, but if you substitute other material from this course or your own material for some of the material offered here, check to see that you have covered all relevant facets of understanding and that you have not missed knowledge or skills required in later units.

Perceive *Optional Learning Experience:* Hook the students' interest with questions from society today.

Reflect *Step 1:* Preassess what the students already know about Revelation, Inspiration, and vocation.

Empathize *Step 2:* Follow this assessment by presenting to the students the handouts "Final Performance Task Options for Unit 2" (Document #: TX001093) and "Rubric for Final Performance Tasks for Unit 2" (Document #: TX001094).

Explain *Step 3:* Introduce the human need for God and ways God reveals himself outside the Scriptures.

Empathize *Step 4:* Invite the students to recognize God's Revelation in one another.

Perceive *Step 5:* Read the Scriptures and discuss God's Revelation to biblical figures.

Reflect *Step 6:* Have the students reflect on how they come to know God.

Apply *Step 7:* Use a movie to lead the students to uncover how God can reveal, inspire, and call his People through ordinary means.

Perceive *Step 8:* Explore the call of Samuel.

Apply *Step 9:* Reinforce the students' thinking about Revelation and Inspiration through a Socratic seminar.

Empathize *Step 10:* Give a quiz to assess student understanding.

Apply *Step 11:* Apply Revelation, Inspiration, and vocation to today.

Apply *Step 12:* Guide the students in reflecting on the role Sacred Scripture plays in the life of the Church.

Step 13: Now that the students are closer to the end of the unit, make sure they are all on track with their final performance tasks, if you have assigned them.

 Step 14: Provide the students with a tool to use for reflecting about what they learned in the unit and how they learned.

Background for Teaching This Content with These Methods

In addition to finding information about the pedagogical approach used in this guide, you will also find background information on these and other topics at *smp.org/LivinginChrist:*

- "Finding God and Being Found by God" (Document #: TX001016)
- "Introduction to Revelation, Inspiration, and Vocation" (Document #: TX001017)

The Web site also has background information on the following teaching methods:

- "How to Lead a Socratic Seminar" (Document #: TX001006)
- "Using the Think-Pair-Share Method" (Document #: TX001019)
- "Using the Barometer Method" (Document #: TX001021)

Student Book Articles

The articles covered in unit 2 are from "Section 1: Revelation" of the student book. If you believe the students would do the reading more successfully with additional structure, see the handout "Student Notes for Unit 2" (Document #: TX001165) at *smp.org/LivinginChrist.*

- "Longing for God" (article 1)
- "God's Invitation" (article 2)
- "Happiness in God Alone" (article 3)
- "Saint Augustine and the Four Objects of Love" (article 4)
- "The Sacred Scriptures and Natural Revelation" (article 5)
- "Natural Revelation and the Wisdom of the Church Fathers" (article 6)
- "Natural Revelation and Scholastic Theology" (article 7)
- "Natural Revelation: Vatican Council I to the Present" (article 8)
- "The Study of the Sacred Scriptures" (article 71)
- "The Centrality of the Scriptures in the Mass and Other Liturgies" (article 72)
- "The Liturgy of the Hours: A Window into the Daily Rhythms of Life" (article 73)

- "The Lord's Prayer: Rooted in Scripture" (article 74)
- "The Scriptures and the Rules of the Saints" (article 75)

Scripture Passages

- Genesis, chapter 12 (the call of Abram)
- Genesis, chapter 15 (God's Covenant with Abraham)
- Genesis, chapter 32 (Jacob wrestles with an angel)
- Exodus, chapter 3 (Moses and the burning bush)
- 1 Samuel 1:1—2:10 (Hannah's prayer for a son)
- 1 Samuel 3:1–21 (God calls Samuel)
- Job, chapters 40–42 (God's response to Job and Job's insight)
- 2 Samuel 7:1–17 (God's promise to David)
- 2 Samuel 7:18–29 (David's response)
- Luke, chapters 1—2 (Elizabeth and Zechariah)
- Luke, chapter 2 (Mary and Elizabeth)
- Acts 9:1–9 (Saul's conversion)

Vocabulary

If you choose to provide a vocabulary list for material covered in both the student book and the teacher guide, download and print the handout "Vocabulary for Unit 2" (Document #: TX001095), one for each student.

desire	natural revelation
Divine Inspiration	papal infallibility
Divine Revelation	salvation
Ecumenical Council	scholastic theology
Fathers of the Church (Church Fathers)	Vatican Council II
Incarnation	vocation
Magisterium	
Middle Ages	

Learning Experiences

Optional Learning Experience

Hook the students' interest with questions from society today.

During this unit the students will learn about Divine Revelation and Inspiration, as well as about their own vocations or calls. Connect the Scriptures with the students' lives to tease out some reflections about the concepts to be covered.

1. Place the students into three roughly equal groups. Ask the groups to answer the following questions:

   - **Revelation** (in the sense of revealing oneself to another person):

     ➤ What should teens safely reveal about themselves on the Internet and especially on social networking sites like Facebook and MySpace?

   - **Inspiration** (in the sense of feeling an energy to create that seems to come from outside oneself):

     ➤ What people, events, truths, or beliefs inspire you? What do they inspire you to do?

   - **Vocation** (in the sense of involvement in a particular line of work):

     ➤ From your knowledge of vocational or technical training, how do these options prepare a person for a career compared with how a liberal arts education prepares a person?

2. Ask the students to share with the large group the answers their small groups came up with. Comment that these terms are used here in the way today's society commonly uses them. This conversation should get the students thinking about the meaning of these terms and prepare them to discuss the terms in a religious context.

Step 1

Preassess what the students already know about Revelation, Inspiration, and vocation.

The learning experiences later in the unit will help the students to unpack and explore these concepts with increasing depth. Several options exist for assessing what the students know and understand before beginning this unit. Note that each option requires preparing different materials.

Option 1: Journaling

Give the students the opportunity to reflect on what they know and understand about their relationship with God. The focus questions below invite the students to think critically about how they have developed, or would like to develop, this relationship. This learning experience will also help you to determine how much to present about God's ability and decision to communicate with humanity.

1. Write the following focus questions on the board:

   • How have I come to know God?

   • If I wanted to know God, how could I do that?

2. Have the students reflect on these questions for about 5 minutes by writing their thoughts in their notebooks. Distribute pens or pencils for this.

3. When time is up, invite the students to share their thoughts with the large group.

4. List the students' answers underneath the questions on the board.

5. After this list is created, ask the students to identify what the suggestions have in common. The definitions for Revelation and Inspiration should naturally surface through their suggestions. If not, lead the students toward the definitions used in this course.

6. Next, use a colored marker to circle those words related to Revelation. Use a different-colored marker to circle those that pertain to Inspiration.

7. Finally, discuss what *Revelation* and *Inspiration* mean as applied to the Bible.

Option 2: Think-Pair-Share

Give the students the opportunity to reflect on what they know and understand about the communication of ideas. The focus questions invite the students to think critically about how they know, or would like to know, certain things. This learning experience will also help you to determine how much material to present about God's ability and decision to communicate with humanity.

> **Teacher Note**
>
> See *smp.org/LivinginChrist* for the background article "Using the Think-Pair-Share Method" (Document #: TX001019).

1. Write the following question on the board. Ask the students to write their answers in their notebooks. Allow 5 minutes for writing. Distribute pens or pencils for this.

   • Can you think of a time when something was revealed to you or you were inspired to do something?

2. When time is up, place the students in pairs. Invite the students to discuss their experiences of Revelation and Inspiration. Allow 5 minutes for discussion.

3. When time is up, ask the students to share with the large group the experiences that illustrate their understanding of Revelation and Inspiration. If the students do not seem to understand the concepts, tell the students you will address them later in the unit.

Option 3: Big Paper

Teacher Note

As background see "Using the Big Paper Exercise" (Document #: TX001018) at *smp.org/LivinginChrist.*

This learning experience will give the students the opportunity to reflect on what they know and understand about the concepts of revelation, inspiration, and vocation. The focus story invites the students to think critically about how they understand these concepts. This will also help you to determine how much to present about these concepts.

1. Prepare by collecting the following items:

   • easel-sized paper (one sheet for each group of three)

   • a story containing an example of personal revelation, inspiration, or vocation (Use the same story for all groups. You will write this story in the center of each sheet of easel paper.)

   • markers, enough for each group

   • a roll of masking tape

2. Place the students in small groups of no more than three. Distribute the easel-sized papers with the story in the center, one to each group.

3. Explain that the groups are to silently read the story.

4. Say that once the students have read the story, the group members will hold a silent "conversation" by writing down their thoughts and comments on the paper around the story. No speaking is allowed during this learning experience. Allow about 10 minutes to complete the learning experience.

5. When time is up, post the groups' papers around the classroom. Ask the students to walk around and read each group's comments.

6. After the students have read the comments, call the students back into the large group. Discuss how a person may be inspired or receive revelation.

7. Finally, collect the big papers when the class is over so you can review them to see whether the students understand the concepts of Revelation and Inspiration.

Empathize

Step 2

Follow this assessment by presenting to the students the handouts "Final Performance Task Options for Unit 2" (Document #: TX001093) and "Rubric for Final Performance Tasks for Unit 2" (Document #: TX001094).

This unit provides you with two ways to assess that the students have a deep understanding of the most important concepts in the unit: creating a biblical exegesis about God's Revelation and call or creating a visual representation of Revelation, Inspiration, or vocation. Refer to "Using Final Performance Tasks to Assess Understanding" (Document #: TX001011) and "Using Rubrics to Assess Work" (Document #: TX001012) at *smp.org/LivinginChrist.*

1. Prepare by downloading and printing the handouts "Final Performance Task Options for Unit 2" (Document #: TX001093), "Rubric for Final Performance Tasks for Unit 2" (Document #: TX001094), and "Biblical Exegesis Worksheet" (Document #: TX001096).

2. Distribute the handouts. Give the students a choice as to which performance task they choose and add more options if you so choose. Review the directions, expectations, and rubric in class, allowing the students to ask questions.

3. Explain the types of tools and knowledge the students will gain throughout the unit so they can successfully complete the final performance task.

4. Answer questions to clarify the end point toward which the unit is headed. Remind the students as the unit progresses that each learning experience builds the knowledge and skills they will need to show you that they understand how God reveals himself and how Jesus is God's Perfect Revelation.

Teacher Note

You will want to assign due dates for the performance tasks.

If you have done these performance tasks, or very similar ones, with students before, place examples of this work in the classroom. During this introduction explain how each is a good example of what you are looking for, for different reasons. This allows the students to concretely understand what you are looking for and to understand that there is not only one way to succeed.

Step 3

Introduce the human need for God and ways God reveals himself outside the Scriptures.

Invite the students to consider their own need for God, using water as an analogy.

- The following articles are important for this step as well as for steps 4–9. Consider assigning the students to read these articles before beginning this step:
  - ○ "Longing for God" (article 1)
  - ○ "God's Invitation" (article 2)
  - ○ "Happiness in God Alone" (article 3)
  - ○ "Saint Augustine and the Four Objects of Love" (article 4)
  - ○ "The Sacred Scriptures and Natural Revelation (article 5)
  - ○ "Natural Revelation and the Wisdom of the Church Fathers" (article 6)
  - ○ "Natural Revelation and Scholastic Theology" (article 7)
  - ○ "Natural Revelation: Vatican Council I to the Present" (article 8)

1. Prepare by bringing in at least one paper cup for each student. Hide some jugs with enough water or the students' favorite beverage for each student to have a small drink.

2. Show one cup and one gallon jug and pour yourself a drink. Drink it with gusto, commenting on how refreshing it is. Make the following points:

    ➤ Water accounts for about 60 to 65 percent of our body weight. Every muscle or tissue cell needs it.

    ➤ Drinking too little water causes thirst and can cause dehydration. Have you ever felt dehydrated? It is miserable.

    ➤ By the time you feel thirsty, you are already on the way to dehydration. Is there a spiritual parallel?

3. Ask the students to read student book article 1, "Longing for God," either as classwork or homework. Note that a big difference between our thirst for God and our thirst for water is that God comes to us and water does not. Make the following additional points:

    ➤ Each one of us is a religious being. Whether we realize it or not, our **vocation** (from the Latin, meaning "to call") as religious beings is to live fully human lives—lives in which we know, love, and freely choose God.

➤ Within the human heart is a place—a God-shaped hole—desiring to be filled with God's infinite love. We have a **desire** for truth and happiness that only God can satisfy.

4. Share the following information about our religious natures and our desire for God. You may want to use the PowerPoint "Finding God and Being Found by God" (Document #: TX001070) at *smp.org/LivinginChrist.*

How Do People Come to Know God or to Search Him Out?

Present the following material about God's invitation to relationship and ways we encounter God:

➤ **God invites us into a relationship.** (See student book article 2, "God's Invitation.")

- God constantly calls us to relationship with him.
- In other words, we are invited into communion with God and to experience the grace of his saving love.
- God wants to know, love, and hold us.

➤ **A. Some people find God in their pursuit of happiness or in the emptiness they feel without something ultimate in their lives.** (See student book article 3, "Happiness in God Alone.")

- The *Catechism* tells us that happiness and truth can be found only when we live "in communion with God" (45).
- God is "our first origin and our ultimate goal" (*CCC,* 229). He is our beginning and our destiny. Thus happiness is found only in a life fully committed to him.
- Jesus provides a framework for happiness through his life, teachings, death, and Resurrection.

➤ **B. The Bible can lead us to know God.**

- *Revelation* comes from a Latin word meaning "to unveil or disclose."
- Divine Inspiration is the divine assistance the Holy Spirit gave the authors of the books of the Bible so the authors could write in human words the salvation message God wanted to communicate.
- The Bible is the Revelation of God, and each of the many writers was inspired.
- Each writer or character in the account heard or understood God's will and message differently.
- God's Covenant is the reason God reveals himself to each of the characters and calls them, and it is the reason they choose to follow God's will.

➤ **C. Other people encounter God through love.** (See student book article 4, "Saint Augustine and the Four Objects of Love.")

- Human beings share a universal capacity and desire for love. Because God is love, true love will ultimately be from him.
- Saint Augustine of Hippo, an early Father and Doctor of the Church, proclaimed that there are four objects we should love: God, our neighbors, ourselves, and our bodies.
  - ○ God deserves love above all created things.
  - ○ Love of God and neighbor are inseparable.
  - ○ Self-love is the realization that God is imprinted on our hearts waiting, wanting to be displayed to the world in a beautiful and magnificent way.
  - ○ Our bodies are one of God's great artistic masterpieces.

➤ **D. Other people come to God through the beauty of creation.** (See student book article 5, "The Sacred Scriptures and Natural Revelation," and article 6, "Natural Revelation and the Wisdom of the Church Fathers.")

- Through creation and reason, we can come to know God. This is called natural revelation, meaning that we can logically and reasonably deduce the existence of God through the natural order.
- God shaped all living things as a sign and symbol of his desire to be known through his magnificent universe.
- Experiences of the natural world or within the world can often bring us a feeling that something is beyond it, or they can cause us to think, "How can someone not believe in God when they see this or hear that or look here?"
- The Scriptures say that God's self-communication and disclosure to humankind are in creation.
- The **Fathers of the Church** further say that the universe provides visible evidence of God's existence.
- Many Church Fathers, especially Saint Athanasius (296–373), Saint Gregory of Nazianzen (325–389), Saint Gregory of Nyssa (395–394), and Saint Augustine of Hippo (354–430), coupled the idea that God can be known through natural revelation with the belief that humanity is the summit of creation. In other words, the Church Fathers saw human beings as the high point of God's creative action in the world.
- Nothing created by God, "even the tiniest insect," is insignificant, says Saint Augustine.

➤ **E. Some people come to, or at least articulate their belief in, God through thought.** (See student book article 7, "Natural Revelation and Scholastic Theology," and article 8, "Natural Revelation: Vatican Council I to the Present.")

- During the **Middle Ages,** new ways of providing logical arguments to demonstrate the existence of God emerged. The centuries with particular influence were the twelfth, thirteenth, and fourteenth centuries.
- The great thinkers of the Middle Ages maintained that through the use of our minds, we could logically develop "converging and convincing arguments" (*CCC,* 31) to attain truth and certainty about God and the human experience.
- According to Saint Thomas Aquinas, the reality of God can be proved, or logically demonstrated, in five ways:
  - The first proof or argument, known as the First Mover, draws on the idea that the universe constantly moves. Because everything continuously moves and changes, human beings can logically deduce or see a need for a "First Mover" who set everything in motion and guides the actions of humanity. We call that First Mover "God."
  - The second proof of God's existence is referred to as Causality, or First Efficient Cause. By reflecting on the cycle of life, we realize that all things are caused by something else. We equally realize that nothing can create itself. Therefore common sense tells us there is an Ultimate Cause or First Efficient Cause, which is uncaused, or not created by something else. This uncaused First Cause is God.
  - The third proof is based on a theory of contingency. This argument states that the universe contains many contingent things— that is, things that came into existence because of something else. But if everything were contingent, there would have to be a time where nothing would exist. This point in time would have been in the past. But things do exist. If they exist, they cannot exist without a Necessary Being. A Necessary Being is one who creates but is not created. That Necessary Being, which gives life to all beings, is God.
  - The fourth proof finds its strength in our understanding of perfection. Most of us can point out the imperfections of the world and humanity. In naming imperfections we acknowledge there are varying degrees of beauty, goodness, and knowledge. The question becomes: "How do we know perfect beauty, goodness, and knowledge?" According to Aquinas, we know perfection because there is one all-perfect being, God, who sets the infinite standard for wisdom and truth.
  - The fifth and final proof asserts that the world is characterized by remarkable order. This proof asserts that it is apparent that there are things in the universe that on their own have no intelligence. Yet regardless of their lack of intelligence, they still act toward and

achieve their end. One can then deduce that if things that lack intelligence still achieve their end, there must be something that does have an intelligence and knowledge of their end and directs all things to their appropriate end. This something can be seen as the intelligent designer behind our complex universe. We name this intelligent designer and magnificent architect God.

- Following is the argument of Saint Anselm of Canterbury (1033–1109) about God's existence:
  - ○ God is "that than which nothing greater can be thought."
  - ○ It is greater to exist in reality than to exist merely in the mind.
  - ○ Then God must exist in reality, not only in mind and understanding.

- At various points in the Church's history, the reality of natural revelation encountered opposition.
  - ○ Large parts of the population challenged the Church's teaching that God can be known in and through creation informed by human reason. Vatican Council I strongly reasserted in the constitution *Dei Filius* (1870) that when people listen "to the message of creation and to the voice of **conscience,** [they] can arrive at certainty about the existence of God" (*CCC,* 46).
  - ○ Philosopher and theologian John Henry Cardinal Newman (1801–1890) developed a theory known as the convergence of probabilities. This theory asserted that a number of probable hints, or indicators, point to the existence of God. These indicators range from people's experiences of beauty and goodness to the mystery of our world, from the voice of conscience to the enjoyment of freedom. The theory also asserted that no indicator alone necessarily proves the existence of God. Instead it claimed that when the indicators are combined, they produce a powerful argument.
  - ○ Karl Rahner (1904–1984), a Jesuit theologian, developed the idea of God as Absolute Mystery. Any time human beings experience limitations in knowledge, freedom, or perfection, there is an underlying awareness of God as Absolute Mystery.

➤ **F. Although we can find God, and God can reveal himself in many different ways, Jesus Christ is God's Perfect Revelation.** (See student book article 2, "God's Invitation.")

- Because God so longs for a relationship with us, he reached out in a radical way. In the Incarnation the Word of God became flesh in the person of Jesus Christ. Through Jesus Christ "God has revealed himself and given himself" (*CCC,* 68) to human beings in a new way so we may heed and understand the message of **salvation.**

- The Church teaches in the *Catechism* that in and through Jesus Christ, God has "provided the definitive, superabundant answer to the questions that man asks himself about the meaning and purpose of life" (68).
- The Incarnation of the Son of God is about God's love for humanity. (*Incarnation:* From the Latin, meaning "to become flesh," referring to the mystery of Jesus Christ, the divine Son of God, becoming man. In the Incarnation, Jesus Christ became truly man while remaining truly God.)

Step 4

Invite the students to recognize God's Revelation in one another.

The song "The Fingerprints of God," by Steven Curtis Chapman, is a nice way to invite the students to reflect on ways they see God's Revelation in others and to help them to see God's Revelation in themselves.

1. Prepare by downloading and printing the handouts "'The Fingerprints of God'" (Document #: TX001097) and "'The Fingerprints of God' Reflection Questions" (Document #: TX001098), one for each student. Also obtain a recording of this song that can be played for the students. See *smp.org/LivinginChrist* for a relevant Web link.

2. Distribute copies of the handouts. Introduce the song with the following or similar words:

> ➤ Sometimes it is easy to forget we are part of God's wonderful creation, because we hear different messages from all sorts of places. This song invites us to consider ourselves as "covered with the fingerprints of God."

   Play the song several times for the students. Ask them to follow the lyrics on the handout as they listen. Allow about 10 minutes for the students to answer the questions on the other handout.

3. When time is up, ask the students to share their insights about God's Revelation through people.

Step 5

Read the Scriptures and discuss God's Revelation to biblical figures.

Help the students to uncover what suggested passages say about Revelation and Inspiration. Consider what you know from the preassessment learning experiences to best prepare for the students' level of need.

1. Prepare by choosing two or three biblical accounts that clearly display God's interaction with humanity. We recommend the following: Genesis, chapters 40 and 41, about Joseph's dreams; Exodus, chapter 3, about Moses and the burning bush; and Luke 1:39–45, about Mary's visit to Elizabeth.

2. Ask several students to read these accounts aloud. Then instruct the students to circle or underline an aspect (a word, phrase, or verse) of each account as it relates most clearly to the concept of Revelation. Encourage the students not to choose an entire paragraph or the complete account itself. If the students are not allowed to write in their Bibles, ask them to write in their notebooks to describe the parts of the account they select.

3. After identifying these aspects, ask the students to share with the large group what they have circled. Repetition of ideas or words is acceptable. Write all these words or phrases on the board and discuss how the figures in the accounts experienced God, how God communicated with the figures, and how the accounts accurately depict the concept of Revelation.

Optional Learning Experience: Explore Revelation and Inspiration Using the Jigsaw Process

In this learning experience, the students will study the content of different biblical passages about Inspiration and Revelation and then work in small groups to apply biblical literary skills to the accounts. (For further explanation of this approach, see the article "Using the Jigsaw Process" [Document #: TX001020] at *smp.org/LivinginChrist.*)

1. To practice the learning experience, we recommend using Genesis 12:1–9, God's self-introduction to Abraham. Assign each student one of four accounts you have previously chosen. Following are four additional passages the students can use for the learning experience:

   • Genesis, chapter 32 (Jacob's struggle with an angel)
   • 1 Samuel 1:1—2:10 (Hannah's prayer)
   • 2 Samuel 7:1–29 (God's promise to David and David's response)
   • 1 Kings 3:4–15 (Solomon's wisdom dream)

   Make copies of the handout "Jigsaw Process" (Document #: TX001161), one for each group of four.

   You also may want to read background material about Revelation, Inspiration, and vocation. See the background article "Introduction to Revelation, Inspiration, and Vocation" (Document #: TX001017) at *smp.org/LivinginChrist.* You may also want to download and use the PowerPoint "Revelation, Inspiration, and Vocation" (Document #: TX001071) to accompany your presentation, either as is or with your own modifications.

2. Demonstrate your expectations for reading comprehension and study of content with the account of God's introducing himself to Abraham, in Genesis 12:1–9.

Model your expectations by asking the students to investigate the account of Abraham with you. Ask:

➤ What is the land of Abram's kinfolk?

Ur—this is mentioned later in the account.

➤ Why does the reading contain both regular text and poetic-type text?

The regular text narrates the account, and the poetic text is God's speech. This might be an attempt to set God's speech apart and above human action.

➤ What were the more specific meanings of blessings and curses?

From Saint Mary's Press® Essential Bible Dictionary:

> *Blessing: A prayer of intention that calls on the power and compassion of God to bestow a grace or empower a healing, or a plea to affect an event through God's intervention. The Bible is filled with blessing prayers.*
> *Curse: A curse could also be a punishment and condemnation by God (Gen 3:14). It could be a shaming device (Gen 9:25) or a condemnation against injustice and crime (Gen 49:7). The curse could serve as a prophetic warning, a priestly teaching against idolatry (Deut 27:15), or a warning to obey a conqueror's orders (Josh 6:26).*

(Pp. 28 and 40)

➤ Who are "the persons they had acquired in Haran"?

Slaves and others that formed the social group under Abraham.

➤ Who are the Canaanites?

From Saint Mary's Press® Essential Bible Dictionary:

> *[People who lived in] the land to which God directed Abraham to make his home, the Promised Land, also called Palestine. It occupied the territory that is modern-day Israel. The people who occupied the land were Canaanites. In the Bible, they were called idolaters because of their worship of Baal and Asherah. Through a series of occupations and wars, the Israelites eventually took over most of Canaan.*

(P. 31)

3. Ask the students to read their passages as homework and to come to the next class period with a one-paragraph summary of the account that reflects some greater study of the text.

Teacher Note

By writing out a paragraph about this passage with the students, you will be able to calm the fears of those who struggle with biblical interpretation and simultaneously challenge those who are skilled. Do not repeat this story account in the learning experience itself.

4. Place the students in groups of four that include one representative for each account. Distribute copies of the handout "Jigsaw Process" (Document #: TX001161) and ask the groups to answer the questions on the handout. Explain that the questions require the students to think critically about not only what each group member has read but also the connections and similarities that exist throughout the Bible. Allow about 10 minutes for the students to complete the questions

5. When time is up, call the students back to the large group to discuss how each account reflects the concepts of Revelation and Inspiration and to discuss similarities and differences among the accounts.

Reflect

Step 6

Have the students reflect on how they come to know God.

The students reflect on questions and acknowledge what they have learned so far. This reflection can be done for the first time here in step 6 or can be done now for the second time if previously done as option 1 in step 1. The learning experience is still valuable if repeated, because it highlights what the students have learned so far.

1. Write the following questions on the board:

   • How can I or have I come to know God?
   • If I wanted to know God, how could I do that?

2. Have the students reflect on these questions in the context of the biblical accounts they have read. Allow about 5 minutes for the students to write their responses to these questions in their notebooks.

3. When time is up, if applicable ask the students to turn to their question responses from step 1 and compare their answers.

4. Finally, invite the students to share their thoughts with the large group, directing them specifically to make connections among their previous responses, their current responses, and the biblical accounts you have read.

5. Conclude with the following points:

   ➤ God calls individuals into relationship with him by using their unique gifts and talents in his service.

➤ This process of using gifts and talents is known as *vocation*, a word that comes from the Latin *vocare,* meaning "to call." It is a function or station in life to which God calls us.

➤ The vocation of each individual implies active participation by human beings in the Covenant created between God and humanity centuries ago.

➤ Recall from unit 1 that *covenant* is a solemn agreement between human beings or between God and a human being in which mutual commitments are made.

Apply

Step 7

Use a movie to lead the students to uncover how God can reveal, inspire, and call his People through ordinary means.

Assist the students in reflecting on how God meets people where they are to communicate with them. Use the movie *Field of Dreams* (1989, 107 minutes, rated PG and A-II).

1. Prepare by gathering the following items:

   • the movie *Field of Dreams* and equipment for showing it. Preview the movie before showing it.

   • copies of the handout "*Field of Dreams* Reflection Questions" (Document #: TX001099), one for each student

2. Distribute the copies of the handout. Review the questions carefully with the students before watching the movie. Explain that at the class period after the movie concludes, the students will turn in the completed handouts, with one-paragraph responses for each question.

3. Next, show the movie. At 107 minutes, showing it may take several class periods. Depending on the time available, you may want to show only selected clips.

4. In the class period after the movie concludes, discuss the students' handout responses. Discuss how God can reveal himself, inspire, and call his People through the most ordinary means.

5. Finally, introduce the idea that God's messages can meet people where they are and that God can use their lives to communicate himself. Note that God uses ordinary means to reach people so they can hear God's call and understand their vocation. You may want to refer back to unit 1 and the Noah account with its parallel in *Evan Almighty* to discuss resistance to God's call. Ask:

   ➤ How do people called by God persist despite challenges?

Step 8

Explore the call of Samuel.

This learning experience can stand alone or be used with the subsequent Socratic seminar. Help the students to explore the call of Samuel as they further uncover the meaning of Revelation, Inspiration, and vocation.

1. Prepare for this learning experience by reminding the students they will need Bibles at home and in class. As homework, assign the account of the call of Samuel (see 1 Samuel 3:1–21). Ask half the students to consider the following question as they read: "What is necessary for people to hear and understand God's Revelation?" Ask the other half to consider the following: "How do other people support Samuel in his ability to hear and follow his vocation?" Tell the students they will write a two-paragraph response to their question.

2. Ask the students to bring the question responses to the following class period. They will use their responses either as tickets into a Socratic Seminar or as a basis for discussing the main concepts in the unit.

Step 9

Reinforce the students' thinking about Revelation and Inspiration through a Socratic seminar.

The Socratic seminar develops the students' analytical discussion and thinking skills. Look at the article "How to Lead a Socratic Seminar" (Document #: TX001006) at *smp.org/LivinginChrist* and look through the Socratic seminar process in unit 1 of this teacher guide.

1. The first group of inner-circle students will address the question "What is necessary for people to hear and understand God's Revelation?" They will switch places with the outer-circle students so the second half of the class can discuss the question "How do other people support Samuel in his ability to hear and follow his vocation?"

Step 10

Give a quiz to assess student understanding.

1. Prepare by downloading and printing the handout "Unit 2 Quiz" (Document #: TX001100), one for each student. Note that the quiz is fairly comprehensive, in part because both you and the students want to learn what they do not now know in preparation for a test or the final performance tasks.

2. On the day of the quiz, provide 5 to 10 minutes for the students to review their books and notes. Distribute the quiz and provide sufficient time for the students to work on it. If time remains when the students are done, collect the quizzes and then redistribute them so everyone has someone else's. Go through the quiz, allowing the students to correct one another's work and also giving them an opportunity to affirm or change their understanding of concepts. Collect the quizzes and further your analysis about topics that may need more coverage.

> **Teacher Note**
>
> To save paper, use the electronic copy of the quiz at *smp.org/LivinginChrist* and put it up in a visual place via projector, overhead, monitor, and so on. If these options are unavailable, read the quiz to the students slowly. In both cases, have the students record their answers on loose-leaf paper.
>
> To save time, ask the students to choose two of the three short-answer questions to complete.

Step 11

Apply Revelation, Inspiration, and vocation to today.

Using the barometer method, have the students uncover how God interacts with human beings today.

1. Prepare for this learning experience by finding the story of a person who has experienced God—either a person from the Bible, a saint, or an ordinary person. Make copies of the story, one for each student. If possible, don't tell the students whom the story is about. That way they will have no preconceptions. (You can use more than one story if you like.) See *smp.org/LivinginChrist* for suggestions and resources for this exercise.

    Create the following two signs. Hang them on facing walls of the classroom:

    - God Revealed Himself
    - God Did Not Reveal Himself

    See the article "Using the Barometer Method" (Document #: TX001021) at *smp.org/LivinginChrist* for an explanation of how to use this learning experience and suggestions on guiding the discussion.

2. On the day of the learning experience, have the students silently read the story of the "anonymous" person. Allow about 5 minutes for the students to finish.

3. When time is up, use the barometer method. Ask the students to stand near the sign that states their position about whether God revealed himself to the person in the story. Students may stand at one end of the spectrum, "God Revealed Himself," or at the other end, "God Did Not Reveal Himself." If they are unsure, they may stand anywhere in the middle.

4. Ask volunteers to share their logic about why they are standing where they are.

5. Conclude this learning experience by revealing the identity of the individual. Lead a discussion on the variety of ways God reveals himself to people outside the Bible.

Step 12

Guide the students in reflecting on the role Sacred Scripture plays in the life of the Church.

As the students approach the end of the second unit, this activity helps them connect their understanding of Scripture with the role Scripture plays in the life of the Church. In this step the students will work in groups to address the topics of Scripture and liturgy, the Liturgy of the Hours, the Lord's Prayer, and Scripture and the saints, and then present their topic to the class. For this activity you will want the students to have copies of the Bible. Also, if your students do not have access to the Internet, you will want to provide two or three copies of the *Roman Missal,* two or three copies of a Liturgy of the Hours book, paper, and markers or colored pencils for drawing.

1. Before class or at the beginning of this step, have the students read student book article 71, "The Study of the Sacred Scriptures."

2. Explain that Scripture is vital to the life of the Church. Scripture is part, either directly or indirectly, of all that the Church teaches and practices. Explain that the students will be working in groups to research and explain the role Scripture plays in different parts of the life of the Church.

3. Divide the class into groups of three to four students.

4. Assign each group one of the following articles from the student book:
   - "The Centrality of the Scriptures in the Mass and Other Liturgies" (article 72)
   - "The Liturgy of the Hours: A Window into the Daily Rhythms of Life" (article 73)

- "The Lord's Prayer: Rooted in the Scriptures" (article 74)
- "The Scriptures and the Rules of the Saints" (article 75)

It is fine to assign an article to more than one group.

5. Explain that each group is to complete the following for their assigned article:

   - "The Centrality of the Scriptures in the Mass and Other Liturgies" (article 72): Read the assigned article and prepare a brief presentation (2 minutes) for the class about the content of the article. Additionally, present two examples from each of the four parts of the Mass (Introductory Rite, Liturgy of the Word, Liturgy of the Eucharist, Concluding Rite) where the language of the Mass is based on Scripture. Provide a written version summarizing the article and the examples from the Mass.

   - "The Liturgy of the Hours: A Window into the Daily Rhythms of Life" (article 73): Read the assigned article and prepare a brief presentation (2 minutes) for the class about the content of the article. Additionally, identify a morning prayer from the Liturgy of the Hours and lead the class in praying that prayer. If you have more than one group addressing this topic, you may want to have one group identify a morning prayer, another a daytime prayer, and another an evening prayer. Provide a written version summarizing the article and a copy of the prayer from the Liturgy of the Hours with its scriptural connections identified.

   - "The Lord's Prayer: Rooted in the Scriptures" (article 74): Read the assigned article and prepare a brief presentation (2 minutes) for the class about the content of the article. Additionally, find or create visual depictions for each of the petitions of the Lord's Prayer. Provide a written version summarizing the article and copies of the images identified or created.

   - "The Scriptures and the Rules of the Saints" (article 75): Read the assigned article and prepare a brief presentation (2 minutes) for the class about the content of the article. Additionally, identify and explain five Scripture passages that could serve as a guide for living a Christian life, the way rules guide religious communities. Provide a written version summarizing the article and include a list of the Scripture passages identified with a brief explanation of how each passage can be a guide for Christian living.

6. Invite the groups to present their assignments to the class. Once they have presented, have them turn in the printed version of their assignment. If class time will not allow for every group to present, you may choose to have the groups simply turn in their assignments and allow one group for each article to present.

Step 13

Now that the students are closer to the end of the unit, make sure they are all on track with their final performance tasks, if you have assigned them.

If possible, devote 50 to 60 minutes for the students to ask questions about the tasks and to work individually.

1. Remind the students to bring to class any work they have already prepared so that they can work on it during the class period. If necessary, reserve the library or media center so the students can do any book or online research. Download and print extra copies of the handouts "Final Performance Task Options for Unit 2" (Document #: TX001093) and "Rubric for Final Performance Tasks for Unit 2" (Document #: TX001094). Review the final performance task options, answer questions, and ask the students to choose one if they have not already done so.

2. Provide some class time for the students to work on their performance tasks. This then allows you to work with the students who need additional guidance with the project.

Step 14

Provide the students with a tool to use for reflecting about what they learned in the unit and how they learned.

This learning experience provides the students with an excellent opportunity to reflect on how their understandings of Revelation, Inspiration, and vocation have developed throughout the unit.

1. To prepare for this learning experience, download and print the handout "Learning about Learning" (Document #: TX001159; see Appendix), one for each student.

2. Distribute the handout and give the students about 15 minutes to answer the questions quietly. Invite them to share any reflections they have about the content they learned as well as their insights into the way they learned.

Final Performance Task Options for Unit 2

The following are the main ideas you are to understand from this unit. They should appear in this final performance task so your teacher can assess whether you learned the most essential content:

- Divine Revelation refers to God's self-communication through which he makes known the mystery of his divine plan.
- God revealed himself in many different ways in the Bible and continues to do so today.
- Divine Inspiration is the divine assistance the Holy Spirit gave the authors of the books of the Bible so the authors could write in human words the salvation message God wanted to communicate.
- Revelation, Inspiration, and vocation are closely connected in scriptural accounts, as well as in our lives today.

Option 1: A Biblical Exegesis about God's Revelation and Call

- Choose an account from the Bible in which God calls someone. Listed below are accounts you may choose. If you would like to use another account, first ask your teacher's permission. The account you choose should have a clear plot with one or more characters who answer God's call to action. For example, because of its poetic nature, a psalm would not be an appropriate choice.
  - Genesis, chapter 12 (the call of Abram)
  - Genesis, chapter 15 (God's Covenant with Abraham)
  - Genesis, chapter 17 (Abraham converses with God)
  - Exodus, chapter 3 (Moses and the burning bush)
  - 2 Samuel 7:1–29 (God's promise to David and David's response)
  - Jeremiah, chapter 1 (God calls Jeremiah)
  - Luke 1:26–38 (announcement of the Birth of Jesus)
  - Luke, chapters 1–2 (Elizabeth and Zechariah)
  - Acts 9:1–9 (Saul's conversion)

- Analyze the account, using the methods and tools of biblical criticism you have learned. Use the handout "Biblical Exegesis Chart" (Document #: TX001090) to identify the questions you want answered. Refer to the handout "Exegesis Online Information Quest" (Document #: TX001092) for online biblical tools but also use resources you may find in class or in the library such as a second translation of the Bible, a Bible dictionary, or a concordance. (Use the handout "Biblical Exegesis Worksheet" (Document #: TX001096) to guide your work.) Ask your teacher for copies of these unit 1 handouts if you no longer have yours.

- Once you have completed the exegesis for your passage, answer the following questions:
  - How does God communicate the divine plan in this account?
  - What are some other ways God reveals himself in the Bible? How does God sometimes reveal himself today?
  - How does God call the person in your account? What does God call this person to do?
  - How does God inspire the biblical person? How can God inspire us through this account today?

Document #: TX001093

- Arrange your written response in one of two ways. Either talk about your exegesis first and then answer these questions in essay form or else structure your essay around the questions and weave the exegesis throughout.

Option 2: Seeing God's Revelation, Inspiration, and Call

- Respond completely to the following directions and questions before beginning your creative project.
    - Name three times God reveals the divine plan in the Old Testament. How does God do this in each case?
    - What are some other ways God reveals himself in the Bible? How does he sometimes reveal himself today?
    - How has God revealed himself to you? What has God called you to do?
    - How has God inspired you? How have you seen God inspire others?

    Reflect on the concepts of Revelation, Inspiration, vocation and the ways they relate to one another. You may want to create a diagram to show the relationships visually.

- Create a visual depiction of how God has revealed himself to you and how he has inspired you and calls you. This could be done through a collage, diagram, painting, drawing, song lyrics, or other visual medium.
- In writing explain or interpret your work so your teacher can clearly see your thought process.

© 2010 by Saint Mary's Press
Living in Christ Series

Document #: TX001093

Rubric for Final Performance Tasks for Unit 2

Criteria	4	3	2	1
Assignment includes all items requested in the instructions.	Assignment includes all items requested, and they are completed above expectations.	Assignment includes all items requested.	Assignment includes more than half of the items requested.	Assignment includes less than half of the items requested.
Assignment shows understanding of the concept *Divine Revelation refers to God's self-communication through which he makes known the mystery of his divine plan.*	Assignment shows unusually insightful understanding of this concept.	Assignment shows good understanding of this concept.	Assignment shows adequate understanding of this concept.	Assignment shows little understanding of this concept.
Assignment shows understanding of the concept *God revealed himself in many different ways in the Bible and continues to do so today.*	Assignment shows unusually insightful understanding of this concept.	Assignment shows good understanding of this concept.	Assignment shows adequate understanding of this concept.	Assignment shows little understanding of this concept.
Assignment shows understanding of the concept *Divine Inspiration is the divine assistance the Holy Spirit gave the authors of the books of the Bible so the authors could write in human words the salvation message God wanted to communicate.*	Assignment shows unusually insightful understanding of this concept.	Assignment shows good understanding of this concept.	Assignment shows adequate understanding of this concept.	Assignment shows little understanding of this concept.
Assignment shows understanding of the concept *Revelation, Inspiration, and vocation are closely connected in scriptural accounts, as well as in our lives today.*	Assignment shows unusually insightful understanding of this concept.	Assignment shows good understanding of this concept.	Assignment shows adequate understanding of this concept.	Assignment shows little understanding of this concept.
Assignment uses proper grammar and spelling.	Assignment has no grammar or spelling errors.	Assignment has one grammar or spelling error.	Assignment has two grammar or spelling errors.	Assignment has more than two grammar or spelling errors.

Document #: TX001094

Vocabulary for Unit 2

desire: From the Latin *desidero,* "to long for what is absent or lost."

Divine Inspiration: The divine assistance the Holy Spirit gave the authors of the books of the Bible so the authors could write in human words the salvation message God wanted to communicate.

Divine Revelation: God's self-communication through which he makes known the mystery of his divine plan. Divine Revelation is a gift accomplished by the Father, Son, and Holy Spirit through the words and deeds of salvation history. It is most fully realized in the Passion, death, Resurrection, and Ascension of Jesus Christ.

Ecumenical Council: A gathering of the Church's bishops from around the world to address pressing issues in the Church. Ecumenical councils are usually convened by the Pope or are at least confirmed or recognized by him.

Fathers of the Church (Church Fathers): During the early centuries of the Church, those teachers whose writings extended the Tradition of the Apostles and who continue to be important for the Church's teachings.

Incarnation: From the Latin, meaning "to become flesh," referring to the mystery of Jesus Christ, the divine Son of God, becoming man. In the Incarnation, Jesus Christ became truly man while remaining truly God.

Magisterium: The Church's living teaching office, which consists of all bishops, in communion with the Pope.

Middle Ages: Also known as the medieval period, the time between the collapse of the Roman Empire in the fifth century AD and the beginning of the Renaissance in the fourteenth century.

natural revelation: The process by which God makes himself known to human reason through the created world. Historical conditions and the consequences of Original Sin, however, often hinder our ability to fully know God's truth through natural revelation alone.

papal infallibility: The dogma declaring the Pope, by the power of the Holy Spirit, free from error when he solemnly declares a dogmatic teaching on faith and morals as being contained in Divine Revelation. Dogmas are teachings that are recognized as central to Church teaching, defined by the Magisterium (the teaching office), and accorded the fullest weight and authority.

salvation: From the Latin *salvare*, meaning "to save," referring to the forgiveness of sins and assurance of permanent union with God, attained for us through the Paschal Mystery—Christ's work of redemption accomplished through his Passion, death, Resurrection, and Ascension. Only at the time of judgment can a person be certain of salvation, which is a gift of God.

scholastic theology: The use of philosophical methods to better understand revealed truth. The goal of scholastic theology is to present the understanding of revealed truth in a logical and systematic form.

Vatican Council II: The ecumenical or general council of the Roman Catholic Church that Pope John XXIII (1958–1963) convened in 1962 and that continued under Pope Paul VI (1963–1978) until 1965.

vocation: A call from God to all members of the Church to embrace a life of holiness. Specifically, it refers to a call to live the holy life as an ordained minister, as a vowed religious (sister or brother), in a Christian marriage, or in single life.

 © 2010 by Saint Mary's Press
Living in Christ Series

Document #: TX001095

Biblical Exegesis Worksheet

Use the questions in this chart to guide your exegesis. (You may not be able to answer all the questions.) Take notes in the blank spaces to the right.

Type of Method	Questions This Method Asks	Exegesis Work
Textual Criticism	• Of the many ancient copies and fragments of Bible books, which ones are the oldest? • Can we identify why there are differences between different copies of the same book? • Can we identify why different translations use different words in passages?	
Historical Criticism	• What was the historical situation during the life of the author / editor or of the author's / editor's community? • How did the historical situation influence the author's writing?	
Literary Criticism	• Did the writer use a particular literary form or device such as a poem, a historical story, a prophecy, a letter, or a gospel? • Did the passage use metaphors, puns, parables, exaggeration, a midrash, or other literary devices? • How did these particular literary forms or devices function in an ancient society?	
Source Criticism	• Are other writings from ancient cultures outside the Scriptures similar to a biblical passage? • What is the meaning of the differences between the way a story is told in the Bible and the way it is told in other sources?	

(This chart is adapted from *Saint Mary's Press*® *Essential Bible Dictionary*, by Sheila O'Connell-Roussell [Winona, MN: Saint Mary's Press, 2005], page 57. Copyright © 2005 by Saint Mary's Press. All rights reserved.)

"The Fingerprints of God"

Steven Curtis Chapman

I can see the tears filling your eyes
And I know where they're coming from
They're coming from a heart that's broken in two
By what you don't see
The person in the mirror
Doesn't look like the magazine
Oh but when I look at you it's clear to me that

I can see the fingerprints of god
When I look at you
I can see the fingerprints of god
And I know it's true
You're a masterpiece
That all creation quietly applauds
And you're covered with the fingerprints of god

Never has there been and never again
Will there be another you
Fashioned by god's hand
And perfectly planned
To be just who you are
And what he's been creating
Since the first beat of your heart
Is a living breathing priceless work of art and

Just look at you
You're a wonder in the making
Oh and god's not through no
In fact he's just getting started.

"The Fingerprints of God" Reflection Questions

Name: _____

1. Where can you see God's work in people you know?

2. How do magazines and other media make it easier to see yourself as God's masterpiece? How do magazines and other media make it more difficult to see yourself as God's masterpiece?

3. Are there people in your life who help you to see yourself as part of God's creation? How do they do this?

4. How might you affirm how special another person is?

5. Does being one of God's masterpieces carry responsibility with it? Explain.

Document #: TX001098

Field of Dreams Reflection Questions

Name: _____

Answer each question with at least one full paragraph. Use the back of this sheet if you require more room. Be sure to properly use the words *Revelation, Inspiration,* and *vocation* in your answers.

1. The movie *Field of Dreams* displays the concepts of Revelation, Inspiration, and vocation throughout. Define these words and explain how and why a character from the movie experiences each in a nonreligious way. Do not use the same character more than once.

2. What is Ray Kinsella's vocation? How does Ray come to know his vocation? Describe the events or people that help Ray to understand who he is and what his purpose in life is.

3. How does "the Voice" communicate with the characters in the movie? Please provide at least two different examples. Although "the Voice" is not necessarily God in the movie, how does "the Voice" show us how God might be able to communicate with humanity? What can "the Voice" teach us about the concept of Revelation?

4. How can a person understand and act on Inspiration? Can a person use his or her own intellect and reason to interpret God's message? If so, does this mean human beings can misinterpret God's message? Provide examples from the movie that support your answer.

© 2010 by Saint Mary's Press
Living in Christ Series

Document #: TX001099

Unit 2 Quiz

Name: _____

Read Job, chapters 40–42. Take notes in the space provided below. After you have finished reading and taking notes, answer the questions. Your response should be eight to ten sentences long and should thoroughly answer all the questions about the passage from Job.

Notes

Questions

1. How does God reveal himself to Job in this passage?
2. Does Job's Revelation inspire him to act? If yes, how? If not, why not?
3. What is Job's vocation? How do you know?

Document #: TX001100

Unit 2 Test

Part 1: Multiple Choice

Write your answers in the blank spaces at the left.

1. _____ What is it that God desires most of us?
- **A.** that we are successful in life
- **B.** that we know him
- **C.** that we receive the Eucharist each Sunday
- **D.** that we read religious books

2. _____ Which of the following statements is false?
- **A.** God reveals himself in many and varied ways.
- **B.** The Sacred Scriptures call attention to God's glory in creation.
- **C.** Divine Revelation helps us to understand more about God.
- **D.** The angels are God's most important works of creation.

3. _____ According to the *Catechism of the Catholic Church,* our inner longing for God is written in _____.
- **A.** the Bible
- **B.** the Beatitudes
- **C.** the human heart
- **D.** the words of the prophets

4. _____ What can hinder our ability to know God more fully?
- **A.** the consequences of Original Sin
- **B.** belief in evolution
- **C.** Divine Revelation
- **D.** mindless TV shows

5. _____ To what is God inviting us?
- **A.** a fulfilled life in our Christian community
- **B.** health and happiness in our careers
- **C.** a position of honor in the Kingdom of Heaven
- **D.** a relationship of mutual love and understanding

6. _____   In Psalm 42 the psalmist compares thirst for God to _____.
   A. a deer searching for water
   B. a man lost in the desert
   C. people on a long trip
   D. someone looking for love

7. _____   Presenting the understanding of revealed truth in a logical and systematic way is the goal of

   _____.
   A. the Church Fathers
   B. the Magisterium
   C. natural revelation
   D. scholastic theology

8. _____   The document *Pastoral Constitution on the Church in the Modern World* (*Gaudium et Spes*, 1965), coming out of Vatican Council II, addressed all of the following except _____.
   A. the best way for the priest to say the Mass
   B. the dignity of the human person
   C. the necessity of community in an individualistic world
   D. human beings' relationship to the universe

9. _____   The document *Pastoral Constitution on the Church in the Modern World* (*Gaudium et Spes*, 1965) also deals with the sanctity of marriage and family life and _____.
   A. capital punishment
   B. economic and social justice
   C. how to increase vocations to the priesthood
   D. whether nuns should wear habits

10. _____   Which of the following statements is not true about moral conscience?
   A. It leads us to act responsibly.
   B. It prompts us to do good.
   C. It gives us an excuse to make poor decisions.
   D. It prompts us to avoid evil.

Document #: TX001296

Part 2: Fill-in-the-Blank

Use the word bank to fill in the blanks in the following sentences. (*Note:* There are two extra terms in the word bank.)

WORD BANK

Beatitudes	Incarnation	parables
Saint Augustine	Fathers of the Church	conscience
Saint Paul	Acts of the Apostles	Sacred Scriptures
Jesus	salvation	Saint Thomas Aquinas

1. "God saves" is the meaning for the word _____.

2. _____ is 'the interior voice" of a person, a God-given sense of the law of God.

3. We find expressions of the desire for truth and happiness in the _____ and in the lives of the saints.

4. _____ are short stories that use everyday images to communicate religious messages.

5. _____ is the restoration of friendship with God.

6. _____ wrote a letter to the Romans in which he affirmed the evidence of God in all creation.

7. _____ wrote about theology and faith in the *Summa Theologica*.

8. The_____ were teachers during the early centuries of the Church whose writings extended the Tradition of the Apostles and who continue to be important for the Church's teachings.

9. Jesus gave us the _____ as a key for living in true happiness.

10. The _____ is about God's love for humanity.

Document #: TX001296

Part 3: Short Answer

Answer each of the following questions in paragraph form on a separate sheet of paper.

1. What is Divine Revelation? How is it made known to us most fully?

2. What is natural revelation? From where can it be drawn?

3. What is Divine Inspiration? How does it relate to the writing of the Sacred Scriptures?

4. What is the one vocation that all human beings share? What roles does Revelation play in fulfilling this vocation?

Unit 2 Test Answer Key

Part 1: Multiple Choice

1. B
2. D
3. C
4. A
5. D

6. A
7. D
8. A
9. B
10. C

Part 2: Fill-in-the-Blank

1. Jesus
2. conscience
3. Sacred Scriptures
4. parables
5. salvation

6. Saint Paul
7. Saint Thomas Aquinas
8. Fathers of the Church
9. Beatitudes
10. Incarnation

Part 3: Short Answer

1. Divine Revelation is God's communication about himself and his plan for humanity. It is made known to us most fully by the Incarnation, the sending of his own Divine Son, Jesus Christ.

2. Natural revelation means that through the natural order of creation we can logically and reasonably deduce the existence of God. Natural revelation is pointed to in the Scriptures and in the wisdom of the Church Fathers, in the "proofs" developed by scholastic theologians and in the teachings of recent Church Councils.

3. Divine Inspiration is the assistance given by the Holy Spirit to perform acts that bring us closer to God. Divine Inspiration is most clearly seen in the assistance the Holy Spirit gave the authors of the books of the Bible so the authors could write in human words the salvation message God wanted to communicate.

4. The one vocation we all share is to live fully human lives, in which we know, love, and freely choose God or to live in communion with God. Revelation helps by showing us the actions of Jesus Christ and the love God has for us by sending Jesus to live among us.

Document #: TX001297

Unit 3

What Is Salvation History?

Overview

This third unit sets the stage for the remaining units in the course by giving an overview of salvation history, an explanation of why salvation was necessary, and a context for understanding the significance of Christ's redemption.

Key Understandings and Questions

At the end of this unit, the students will possess a deeper understanding of the following important concepts:

- Salvation history is the pattern of specific events in human history in which God clearly reveals his presence and saving actions. In one sense we can say that all human history is salvation history. By this we mean that the one true God—Father, Son, and Holy Spirit—has been present and active in the lives of his People since the beginning of time.
- Salvation history began with humanity's first sin and ended in the Resurrection of Jesus Christ.
- Original Sin led to the loss of original holiness, made humans subject to death, and made sin universally present in the world. This universally present sin led to further sin among God's People. The sins of his People resulted in broken communities and families and in separation from God, one another, the natural world, and even themselves. Christ's saving death and Resurrection gave human beings the grace to be in communion with God.
- Although human beings may have turned from their relationship with God during salvation history, God always remains faithful to them.

At the end of this unit, the students will have answered these questions:

- Why do we need to be saved?
- What is salvation history?
- Why did God allow Original Sin?
- How does salvation history help me to better understand the Bible?

How Will You Know the Students Understand?

These tools will help you to assess the students' understanding of the main concepts:

- handout "Final Performance Task Options for Unit 3" (Document #: TX001101)

- handout "Rubric for Final Performance Tasks for Unit 3" (Document #: TX001102)
- handout "Unit 3 Test" (Document #: TX001298)

The Suggested Path to Understanding

This teacher guide provides you with one path to take with the students, enabling them to begin their study of Jesus by deepening their understanding of salvation history. It is not necessary to use all the learning experiences, but if you substitute other material from this course or your own material for some of the material offered here, check to see that you have covered all relevant facets of understanding and that you have not missed knowledge or skills required in later units.

Reflect

Step 1: Preassess what the students already know about Revelation, Inspiration, and vocation in salvation history.

Empathize

Step 2: Follow this assessment by presenting to the students the handouts "Final Performance Task Options for Unit 3" (Document #: TX001101) and "Rubric for Final Performance Tasks for Unit 3" (Document #: TX001102).

Perceive

Step 3: Connect theology to history.

Apply

Step 4: Introduce salvation history.

Perceive

Step 5: Explain what the students will look for in salvation history through exegesis.

Perceive

Step 6: Introduce why salvation history was necessary and how it began.

Perceive

Step 7: Introduce original blessing and Original Sin.

Apply

Step 8: Do a sprint through salvation history.

Empathize

Step 9: Give a quiz to assess student understanding.

Perceive

Step 10: Brainstorm the relationship between Judaism and Christianity.

Apply

Optional Learning Experience: Direct an information quest.

Step 11: Use a stations exercise to assess student understanding.

Step 12: Now that the students are closer to the end of the unit, make sure they are all on track with their final performance tasks, if you have assigned them.

Step 13: Provide the students with a tool to use for reflecting about what they learned in the unit and how they learned.

Background for Teaching This Content with These Methods

In addition to finding information about the pedagogical approach used in this guide, you will also find background information on these and other topics at *smp.org/LivinginChrist:*

- "Salvation History" (Document #: TX001027)
- "Original Sin" (Document #: TX001028)
- "The Book of Genesis" (Document #: TX001025)
- "Introduction to the Pentateuch" (Document #: TX001024)
- "Understanding Genres and Literary Forms" (Document #: TX001026)

The Web site also has background information on the following teaching methods:

- "Using Final Performance Tasks to Assess Understanding" (Document #: TX001011)
- "Using Rubrics to Assess Work" (Document #: TX001012)

Student Book Articles

The articles covered in unit 3 are from "Section 1: Revelation" and "Section 3: Revelation in the Old Testament" of the student book. If you believe the students would do the reading more successfully with additional structure, see the handout "Student Notes for Unit 3" (Document #: TX001029) at *smp.org/LivinginChrist.*

- "Salvation History: God's Revelation" (article 9)
- "Salvation History in the Old Testament" (article 10)
- "Jesus Christ: The Fullness of All Revelation" (article 11)
- "The Transmission of Divine Revelation" (article 12)
- "Creation: In the Beginning" (article 31)
- "Sin and God's Response" (article 32)

Scripture Passages

- Genesis 1:1—2:4 (the creation of the world)
- Genesis 2:5–3 (the creation of humanity)
- Genesis 2:7; 15:1,23 (God breathes life into man, gives him the garden to care for)
- Genesis 3:1–24 (the Fall of humanity)
- Genesis 4:1–16 (Cain and Abel)
- Genesis 6:5–13 (introduction to the Flood)
- Genesis 11:1–9 (the Tower of Babel)
- Genesis 12:1–7, 15:1–21 (Abraham's call)

Vocabulary

If you choose to provide a vocabulary list for material covered in both the student book and the teacher guide, download and print the handout "Vocabulary for Unit 3" (Document #: TX001103), one for each student.

Apostolic Succession	patriarch
covenant	primeval history
creed	prophet
Deposit of Faith	Sacred Tradition
Divine Revelation	salvation history
dogma	sin
Logos	theophany
Magisterium	Trinity
mortal sin	venial sin
Original Sin	wisdom literature

Learning Experiences

Reflect

Step 1

Preassess what the students already know about Revelation, Inspiration, and vocation in salvation history.

Assess the students' prior knowledge of Revelation, Inspiration, and vocation and of humanity's history of relationship with God.

Option 1: Journaling

> **Teacher Note**
>
> This journaling exercise uses the same question as the think-pair-share exercise in option 2 of the unit 2 preassessment exercise. Do not repeat it unintentionally.

Give the students the opportunity to reflect on what they know and understand about salvation history. The focus questions invite the students to consider the influence of Divine Inspiration in their own lives, reminding them of the effect of God's Inspiration on the major figures of salvation history.

1. Write the following question on the board. Distribute pens or pencils and ask the students to write their answers in their notebooks. Allow 5 minutes for writing.

   • Can you think of a time when something was revealed to you or you were inspired to do something?

2. When time is up, have the students form pairs. Invite the students to discuss their experiences of Revelation and Inspiration. Allow 5 minutes for discussion.

3. When time is up, ask the students to share with the large group the experiences that illustrate their understanding of Revelation and Inspiration. If the students do not seem to understand the concepts, tell the students you will address them later in the unit.

4. After the large-group discussion, introduce the focus questions for the unit.

> **Teacher Note**
>
> This exercise introduces the concept of covenant, which will be reintroduced in this unit and further elaborated in unit 4.

Option 2: A Person of Inspiration

Build on the students' understanding of Inspiration, Revelation, and vocation to apply those concepts outside scriptural study.

1. Ask the students to name a person from history or someone they know who inspires them. Tell the students this person need not be a biblical figure. This exercise is meant to personalize the students' understanding of inspiration in their daily lives.

2. Write the following questions on the board. Distribute pens or pencils and ask the students to write their answers in their notebooks. Allow about 10 minutes for writing.

   - Who inspires you?
   - Why does this person inspire you?
   - What lessons does this teach you?
   - How do you act based on this inspiration?
   - Compare this aspect of inspiration and revelation to what we discussed in the previous unit.

3. When time is up, ask the students to share their ideas with the large group. Note that the variety of answers will illustrate the effect of individuals on larger groups and the actions their inspiration motivates.

4. After the students have shared, ask them to answer the following questions with the large group:

   ➤ How do past events and people influence us?
   ➤ Why do these events and people influence us?

5. To conclude, highlight the following points:

   ➤ People and events of the past teach us lessons, some positive and some negative.
   ➤ We learn from the behaviors of inspiring people and may feel called to imitate them.
   ➤ Often people who have overcome challenges inspire us.
   ➤ Our decision to learn from the examples of others puts us into a relationship with them—we commit ourselves to live by the lessons they have taught us.

Empathize

Step 2

Follow this assessment by presenting to the students the handouts "Final Performance Task Options for Unit 3" (Document #: TX001101) and "Rubric for Final Performance Tasks for Unit 3" (Document #: TX001102).

This unit provides you with two ways to assess that the students have a deep understanding of the most important concepts in the unit: performing a creative writing task with biblical exegesis or researching Jewish rituals, festivals, or holidays to commemorate key moments in salvation history. Refer to "Using Final Performance Tasks to Assess Understanding" (Document #: TX001011) and "Using Rubrics to Assess Work" (Document #: TX001012) at *smp.org/ LivinginChrist*.

Teacher Note

You will want to assign due dates for the performance tasks.

If you have done these performance tasks, or very similar ones, with students before, place examples of this work in the classroom. During this introduction explain how each is a good example of what you are looking for, for different reasons. This allows the students to concretely understand what you are looking for and to understand that there is not only one way to succeed.

1. Prepare by downloading and printing the handouts "Final Performance Task Options for Unit 3" (Document #: TX001101) and "Rubric for Final Performance Tasks for Unit 3" (Document #: TX001102), one for each student.

2. Distribute the handouts. Give the students a choice as to which performance task they choose and add more options if you so choose. Review the directions, expectations, and rubric in class, allowing the students to ask questions.

3. Explain the types of tools and knowledge the students will gain throughout the unit so that they can successfully complete the final performance task.

4. Answer questions to clarify the end point toward which the unit is headed. Remind the students as the unit progresses that each learning experience builds the knowledge and skills they will need to show you that they understand how God reveals himself and how Jesus is God's Perfect Revelation.

Step 3

Connect theology to history.

Provide the students with a historical context so they understand that the Bible conveys a history of events and religious truths relevant to their daily lives.

1. Prepare by choosing historical events from the students' current or previous courses of study. Familiarity with historical periods and documents will help to make the connection clear for the students. Download and print the handout "Vocabulary for Unit 3" (Document #: TX001103) and "Why Do We Study History?" (Document #: TX001104), one for each student. The history handout refers to documents from U.S. history, such as the *Declaration of Independence*, the *Gettysburg Address*, and Martin Luther King Jr.'s "I Have a Dream" speech. You may choose to make copies of excerpts of these speeches to go with the handout. See *smp.org/LivinginChrist* for links to these three American speeches.

2. Write the following question on the board:

   • Why do we study history?

   Ask the students to respond as a large group. Write their answers on the board. List the students' suggestions or ask a volunteer or two to help you. If the question is difficult for the students, ask them to name someone from history and then follow up by asking: "How do you know this person? What did the person do?" Allow 5 to 10 minutes for discussion.

3. When time is up, distribute the copies of the handouts. If you choose, distribute copies of excerpts from the historical documents or project them to help the students complete the history handout. Allow 10 to 15 minutes (or more if you distribute excerpts) for the students to fill out the handout.

4. When time is up, project a copy of the handout "Why Do We Study History?" (Document #: TX001104) on the board. Ask the students to help you fill it in, drawing from their individual work.

5. Ask the students the following questions:

   ➤ What theme is illustrated here?

   ➤ How do the documents teach similar lessons but in different time periods?

6. Next, discuss the similarities and differences between studying documents like these and studying the Bible. Ask the following questions. Recall material from unit 1.

   ➤ How are the documents similar to and different from the Bible?

   ➤ What historical information must you know before you study the Bible?

7. Conclude by noting that the students will use some of the skills from history class when studying salvation history. They will use other skills, such as biblical exegesis, that are unique to biblical studies.

Apply

Step 4

Introduce salvation history.

Student book articles 9–12 contain many complicated theological concepts related to Divine Revelation and salvation history. The handout "Reading Notes and Questions for Student Book Articles 9–12" (Document #: TX001105) is a helpful tool if you want the students to read this material on their own.

• This step utilizes the following student book articles:

   ○ "Salvation History: God's Revelation" (article 9)

   ○ "Salvation History in the Old Testament" (article 10)

      ○ "Jesus Christ: The Fullness of All Revelation" (article 11)

      ○ "The Transmission of Divine Revelation" (article 12)

Assign the students to read these articles before the step as preparation. You may also consider having the students reread the articles following the step as review.

1. Prepare by setting up equipment to show the PowerPoint presentation "Introduction to Salvation History" (Document #: TX001072) at *smp.org/LivinginChrist.* If you choose, download and print the handout (Document #: TX001105) and follow it with the students as you read the student book articles as a large group. (The material in the following steps contains the most important points from the handout.)

2. Present the following material from student book article 9, "Salvation History: God's Revelation":

    ➤ **Salvation history** is the pattern of events in human history in which God clearly reveals his presence and saving actions. Salvation was accomplished once and for all through Jesus Christ, a truth foreshadowed and revealed throughout the Old Testament.

    ➤ God's saving hand has been at work in and through human history. In one sense we can say that all human history is salvation history. By this we mean that the one true God—Father, Son, and Holy Spirit—has been present and active in the lives of his People since the beginning of time.

    ➤ Divine Revelation culminates in Jesus Christ.

    ➤ In the unfolding of salvation history, God invites us into communion with the blessed Trinity.

3. Present the following material from article 10, "Salvation History in the Old Testament" in the student book:

    ➤ Salvation history, as written about in the Scriptures, reveals God's love for his people. Every time we read or hear the Word of God, we are led ever deeper into the mystery and wonder of God.

    ➤ God invited our first parents, Adam and Eve, into intimate communion with him when he created them.

    ➤ Although God revealed his will and plan to Adam, Eve, Abraham, and Moses, humanity's inclination to sin stood in the way of God's plan. The Israelites continued to turn away from the Covenant and the Law. In response, God revealed himself to the **prophets,** men like Isaiah, Jeremiah, and Ezekiel.

    ➤ God remains faithful to the Covenant even when the people of Israel do not.

4. Present the following material from article 11, "Jesus Christ: The Fullness of All Revelation," in the student book:

- ➤ Jesus Christ fully reveals God to us.

- ➤ The Gospel of John uses the Greek word *Logos* (translated in English as *Word*) for Jesus Christ.

- ➤ Because the Word (Jesus Christ) is God, we read about the Word in the Old Testament even before he becomes human as described in the New Testament.

- ➤ In the life of Jesus Christ, we see the glory of God.

- ➤ In studying the life of Jesus Christ, who reveals the New Covenant, we come to know the fullness of salvation.

5. Present the following material from article 12, "The Transmission of Divine Revelation," in the student book:

- ➤ Jesus Christ, the fullness of Divine Revelation, commanded the Apostles to tell all people and all nations what they had heard and seen regarding the salvation of God.

- ➤ This handing on, or transmission, of the truths that Jesus Christ taught is known as **Sacred Tradition** and will continue "under the inspiration of the Holy Spirit, to all generations until Christ returns in glory" (*CCC*, 96).

- ➤ Once the time had come to finish their work on this earth, the Apostles chose their successors, who are given the title bishop. To these successors the Apostles passed on the authority to teach and interpret the Scriptures and Tradition. This process is known as **Apostolic Succession.**

- ➤ These two pillars, the written, inspired Word of God and the living transmission of the Word of God, communicate effectively the whole of God's Revelation. Neither pillar can be understood without the other.

- ➤ The **Deposit of Faith** is the heritage of faith contained in Sacred Scripture and Sacred Tradition.

- ➤ The task of interpreting the Deposit of Faith is entrusted to the **Magisterium,** the living teaching office of the Church, made up of the Pope and all the bishops in communion with him, under the guidance of the Holy Spirit.

- ➤ The Magisterium, rooted in its teaching authority and moved by the Holy Spirit, defines the **dogma,** or doctrine, of faith.

6. Invite the students to ask questions about all they have just learned.

Step 5

Perceive

Explain what the students will look for in salvation history through exegesis.

Though salvation history resembles other studies of history, it is also uniquely interested in religious truth rather than other types of historical or scientific truth. Form criticism can help the students to identify the meaning the authors were trying to convey and so to read the selections appropriately.

1. Write all or some of the following examples on the board. Ask the students to tell you what information the examples provide.

> **Teacher Note**
> An answer is provided for you in italic. Do not write the answer initially. Add your own local or school words, abbreviations, and so on, to make this fun.

- 98407 *(ZIP code)*
- 77–65 *(the score of a game such as basketball)*
- 25–37 *(a range of pages in a book, such as "Read pages 25–37 for homework.")*
- 301-256-7821 *(phone number)*
- 50° *(temperature)*
- www. *(Internet address)*
- Mrs. *(woman's title)*
- jpg *(type of electronic file)*
- chrischristianson@ *(e-mail address)*
- 50% off *(sale)*
- 4.0 *(GPA)*
- S&P 500 *(financial Index)*
- NBC *(media network)*
- NHL *(hockey league)*
- CHA @ CLE 7:00 ET *(basketball game announcement: Charlotte Bobcats at Cleveland Cavaliers, 7:00 eastern time)*

Ask how the students know what each group of characters means. They should be able to say that the form of each group and its familiarity helped them to decide what the item meant.

2. Make the following points:

   ➤ We look for specific information contained in the form of the writing and by knowing the author's intent. Examples include Social Security numbers, obituaries, homilies, and student-parent handbooks. We do not look in an obituary for homework help. We do not try to learn about someone's death from a handbook.

➤ The Bible tells us about salvation history. It is not a history book, a scientific article, a novel, or a phone book. Because of the forms of literature in the Bible, we know not to look in it for historical or scientific truth, as if it wasn't Sacred Revelation about God. In this way salvation history is different from U.S. history or world history. The Bible focuses on God's action in saving us and on religious truth.

➤ We may not realize that we often think something can be true only if it falls into the categories of scientific truth or historical fact. If we are used to thinking this way, our biblical studies will challenge our assumptions.

Perceive

Step 6

Introduce why salvation history was necessary and how it began.

Have the students examine passages from the Book of Genesis that help them to define and establish a basic understanding of the initiating acts of salvation history.

1. Prepare by downloading and printing the handout "Why Is Salvation History Necessary?" (Document #: TX001106), one for each student. Have available sheets of newsprint, one for each of six small groups. Write the following on the board:

   • Briefly describe this event.

   • Who was involved?

   • How did God interact with humanity?

   • Why did God interact with humanity?

     As homework, you may want to assign student book articles 31 and 32, "Creation: In the Beginning" and "Sin and God's Response."

> **Teacher Note**
>
> The use of charts in steps 3 and 4 of this learning experience will allow the students to easily compare the groups' work. If you prefer to vary the learning experience, post six sheets of newsprint around the classroom, each headed by one of the scriptural passages from the chart on the handout.

2. Distribute the copies of the handout. During the next class period, divide the class into six small groups. Assign each group one of the following Scripture passages to read and present to the class:

   • Genesis 1:1—2:4 (the creation of the world)

   • Genesis 2:5–25 (the creation of humanity)

   • Genesis 3:1–24 (the Fall of humanity)

   • Genesis 4:1–16 (Cain and Abel)

   • Genesis 6:5–13 (introduction to the Flood)

   • Genesis 11:1–9 (the Tower of Babel)

3. Ask the students to read the assigned passages in their small groups and to fill in only the first two rows on the handout. Tell them they will fill out the last two rows at the end of class. Allow about 10 minutes for the groups to work. If the groups are working on charts using the newsprint, ask them to read the questions on the board, fill in their charts, and post them around the classroom.

4. As the students work, project the handout on the board.

5. When time is up, ask a representative from each group to present its information. Ask the rest of the students to fill in their charts or to take notes in their notebooks as each student presents. Invite the students to ask questions for clarification. After the presentations all the students should have the first three rows of the chart filled in.

6. After all six of the small groups have presented, ask the students to discuss the following questions in their groups:

- How did God interact with humanity?
- Why did God interact with humanity?

Remind the students to refer to their charts or notebooks and to consider how the order of the events might influence the answers to the questions. Allow about 5 minutes for this small-group discussion.

7. When time is up, call the students back into the large group. Discuss how and why God interacted with humanity in each passage. Write the best suggestions for each passage at the bottom of the projected chart and remind the students to write these notes down on their charts as well. They will be filling in the columns for all the Bible passages, not just their own.

8. Remind the students that although salvation history is history, it is a history of God's interaction with human beings. It records religious truth rather than historical truth.

Teacher Note

This learning experience intentionally parallels the previous one to connect the cross-curricular skills needed for interpreting and understanding the Scriptures.

Step 7

Perceive

Introduce original blessing and Original Sin.

The first eleven chapters of Genesis contain important principles. The Book of Genesis explains why we humans need salvation and how God still cares for us even after we sin. Although unit 4 focuses on the leaders from the Books of Genesis and Exodus, it does not provide an overview of this first book of the Bible. Consider using the PowerPoint "Introduction to the Book of Genesis" (Document #: TX001074) at *smp.org/LivinginChrist*. It can supplement your presentation and review of the background article "The Book of Genesis" (Document #: TX001025) for your own enrichment. Before presenting each section of the PowerPoint, ask one or two students to read the relevant passages aloud to the class.

1. Prepare by gathering equipment to present the PowerPoint. Because there are several stories to cover, you may want to pick and choose stories to cover or break up the stories in some way. The following material is a brief overview of Genesis.

   ➤ The Book of Genesis is not meant to be read as a detailed, chronological account of history but rather as an account steeped in truth and meaning.

   ➤ Genesis, chapters 1–11, contain stories known as **primeval history.** The term refers to the time period before the invention of writing and recording of historical data.

   ➤ Genesis, along with the other four books in the Pentateuch:

      • illustrates God as the source of all creation

      • explains the role of humans in the origin of sin and its many devastating effects

      • shows God's desire to be in communion with people

      • emphasizes the lasting effect of the Covenant God formed with Abraham

2. Continue by focusing on the theology and truths found in the Creation stories. Ask a student to read aloud Genesis 1:1—2:4. The following material is from student book article 31, "Creation: In the Beginning":

   ➤ The Father, Son, and Holy Spirit (the Trinity) were intimately involved in creation, but "the work of creation is attributed to the Father in particular" (*CCC,* 316).

   ➤ "God alone created the universe freely, directly, and without any help" (317).

   ➤ Creation illuminates the holiness and goodness of all that was created. This is especially visible in human beings, who were formed "in his image" (Genesis 1:27).

   ➤ The glory of God lies within each of these creations. Sometimes God's glory is visible and other times it is invisible.

   You may want to emphasize some of the following implications of the Creation stories:

   ➤ We are God's holy and good creation, even when we do not feel like it.

   ➤ All creation bears the mark of God. God is present in our world. There is no place God cannot be, even in difficult times or times of great mistakes. We are never completely alone.

   ➤ All creation is the good work of God. When people disrespect God's creation, they also disrespect God.

3. Ask one or two students to read aloud Genesis 2:5—3:24, about Creation and the Fall of humanity. Make the following points:

   ➤ God made the first person from the earth and breathed life into him (see Genesis 2:7).

   ➤ God "took the man and settled him in the garden of Eden, to cultivate and care for it" (Genesis 2:15).

   ➤ God created woman from man, and the man said, "This one . . . is bone of my bones / and flesh of my flesh" (Genesis 2:23).

   ➤ God "gave man this order: 'You are free to eat from any of the trees of the garden except the tree of knowledge of good and bad. From that tree you shall not eat; the moment you eat from it you are surely doomed to die'" (Genesis 2:16–17).

   You may want to emphasize the following implications of the Creation stories:

   ➤ The Creation stories teach us that free will is essential to being human.

   ➤ They also show us what God had originally planned for us before we sinned. God wanted us to be close and live in paradise but did not want to force our choice.

4. After learning about what God wanted for humanity, ask a student to read aloud Genesis 3:1–24, about the Fall of humanity, to look at the basis for salvation history. Make the following points:

   ➤ The serpent tempts: "You certainly will not die! No, God knows well that the moment you eat of it your eyes will be opened and you will be like gods who know what is good and what is bad" (Genesis 3:4–5).

   ➤ We were created to live according to God's laws. In other words, we are created to be in right relationship with God and others.

   ➤ God gave man and woman all they needed, including life itself. Their disobedience to God's one rule disrespected their Creator and showed a desire to be equal to him.

   The following material is based on student book article 32, "Sin and God's Response":

   ➤ Missing the mark, falling short, brokenness, wrongdoing, misdeed, an offense against truth: these are all ways of describing the reality of sin.

   ➤ Sin is any deliberate offense, in thought, word, or deed, against the will of God.

   ➤ We were created to live in right relationship with God.

   ➤ The choice to give in to the Devil's temptation and disobey God marks the first sin in salvation history. Adam and Eve's sin is called Original Sin and is often referred to as "the Fall."

➤ By Original Sin the first humans disobeyed God and thereby lost their original holiness and became subject to death.

➤ The term *Original Sin* comes from the Latin *origo,* meaning "beginning" or "birth." The term has two meanings: (1) the sin of the first human beings, who disobeyed God's command by choosing to follow their own will and thus lost their original holiness and become subject to death, (2) the fallen state of human nature that affects every person born into the world.

➤ Original Sin also describes the *"fallen state"*[1] (*CCC,* 404) in which all the descendants of Adam and Eve, with the exception of Jesus and his mother, Mary, are deprived of original holiness and justice.

➤ There are two kinds of sins: venial and mortal.

  • Sin is considered venial when it is less serious and reparable by charity.

  • Mortal sin is a serious transgression of a person's relationship with God and neighbors. It hinders an individual's potential for love and eternal life.

➤ Before there was sin, humans were comfortable with themselves, close to God, each other, and nature. After sin, humans realized they were naked, were further from God and each other, and had an adversarial role with nature. Sin works the same way today.

➤ Despite humanity's sin and Fall, God still "promised them salvation (cf. *Genesis* 3:15) and offered them his covenant" (*CCC,* 70). God punishes his children justly but continues to love and protect them.

➤ According to Saint John of God (1495–1550), patron saint of hospitals and the sick, "Just as water extinguishes fire, so love wipes away sin."

➤ God's love, as revealed in Jesus Christ, is the only way to end the cycle of sin and evil. Jesus Christ redeemed humanity and broke the bonds of Original Sin.

5. Continue your reading in Genesis, chapters 4–16, asking the students to observe the qualities of sin that the story of Cain and Abel reveals. Include the following points during the reading:

  • The effects of Original Sin continue into the story of Cain and Abel.

  • Eve recognizes God's blessing in Cain's birth (see Genesis 4:1).

  • God warns Cain against resentment and anger (see 4:6–7).

  • Cain kills Abel despite God's warning (see 4:8).

  • Cain lies to God (see 4:9).

  • Cain is banned from farming, paralleling Adam and Eve's banishment from the Garden (see 4:12–14).

- God neither kills Cain himself nor allows others to kill him—revenge would be the same sin Cain committed.

6. If you worked with the Flood story in unit 1, please skip the following section. Otherwise ask your students to notice the qualities of Noah, who is a good man in a sinful world. Include the following material, based on student book article 32, "Sin and God's Response," in your discussion:

   ➤ In the story of Noah and the Flood (see Genesis, chapters 6–9), human beings fall prey to the sinful and evil ways.

   ➤ Following the Flood a rainbow appears as a sign of God's Covenant with Noah and all living beings. God's Covenant with Noah is an "everlasting covenant" that "will remain in force as long as the world lasts" (*CCC*, 71).

   ➤ The Covenant God forms with Noah foreshadows God's Covenant with Abraham.

   ➤ Like Adam, Eve, and Cain, humanity has fallen away from the divine image in which it was created.

   ➤ God chooses Noah to escape the Flood because of his obedience to God's law and his respect for creation.

7. Unfortunately the Tower of Babel is a story without a happy ending. Ask your students to discern why they think God did not like the tower the people were building. Include the following points, which are based on student book article 32, "Sin and God's Response":

   ➤ In the account of the Tower of Babel (see Genesis 11:1–9), power-hungry people attempt to build a tower that will reach the heavens.

   ➤ Longing to be like God, lured by the hope to be famous, and forgetting about their covenantal relationship with God, nothing will stop the people from building a self-serving tower of greed—nothing except the hand of God.

   ➤ God stops the people from building the tower by confusing their speech, making it impossible for them to communicate and effectively carry out their plan.

8. Conclude by asking the students to identify important teachings that come from Genesis, chapters 1–11. If they miss any of the following points, include them or others you think are significant:

   - God created the earth and humanity as good.
   - The history of our interactions with God began with God's initiative in the Creation.
   - Disobedience caused Original Sin, leading to humanity's Fall.
   - Disrespect for humanity and life is disrespect for God, the Creator, as shown, for example, in the story of Cain and Abel.

- God respects those who respect his creation and law (rules), as shown, for example, in the story of Noah.
- God desires to be in relationship with humanity, as shown, for example, by the stories of Adam and Eve and Noah.
- These stories are the opening moments of salvation history and the reason for it.
- God did not abandon humanity at the Fall. Instead salvation history began at this point to help humanity return to a committed relationship with God.
- Salvation history records humanity's relationship with God through a series of promises, or covenants, in which both God and humanity have responsibilities.

Apply

Step 8

Do a sprint through salvation history.

Present the major events of salvation history. This learning experience may require two or three class periods to complete.

1. Prepare by downloading and printing the handouts "Sprint Through Salvation History" (Document #: TX001107) and "Sprint Through Salvation History: Scriptural Passages" (Document #: TX001108), one for each student. Reserve a computer lab or library with Internet access for at least one day during this learning experience. The students' research of an assigned segment of salvation history will build on the skills they learned in units 1 and 2 about evaluating reliable material online, locating scriptural study aids, and citing their research. You might choose to have the students read the handout "Sprint Through Salvation History" (Document #: TX001107) as homework. If so, distribute copies of the handout before the next class period.

2. At the next class period, tell the students they will be placed in small groups. Each group will share with the class the following information about their assigned segment. Each group will present a 2-minute visual accompaniment—pictures, a PowerPoint presentation, or another visual medium—and hand in a one- to one-and-a-half-page written report. The presentation will answer the following questions:

- Where did you find information about your scriptural time period (cite three passages)?
- When did the events take place?
- What major events occurred?
- Did the story take place in a time or place when something significant was happening? What was the situation in which these events occurred?

- Who was involved?
- Where did this occur?
- What was God doing?

3. Place the students into small groups of no more than four and assign each small group one segment of salvation history as follows:
   - The Founders and the Promise
   - The Exodus of the Israelites and the Covenant
   - Taking Over the Promised Land
   - The Nation and the Temple
   - The Kings and the Prophets
   - The Babylonian Exile and the Jewish Dispersion
   - More Oppressors
   - Jesus, the Savior

4. Distribute the copies of the handout "Sprint Through Salvation History" (Document #: TX001107). Have the small groups complete the handout at the start of class. (If you assigned the handout as homework, allow 3 to 5 minutes before class starts for the students to review their notes.)

5. Distribute the copies of the handout "Sprint Through Salvation History: Scriptural Passages" (Document #: TX001108). Allow 10 to 15 minutes for the students to read and take notes as directed on the handout. The students should look up at least three major scriptural passages that explain or describe their assigned segments of salvation history, as well as using other reliable Internet and other research sources to draw historical information.

6. The small groups will present their projects in chronological order (that is, the students whose events took place first in the Bible will present first). The students who are not presenting should take careful notes in their notebooks. At the end of each presentation, allow a few minutes for the class to ask questions for clarification. Remind the students to fill in their handouts with the major scriptural passages each group highlights in its presentation.

7. After each small group finishes presenting, discuss any common characteristics the people or God display in the stories and ask if there were any other trends.

8. Collect the reports and handouts to be graded and returned. Let the students know that this learning experience provides an outline for the rest of the course.

Step 9

Give a quiz to assess student understanding.

1. Prepare by downloading and printing the handout "Unit 3 Quiz" (Document #: TX001109), one for each student. Note that the quiz is fairly comprehensive, in part because both you and the students want to learn what they do not now know in preparation for a test or the final performance tasks.

2. On the day of the quiz, provide 5 to 10 minutes for the students to review their books and notes. Distribute the quiz and provide sufficient time for the students to work on it. If time remains when the students are done, collect the quizzes and then redistribute them so everyone has someone else's. Go through the quiz, allowing the students to correct one another's work and also giving them an opportunity to affirm or change their understanding of concepts. Collect the quizzes and further your analysis about topics that may need more coverage.

> **Teacher Note**
>
> To save paper, use the electronic copy of the quiz from *smp.org/LivinginChrist* and put it up in a visual place via projector, overhead, monitor, and so on. If these options are unavailable, read the quiz to the students slowly. In both cases, have the students record their answers on loose-leaf paper.
>
> To save time, ask the students to choose two of the ten Bible passages.

Step 10

Brainstorm the relationship between Judaism and Christianity.

Discuss the connections between Judaism and Christianity to provide a period of reflection following the quiz. Use it as a starting point to examine the relationship between Judaism and Christianity in salvation history. Briefly introduce the concept of covenant, which will be further explored in the following units.

1. Prepare by reminding the students that they will need their Bibles.

2. At the next class period, return the students' graded quizzes from step 9. Allow 3 to 5 minutes for the students to look over their work.

3. Ask the students to silently read Genesis 12:1–7, which is about Abraham's call.

4. Invite one of the students to read the passage aloud.

5. Ask the following question: "What theme is introduced in this passage about Abraham that continues throughout salvation history?"

> **Teacher Note**
>
> This passage is the essential starting point for understanding God's call to follow him as traced through salvation history into the Gospels, which mark the separation point of Christianity from Judaism.

If the students have trouble identifying the theme, ask them to look at the scriptural passages on their quizzes and think about how these reflect the theme. The students should identify and revisit the concept of vocation from unit 2 in the passage on Abraham's call and see how salvation history includes events in which individuals and groups are called to listen to God or act on his behalf. Some of the quiz passages illustrate the countertheme of failure to listen to the call—an equally important recognition.

6. After discussing how a few passages illustrate the theme of being called, ask the students: "Why would generations of people respond to this call?" Brainstorm for a few minutes.

7. Write the word *covenant* on the board or overhead. Then discuss as follows:

    ➤ *Covenant* refers to a solemn agreement between human beings or between God and a human being in which mutual commitments are made.

    ➤ A covenant is like a promise between two people or groups.

    ➤ Every relationship has responsibilities for those involved.

    ➤ When those involved do not uphold their responsibilities, consequences usually follow. Consider a friendship. If you always help out your friend, but the friend does not help you in return, the friendship will likely not last long.

8. Ask the following questions about the handout "Sprint Through Salvation History" (Document #: TX001107) (from step 8). Write the student responses on the board.

    ➤ What are some examples of positive interactions between God and humanity? What makes them positive?

    ➤ What are some examples of negative interactions between God and humanity? What makes them negative?

    ➤ These positive and negative examples from salvation history illustrate times when humanity honored or neglected its promise, or covenant, with God.

    ➤ Both Jews and Christians recognize four major covenantal events in salvation history.

    Ask the students to suggest the ones they know.

    • The first Covenant was the one God made with Noah to never again destroy the earth with a flood (see Genesis 9:1–17). God promised he would never abandon humanity.

    • The second Covenant God made was with Abraham and his wife, Sarah (or Abram and Sarai, as they were known at that point). In this important Covenant, God promised to give them descendants who would become a great nation (see Genesis 12:1–3, 15:1–21).

This Covenant was to be marked by the circumcision of all male descendants of Abraham and Sarah.

- At Mount Sinai God renewed the Covenant with Abraham's descendants, giving the Ten Commandments. The Sinai Covenant established the Israelite people as God's Chosen People (see Exodus, chapters 19–20). A system of laws and rituals of sacrifice was the outward sign of the Sinai Covenant.
- Again God renewed the Sinai Covenant with King David and affirmed the promise that the House of David would stand forever (see 2 Samuel 7:8–17).

➤ The New Covenant was made with humanity through Jesus Christ and is recorded in the Bible as the New Testament. The Christian Bible is divided into two testaments, one that records God's covenant relationship with the people of Israel and one that records the promises of Jesus Christ to all humanity.

9. For about 5 minutes, brainstorm the following question: "How do we participate in these covenants today?" Ask the students for examples and write them on the board. If the students do not provide the following answers or other ways you would like to emphasize, add them:

- One important way both Jews and Christians celebrate their covenant relationship with God is through rituals, holidays, and festivals.
- Rituals and festivals are ways to remember and celebrate major events of salvation history.
- In addition, there are significant connections between Jewish rituals and festivals and Christian rituals and festivals, because we share part of the same history and because Jesus and many early followers were Jewish.

Teacher Note

These connections will be the focus of the optional learning experience. Encourage the students to keep their notes from this step for reference during the information quest.

Apply

Optional Learning Experience

Direct an information quest.

See *smp.org/LivinginChrist* for a Web link with information about Jewish holidays. Help the students to identify the links between Jewish practice and salvation history by examining the festivals of Passover and Shavuot. Assign the students to write a reflection on how these holidays illustrate the Israelites' and Jews' commitment to the Old Covenant and how Christians have understood and transformed the meanings of these holidays in light of the New Covenant.

Step 11

Use a stations exercise to assess student understanding.

This learning experience provides the students with the opportunity to help one another to understand the material, as well as to identify where clarification or further study is needed.

1. Prepare by creating five different lists of four vocabulary terms each (a total of twenty different terms), including people, places, events, and terms from this unit that will help the students to review for the final performance tasks. Make five copies of each list. Under each term, write the following:

    1. Define the term.
    2. Make connections between this term and the other terms.
    3. Identify the term in the context of salvation history.

    To further prepare, organize the classroom into five stations. At the center of every station, place a folder containing the five prepared word lists. The students will share these lists with their group members. (See *smp.org/LivinginChrist* for the sample handout "Check Your Understanding" [Document #: TX001040].) Make copies of another list that includes all twenty terms, one for each student. You will distribute this list at the end of the learning experience for the students to fill out during the class discussion.

2. On the day of the learning experience, place the students into five small groups and assign each group to one of the stations. Allow 5 minutes for the groups to fill out one sheet at the group's first station. As the students work, write the vocabulary words on the board as you have grouped them for the stations.

3. When time is up, rotate the small groups. They should bring the sheet from each station with them as they move. Allow 5 minutes for the groups to fill out a sheet at each station.

4. After the groups have visited every station, call the students back into the large group. One student from each small group will keep its group's paper and act as the group's reporter.

5. Distribute the master list of twenty terms and invite the students to discuss how they defined the words, made connections between the words, and identified the role of the words in the context of salvation history. Encourage the students to fill in the master terms list during the discussion.

Step 12

Now that the students are closer to the end of the unit, make sure they are all on track with their final performance tasks, if you have assigned them.

If possible, devote 50 to 60 minutes for the students to ask questions about the tasks and to work individually.

1. Remind the students to bring to class any work they have already prepared so that they can work on it during the class period. If necessary, reserve the library or media center so the students can do any book or online research. Download and print extra copies of the handouts "Final Performance Task Options for Unit 3" (Document #: TX001101) and "Rubric for Final Performance Tasks for Unit 3" (Document #: TX001102). Review the final performance task options, answer questions, and ask the students to choose one if they have not already done so.

2. Provide some class time for the students to work on their performance tasks. This then allows you to work with the students who need additional guidance with the project.

Step 13

Provide the students with a tool to use for reflecting about what they learned in the unit and how they learned.

This learning experience provides the students with an excellent opportunity to reflect on how their understandings of Revelation have developed throughout the unit.

1. Prepare by downloading and printing the handout "Learning about Learning" (Document #: TX001159; see Appendix), one for each student.

2. Distribute the handout, and give the students about 15 minutes to answer the questions quietly. Invite them to share any reflections they have about the content they learned as well as their insights into the way they learned.

Final Performance Task Options for Unit 3

The following are the main ideas you are to understand from this unit. They should appear in this final performance task so your teacher can assess whether you learned the most essential content:

- Salvation history is the pattern of specific events in human history in which God clearly reveals his presence and saving actions. In one sense we can say that all human history is salvation history. By this we mean that the one true God—Father, Son, and Holy Spirit—has been present and active in the lives of his People since the beginning of time.

- Salvation history began with humanity's first sin and ended in the Resurrection of Jesus Christ.

- Original Sin led to the loss of original holiness, made humans subject to death, and made sin universally present in the world. This universally present sin led to further sin among God's People. The sins of his People resulted in broken communities and families and in separation from God, one another, the natural world, and even themselves. Christ's saving Death and Resurrection gave human beings the grace to be in communion with God.

- Although human beings may have turned from their relationship with God during salvation history, God always remains faithful to them.

Option 1: "My History," a Creative Writing Performance Task with Biblical Exegesis

Read the following writing prompts. You will create at least a two-page personal reflection and exegesis that will illustrate the connection between an event or a time in your life during which you felt God's presence and a similar event in salvation history.

- Begin by thinking about an important time in your life, perhaps a challenge, when God called you or you felt his presence.

- Take some notes. When was this event? What were you doing or experiencing at the time? How did you feel God's presence or call? Did you understand it at the time? Were others involved?

- Next look back through your class notes (especially the handout "Sprint Through Salvation History" [Document #: TX001107]) to find a period of salvation history that illustrates a similar situation. (If you need some help with this, consult an older relative or your teacher.)

- Now look through your Bible to find two or three passages about that similar situation.

- Read over the passages a few times and take notes. Ask a few questions about them from the unit 1 handout "Biblical Exegesis Chart" (Document #: TX001090). Use biblical tools such as a concordance, biblical dictionary, or commentary to explore these questions and write down your observations. (This will be the exegesis portion of your reflection.) Be sure to include appropriate citations for your sources.

- Reflect on the similarities and differences between the events from salvation history and your experience.

© 2010 by Saint Mary's Press
Living in Christ Series

Document #: TX001101

- Write about your experience. In your reflection include the passages, either fully or partially, to make a direct connection between your life and the passages.

- After you have written your reflection, proofread it for spelling, grammar, and punctuation errors. Write your name at the top of the first page.

- Create a visual accompaniment with your reflection—a collage, a scene, or another visual representation of the connection you have just written about. (It will be displayed for others to view.)

- Turn in the completed, proofread reflection and visual accompaniment.

Option 2: Commemorating Key Moments in Salvation History by Researching a Jewish Ritual, Festival, or Holiday

- Choose a Jewish ritual, festival, or holiday to research. Check your selection with your teacher. You will identify the historical basis and the contemporary observance of the ritual, festival, or holiday.

- Next, look through your Bible to find information about your chosen ritual, festival, or holiday.

- Begin your research. You may use biblical resources such as a concordance, commentary, or Bible dictionary or any other reliable source from the Internet. Be sure to include appropriate citations for your sources.

- Find at least three scriptural passages that explain or provide a context for the ritual, festival, or holiday. Ask: "At the beginning of the story, are the people close to or far from God? By the end of the story, has their relationship with God changed? How do the people act? How does God act? How does the celebration today celebrate God's saving presence?"

- When you have adequately researched, write a two- to three-page report on your ritual, festival, or holiday. Explain the historical roots and the scriptural passages that refer to the festivity, or provide a context for it and explain the role the festivity played in Jewish life in biblical times, in salvation history, and today.

- After you have written your report, proofread it for spelling, grammar, and punctuation errors.

- Create a 2-minute presentation about your festivity with a visual medium such as PowerPoint, poster board, a skit, a song, and so on.

- You will present your findings to the class, after which the other students will be allowed to ask clarification questions, so be sure to review your report!

© 2010 by Saint Mary's Press
Living in Christ Series

Document #: TX001101

Rubric for Final Performance Tasks for Unit 3

Criteria	4	3	2	1
Assignment includes all items requested in the instructions.	Assignment not only includes all items requested but they are completed above expectations.	Assignment includes all items requested.	Assignment includes over half of the items requested.	Assignment includes less than half of the items requested.
Assignment shows real connections between the biblical stories and events of today.	Assignment shows exceptional connections between the biblical stories and events of today.	Assignment shows real connections between the biblical stories and events of today.	Assignment shows some real connection between the biblical stories and events of today.	Assignment shows little connection between the biblical stories and events of today.
Assignment shows understanding of the concept *salvation history is the pattern of specific events in human history in which God clearly reveals his presence and saving actions. In one sense we can say that all human history is salvation history. By this we mean that the one true God—Father, Son, and Holy Spirit—has been present and active in the lives of his People since the beginning of time.*	Assignment shows unusually insightful understanding of this concept.	Assignment shows good understanding of this concept.	Assignment shows adequate understanding of this concept.	Assignment shows little understanding of this concept.
Assignment shows understanding of the concept *salvation history began with humanity's first sin and ended in the Resurrection of Jesus Christ.*	Assignment shows unusually insightful understanding of this concept.	Assignment shows good understanding of this concept.	Assignment shows adequate understanding of this concept.	Assignment shows little understanding of this concept.

Document #: TX001102

Assignment shows understanding of the concept *Original Sin led to the loss of original holiness, made humans subject to death, and made sin universally present in the world. This universally present sin led to further sin among God's People. The sins of his People resulted in broken communities and families and in separation from God, one another, the natural world, and even themselves. Christ's saving Death and Resurrection gave human beings the grace to be in communion with God.*	Assignment shows unusually insightful understanding of this concept.	Assignment shows good understanding of this concept.	Assignment shows adequate understanding of this concept.	Assignment shows little understanding of this concept.
Assignment shows understanding of the concept *although human beings may have turned from their relationship with God during salvation history, God always remains faithful to them.*	Assignment shows unusually insightful understanding of this concept.	Assignment shows good understanding of this concept.	Assignment shows adequate understanding of this concept.	Assignment shows little understanding of this concept.
Assignment uses proper grammar and spelling.	Assignment has no grammar or spelling errors.	Assignment has one grammar or spelling error.	Assignment has two grammar or spelling errors.	Assignment has more than two grammar or spelling errors.
Assignment properly cites both biblical passages and other outside sources.	Assignment perfectly cites both biblical passages and other outside sources.	Assignment properly cites both biblical passages and other outside sources.	Assignment properly cites some biblical passages and other outside sources.	Assignment properly cites few biblical passages and other outside sources.
The element of the assignment that is for the class is done neatly and creatively.	The element of the assignment that is for the class is done in an unusually neat or creative way.	The element of the assignment that is for the class is done neatly and creatively.	The element of the assignment that is for the class is done somewhat neatly and creatively.	The element of the assignment that is for the class is not done neatly and creatively.

Vocabulary for Unit 3

Apostolic Succession: The uninterrupted passing on of apostolic preaching and authority from the Apostles directly to all bishops. It is accomplished through the laying on of hands when a bishop is ordained in the Sacrament of Holy Orders. The office of bishop is permanent, because at ordination a bishop is marked with an indelible, sacred character.

covenant: A solemn agreement between human beings or between God and a human being in which mutual commitments are made.

creed: A short summary statement or profession of faith. The Nicene and Apostles' Creeds are the Church's most familiar and important creeds.

Deposit of Faith: The heritage of faith contained in the Sacred Scriptures and Tradition. It has been passed on from the time of the Apostles. The Magisterium takes from it all that it teaches as revealed truth.

Divine Revelation: God's self-communication through which he makes known the mystery of his divine plan. Divine Revelation is a gift accomplished by the Father, Son, and Holy Spirit through the words and deeds of salvation history. It is most fully realized in the Passion, death, Resurrection, and Ascension of Jesus Christ.

dogma: Teachings recognized as central to Church teaching, defined by the Magisterium and accorded the fullest weight and authority.

Logos: A Greek word meaning "word," used to refer to the Second Person of the Trinity, Jesus Christ.

Magisterium: The Church's living teaching office, which consists of all bishops, in communion with the Pope.

mortal sin: A serious transgression of a person's relationship with God and neighbors. Mortal sin hinders an individual's potential for love and eternal life.

Original Sin: From the Latin *origo,* meaning "beginning" or "birth." The term has two meanings: (1) the sin of the first human beings, who disobeyed God's command by choosing to follow their own will and thus lost their original holiness and became subject to death, (2) the fallen state of human nature that affects every person born into the world.

patriarch: The father or leader of a tribe, clan, or tradition. Abraham, Isaac, and Jacob were patriarchs of the Israelite people.

primeval history: The time period before the invention of writing and recording of historical data.

prophet: A person God chooses to speak his message of salvation. In the Bible, primarily a communicator of a divine message of repentance to the Chosen People, not necessarily a person who predicted the future.

Sacred Tradition: From the Latin *tradere,* meaning "to hand on." Refers to the process of passing on the Gospel message. It began with the oral communication of the Gospel by the Apostles, was written down in the Scriptures, and is interpreted by the Magisterium under the guidance of the Holy Spirit.

salvation history: The pattern of specific events in human history in which God clearly reveals his presence and saving actions. Salvation was accomplished once and for all through Jesus Christ, a truth foreshadowed and revealed throughout the Old Testament.

sin: Any deliberate offense, in thought, word, or deed, against the will of God.

theophany: God's manifestation of himself in a visible form to enrich human understanding of him. An example is God's appearance to Moses in the form of a burning bush.

Trinity: From the Latin *trinus,* meaning "threefold," referring to the central mystery of the Christian faith that God exists as a communion of three distinct and interrelated divine Persons: Father, Son, and Holy Spirit. The doctrine of the Trinity is a mystery that is inaccessible to human reason alone and is known through Divine Revelation only.

venial sin: Sin that is less serious and reparable by charity.

wisdom literature: The Old Testament Books of Proverbs, Job, Ecclesiastes, Sirach, and Wisdom.

Why Do We Study History?

A Cross-Curriculum Activity Worksheet

Name: _____

Below are listed three major American historical documents with important lessons. For each prompt or question in the left-hand column, provide a short response in the spaces provided.

	Declaration of Independence	*Gettysburg Address*	Martin Luther King Jr.'s "I Have a Dream" Speech
Briefly summarize this document.			
Who wrote it?			
When was it written? (Describe the historical events it spoke of.)			
What effect did it have at the time it was written?			
How can we apply this lesson today?			

Reading Notes and Questions for Student Book Articles 9–12

Name: _____

This handout is meant to aid you as you read through the following articles in your student book. Various phrases mean different things. "Look" means you should find the answer to a question or fill in blanks from your text. "Know" means you are reading a summary statement that should help you understand difficult concepts. "Research" means you should consult a source outside your student book.

Article 9: "Salvation History: God's Revelation"

This article introduces some new terms and concepts. There are two main points in bold.

Know: God saves us through human history.

Look: What is the heart of salvation history?

Look: What adverb is used to describe the "speed" at which Divine Revelation occurred?

Know: Through salvation history God invites us into communion with the blessed Trinity.

Research: Look up the meaning of the word *communion* and write it down.

Know: The word *Trinity* comes from the Latin *trinus,* meaning "threefold," referring to the central mystery of the Christian faith that God exists as a communion of three distinct and interrelated divine Persons: Father, Son, and Holy Spirit. The doctrine of the Trinity is a mystery that is inaccessible to human reason alone and is known through Divine Revelation only.

Know: God invites us to be in relationship with him in a way that is like the way the Father, Son, and Holy Spirit relate to one another. (It is okay if you have questions about this, because it is a mystery.)

Look: Where can people gain answers to the questions they ask about the meaning and purpose of life?

Look: God, who "remains a _____ beyond words" (*CCC*, 230), _____our hearts and minds so there is immeasurable space for divine _____ and _____. We can never fully _____God. Human words and language can never capture the magnificence of our transcendent God.

Look: What is prayer?

Look: What is Revelation?

© 2010 by Saint Mary's Press
Living in Christ Series

Document #: TX001105

Article 10: "Salvation History in the Old Testament"

Know: Salvation history, as written about in the Scriptures, is an unfolding story of God's love.

Know: God remains faithful to the Covenant even when the people of Israel do not.

Look: What did God want for our first parents, symbolically called Adam and Eve?

Look: How was God faithful to his People even when Adam and Eve turned away from him in sin?

Look: What are three effects of Original Sin?

Look: True or false: Sin spreads.

Look: What do the instructions and rainbow that appear at the end of the Flood symbolize?

Look: To whom did God appear in a vision and promise him descendants more numerous than the stars?

Look: What are the names of three patriarchs mentioned in the article?

Research: What does the word *liberator* mean?

Research: What does the word *propensity* mean?

Look: True or false: The prophets announce redemption, purification, and salvation.

Look: Name one book from wisdom literature.

Article 11: "Jesus Christ: The Fullness of All Revelation"

Know: Jesus Christ fully reveals God to us.

Know: The Gospel of John uses the Greek word *Logos,* or *Word,* for Jesus Christ.

Know: Because the Word (Jesus Christ) is God, we read about the Word in the Old Testament even before he became human as described in the New Testament.

Know: In the life of Jesus Christ, we see the glory of God.

Look: How do we know God's saving plan?

Look: True or false: We can fully understand this plan.

Look: Who can free us from all that enslaves us and takes away our freedom?

Document #: TX001105

Article 12: "The Transmission of Divine Revelation"

Know: Jesus Christ, the fullness of Divine Revelation, commanded and entrusted the Apostles to tell all people and all nations what they had heard and seen regarding the salvation of God.

Look: The handing on, or transmission, of the truths of Jesus Christ taught is known as _____ and will continue "under the inspiration of the Holy Spirit, to all _____ until Christ _____ in glory" (*CCC*, 96).

Look: True or false: The Apostles gave the authority to teach and interpret the Scriptures and Tradition to the bishops.

Look: What are three ways the Church transmits or passes on all that she is and what she believes (see *CCC*, 78)?

Look: Through whom does God continue to talk with men and women?

Look: Who is the "Word made flesh"?

Look: What are two nouns that describe the Holy Spirit?

Research: What is the meaning of the noun *Advocate?*

Look: What two "pillars" communicate effectively the whole of God's Revelation?

Look: True or false: These two "pillars" are equal to each other.

Look: The Deposit of Faith unites all the _____.

Look: The Magisterium of the Church includes the _____ in communion with the _____.

Look: Because they are _____, _____ charges the Pope and bishops with the _____ interpretation and teaching of all that has been handed down. The Magisterium, rooted in its _____ and moved by the _____, defines the _____ teachings of the Catholic Church, known as _____.

Look: True or false: By nature of our Baptism, we are all called to treasure our faith as a priceless gem.

Look: True or false: Mary played a significant role in salvation.

Document #: TX001105

Why Is Salvation History Necessary?   Name: _____

In your group look up your assigned passages and fill in the chart for your section only. You will fill in the rest of the chart during class discussion. Keep this chart for reference for the final performance task.

	The Creation of the World: Genesis 1:1—2:4	The Creation of Humanity: Genesis 2:5–25	The Fall of Humanity: Genesis 3:1–24	Cain and Abel: Genesis 4:1–16	Introduction to the Flood: Genesis 6:5–13	The Tower of Babel: Genesis 11:1–9
Briefly describe this event.						
Who was involved?						
How did God interact with humanity?						
Why did God interact with humanity?						

Document #: TX001106

Sprint Through Salvation History

The God revealed in the Old Testament is not aloof or distant from human affairs; this God acts within human history. Salvation History is the pattern of events in human history that exemplify God's presence and saving actions. In Catholic thought *all* of history is salvation history, even though God's presence may not be recognized.

It will help to keep the big picture of that history in mind as we set out to discover the meaning of the Old Testament, because the history and the Scriptures of ancient Israel were intertwined. Do not be concerned about memorizing names and events at this point; they will come up again in this course. Instead simply try to recognize the broad pattern of history.

About 3000 BC, history as we know it began, with the development of early forms of writing. The biblical period—from the beginnings of Israel as a people through the time of Jesus and the earliest years of the Church—went from about 1850 BC until about AD 100. It lasted almost two thousand years. That is about the same amount of time as has elapsed from the time of Jesus until today.

What follows is a brief overview of the events of the biblical period.

The Founders and the Promise

The history and the religion of the Israelites began with Abraham. Abraham was a wandering herdsman, or nomad, who lived in the region now called Iraq, around 1850 (BC). According to the Book of Genesis, God made an agreement with Abraham. God promised to make Abraham's descendants a blessing to the world and to give them the land of Canaan, later known as Palestine. The Promise, as this is called, was that Abraham's descendants would reveal the one God to the world. Christians believe this Promise reached its fulfillment in the coming of Christ.

Abraham's descendants and their families inherited the Promise. Abraham, his son Isaac, and his grandson Jacob would be called the patriarchs, or founders, of the Jewish faith. Their wives—Sarah, Rebekah, and Rachel—would be called the matriarchs.

The Exodus of the Israelites and the Covenant

At the close of the Book of Genesis, the descendants of Abraham are living in Egypt, having traveled there from Canaan in order to survive a famine. Yet as the Book of Exodus opens, we find them enslaved by the Egyptians. Practically nothing is known about the Israelites in Egypt from about 1700 to 1290 (BC).

Moses, the main character in the story of the Exodus, was one of the greatest religious leaders in history. About 1290 (BC), the understanding that one God was above all other gods came to Moses when God revealed God's name—Yahweh, meaning "I am the One who is always present." With God's power the Israelites, led by Moses, made a daring escape from Pharaoh's army through the sea—the Exodus— and were thus freed from slavery.

After a dramatic encounter between Moses and God on Mount Sinai, a covenant, or agreement, between Yahweh and the Israelites was confirmed. The Israelites' part of the Covenant was to keep the Ten Commandments, which God had presented to Moses. God's part was to make the Israelites "the People of God" and to be with them as long as they kept the Covenant. Once again God promised that they would be given the land of Canaan. But before they entered Canaan, they wandered for forty years in the desert as they learned to trust God's care for them.

Document #: TX001107

Taking Over the Promised Land

After Moses' time the Israelites, led by Joshua, entered Canaan. Over the next centuries—from about 1250 to 1000 (BC)—they fought against the people who lived in that region. In these battles the Israelites were led by military leaders called judges. During this time the Israelites abandoned their nomadic ways for the more settled agricultural life that was native to the region.

The Nation and the Temple

Around 1000 (BC) Israel became recognized as a nation, with David as its anointed king and Jerusalem as its capital city. God made a promise to David that his royal line would endure forever. (Later Jews put their hopes in a descendant of David to save them from oppression.)

David's son Solomon built the Temple in Jerusalem, and it became the principal place of worship for the nation. As both a political and a religious capital, Jerusalem became a great and holy city.

The Kings and the Prophets

After Solomon's death in 922 (BC), the nation divided, with the kingdom of Israel in the north and the kingdom of Judah in the south. Heavy taxes and forced service in both kingdoms created hardships for the people. In addition, the kings often practiced idolatry—the worship of idols (images of other gods).

Prophets spoke out against both kingdoms' injustices to the people and infidelity to God. They questioned the behavior of the kings and called them and their people back to the Covenant. Yet the kingdoms continued to oppress the poor and worship pagan gods until eventually both kingdoms were crushed by powerful conquerors. The Assyrians obliterated the northern kingdom of Israel in 721 (BC) and took its people into exile. In 587 (BC) the Babylonians destroyed Judah, including the city of Jerusalem, and took its people to Babylon as captives.

The Babylonian Exile and the Jewish Dispersion

While the people were exiled in Babylon, still other prophets encouraged them to repent of their sins and turn back to God. During this time the prophet known as Second Isaiah proclaimed that God was the one and only God. Monotheism, the belief in one God, was now the revelation of this people to the world, their blessing to the nations.

After fifty years in Babylon, the exiles were released from captivity by the conquering Persians and allowed to return home. Judah, no longer a politically independent kingdom, had become a district within the Persian Empire, and the returned exiles became known as Jews, from the word *Judah*. They rebuilt the Temple, and under Ezra and Nehemiah, they re-established the Law and restored Jerusalem. That city became the religious capital for the Jews who had resettled all over the world—that is, the Jews of the Dispersion.

During the Exile the Jewish leaders had begun collecting and reflecting on their ancestral writings, forming the core of what would later become their Bible, known to Christians as the Old Testament.

More Oppressors

The Persian Empire was conquered in 330 (BC) by the armies of Alexander the Great, leader of the Greek Empire. This made the Greeks overlords of the Jews for nearly three hundred years, with the exception of a brief period of independence after a revolt led by the Maccabees family. The Greeks were followed by the Romans, who captured Jerusalem in 63 (BC). Although tolerant of other cultures and religions, the Roman Empire severely punished its subjects for revolts.

It was a dark time for the people of the Promise, who longed for release from oppression and for the day when all their hopes for a good and peaceful life would be fulfilled. Many Jews looked toward the coming of a messiah, one sent by God to save them; some expected this messiah to be from the family line of David.

It is at this point in the history of Israel that the Old Testament accounts end. . . .

Jesus, the Savior

Into a situation of defeat and darkness for the people of Israel, Jesus was born, one of the house, or family line, of David. Christians see Jesus as the long-awaited Messiah—the fulfillment of all God's promises to Israel and the Savior of the world. With his Death and Resurrection, Jesus' followers recognized that he was the Son of God. The community of believers began to grow, first among Jews but later among Gentiles, or non-Jews. The story of Jesus and the growth of the early Church is told in the New Testament.

(This handout is adapted from *Written on Our Hearts: The Old Testament Story of God's Love,* Third Edition, by Mary Reed Newland [Winona, MN: Saint Mary's Press, 2009], pages 18–24. Copyright © 2005 by Saint Mary's Press. All rights reserved.)

Sprint Through Salvation History: Scriptural Passages

Name: _____

Find at least three major scriptural passages that refer to your assigned segment of salvation history. Write down the book, chapter, and verses you find and take notes on the essential information of each passage. For example, answer the following questions for each passage:

- Who is mentioned?
- What happens?
- Why?
- Where?
- How?

Fill out the remainder of the handout during your classmates' presentations or as your teacher directs. Keep this handout for later reference.

- The Founders and the Promise:

  _____   _____   _____

- The Exodus of the Israelites and the Covenant:

  _____   _____   _____

- Taking Over the Promised Land:

  _____   _____   _____

- The Nation and the Temple:

  _____   _____   _____

- The Kings and the Prophets:

  _____   _____   _____

- The Babylonian Exile and the Jewish Dispersion:

  _____   _____   _____

- More Oppressors:

  _____   _____   _____

- Jesus, the Savior:

  _____   _____   _____

Document #: TX001108

Your group presentation should answer the following questions:

1. Where did you find information about your scriptural time period (three passages)?

2. When did the events take place?

3. What major events occurred?

4. Did the story take place in a time or place when something significant was happening? What was the situation in which these events occurred?

5. Who was involved?

6. Where did this occur?

7. What was God doing?

Document #: TX001108

The Bible: The Living Word of God

Unit 3 Quiz

Name: _____

Choose five of the following ten passages. In the spaces provided, identify the passage you chose and answer the following questions for each of your five choices:

- What is the salvation history event the passage refers to?
- Briefly describe this event.
- Why is this event important for salvation history?

Passages
- Genesis 1:27,31
- Genesis 2:7,15
- Genesis 12:1–7
- Exodus 12:31–42
- Exodus 20:1–17
- Joshua 24:1,13–28
- 2 Samuel 7:1–7
- 2 Samuel 7:8–29
- 2 Kings 17:5–18
- Matthew 1:1,17

_____ (Passage)

_____

_____

_____

_____

_____

_____ (Passage)

_____

_____

_____

_____

_____

_____ (Passage)

_____

_____

_____

_____

_____ (Passage)

_____

_____

_____

_____

_____ (Passage)

_____

_____

_____

_____

Document #: TX001109

Unit 3 Test

Part 1: Multiple Choice

Write your answers in the blank spaces at the left.

1. _____ The most exquisite moment in the Revelation of God took place _____.
   A. at the Last Supper
   B. when the Word of God, the Second Person of the Trinity, became flesh
   C. in the garden at Gethsemane
   D. with the parting of the Red Sea

2. _____ _____ are the means by which Divine Revelation is transmitted to every generation.
   A. The lives of the saints
   B. The encyclicals of the Magisterium
   C. The prayers and deeds of every Christian
   D. The Sacred Scriptures and Sacred Tradition

3. _____ The Book of Genesis does all of the following except _____.
   A. explain the role of humans in the origin of sin and its devastating effects
   B. describe life as it was between 200 and 1500 BC
   C. show God's desire to be in communication with his People
   D. emphasize the lasting effect of the Covenant God formed with Abraham

4. _____ Saints, who are highly esteemed for their theological writings as well as their holiness, are given the title _____ by the Church.
   A. Patriarch
   B. Theological Expert
   C. Defender of the Faith
   D. Doctor of the Church

5. _____ God alone has revealed to us the central mystery of the Christian faith, which is _____.
   A. the mystery of the Most Holy Trinity
   B. why we were born
   C. the love of Christians for one another
   D. where we came from in a previous existence

Document #: TX001298

6. _____ God stops the people from building the Tower of Babel by _____.
    A. causing a fire that destroys the tower
    B. striking the main builders of the tower with lightning
    C. confusing their speech
    D. having a war start

7. _____ Sin that is a serious transgression of a person's relationship with God and neighbors is called _____.
    A. venial
    B. mortal
    C. heresy
    D. unforgivable

8. _____ _____ is the passing on of the authority to teach and interpret the Scriptures and Tradition to the bishops.
    A. Apostolic Succession
    B. Inspiration
    C. Faith and Morals
    D. The Acts of the Apostles

9. _____ God's relationship with his People throughout the Book of Genesis is much like a(n) _____.
    A. king
    B. uncle
    C. friend
    D. parent

10. _____ Genesis presents in figurative or symbolic language the beginning of _____.
    A. the history of the whole world
    B. evolution
    C. salvation history
    D. papal infallibility

Document #: TX001298

Part 2: Matching

Match each statement in column 1 with a term from column 2. Write the letter that corresponds to your choice in the space provided. (*Note:* There are two extra items in column 2).

Column 1

1. _____ The heritage of faith contained in the Sacred Scriptures and Tradition.

2. _____ Teachings recognized as central to Church teaching.

3. _____ Referring to the process of passing on the Gospel message.

4. _____ The Church's living teaching office, which consists of all the bishops, in communion with the Pope.

5. _____ The Old Testament books of Proverbs, Ecclesiastes, Job, Sirach, and the Wisdom of Solomon.

6. _____ The father or leader of a tribe, clan, or tradition.

7. _____ A solemn agreement between human beings or between God and a human being.

8. _____ A short summary statement or profession of faith.

9. _____ God's appearing to Moses in the burning bush is an example of this.

10. _____ Another name for Original Sin.

Column 2

A. Magisterium

B. Book of Genesis

C. wisdom literature

D. dogma

E. covenant

F. the Fall

G. Deposit of Faith

H. solemn vow

I. theophany

J. patriarch

K. creed

L. Sacred Tradition

Document #: TX001298

Part 3: Short Answer

Answer each of the following questions in paragraph form on a separate sheet of paper.

1. What is meant by the term *salvation history?* Of what does it consist?

2. What is Original Sin and what were its effects?

3. How can Original Sin be termed our "happy fault"?

4. Retell the story of Noah (or Moses and the golden calf) as an example of how God remained faithful to his People despite their turning from him.

Document #: TX001298

Unit 3 Test Answer Key

Part 1: Multiple Choice

1. B	**6.** C
2. D	**7.** B
3. B	**8.** A
4. D	**9.** D
5. A	**10.** C

Part 2: Matching

1. G	**6.** J
2. D	**7.** E
3. L	**8.** K
4. A	**9.** I
5. C	**10.** F

Part 3: Short Answer

1. Salvation history is the pattern of specific events in human history in which God clearly reveals his presence and saving actions. In a sense, all human history is salvation history in that the one true God—Father, Son, and Holy Spirit—has been present and active in the lives of his People since the beginning of time.

2. Original Sin was the sin of our first parents, Adam and Eve, who disobeyed God's command by choosing to follow their own will and so losing their original holiness and becoming subject to death. It also made humans subject to death and made sin universally present in the world.

3. Salvation history began with humanity's first sin and ended in the Resurrection of Jesus Christ. The sins of God's People resulted in broken communities and families, and in separation from God, one another, the natural world, and even themselves. However, without this condition, there would have been no need for a Redeemer. Christ's saving death and Resurrection gave human beings not only the grace to be in communion with God but also visual and faithful proof of God's love for us, thus making Original Sin a "happy fault" for bringing an awareness of God's love before us.

4. *Answers should emphasize the Covenant made between God and Noah (or God and Moses), and how God saves those who are faithful to him.*

Unit 4 God Calls the Early Leaders of Israel

Overview

This fourth unit focuses on God's call to the patriarchs and their wives, and to Moses, Aaron, and Miriam, asking them to lead the people of Israel. These calls were significant for forming the people of Israel and can give us insight into God's call to us today.

Key Understandings and Questions

At the end of this unit, the students will possess a deeper understanding of the following important concepts:

- The first leaders of Israel had a unique calling from God.
- The people of Israel became who they were through significant events such as the call of Abraham and the other patriarchs, the Exodus, and the Covenant at Mount Sinai.
- We can look to the early leaders of Israel for inspiration in our lives today.
- From the beginning of their covenant relationship with God, the people of Israel had a specific pattern. This was the cycle of redemption, in which they sinned and moved away from the covenant but were able to return to God because of God's faithfulness and love.

At the end of this unit, the students will have answered these questions:

- Who were the first leaders of Israel that God called?
- What role did these leaders play in founding Israel?
- What role did these leaders play in the covenant relationship with God?
- What characteristics do these early leaders model for us today?

How Will You Know the Students Understand?

These tools will help you to assess the students' understanding of the main concepts:

- handout "Final Performance Task Options for Unit 4" (Document #: TX001110)
- handout "Rubric for Final Performance Tasks for Unit 4" (Document #: TX001111)
- handout "Unit 4 Test" (Document #: TX001300)

The Suggested Path to Understanding

This teacher guide provides you with one path to take with the students, enabling them to learn about God's call to the patriarchs and how these calls can help us to understand God's call to us today. It is not necessary to use all the learning experiences, but if you substitute other material from this course or your own material for some of the material offered here, check to see that you have covered all relevant facets of understanding and that you have not missed knowledge or skills required in later units.

Interpret *Optional Step:* Hook the students' interest with a question.

Explain *Step 1:* Preassess what the students already know about the first leaders of Israel.

Empathize *Step 2:* Follow this assessment by presenting to the students the handouts "Final Performance Task Options for Unit 4" (Document #: TX001110) and "Rubric for Final Performance Tasks for Unit 4" (Document #: TX001111).

Explain *Step 3:* Familiarize the students with the early leaders of Israel, using comic book–style short stories.

Explain *Step 4:* Present material about the relationship between covenant and the early leaders of Israel.

Explain *Step 5:* Present information about Moses and the Exodus.

Interpret *Step 6:* Explore Moses' leadership qualities.

Explain *Step 7:* Present the cycle of redemption.

Apply *Step 8:* Use the Middle East as a model for the ups and downs of faith.

Apply *Step 9:* Have the students uncover the relevance of the leaders of the Pentateuch in their own lives.

Empathize *Step 10:* Give a quiz to assess student understanding.

Interpret *Step 11:* Encourage the students to think independently by considering a modern patriarch from the Jewish faith.

Empathize *Step 12:* Now that the students are closer to the end of the unit, make sure they are all on track with their final performance tasks, if you have assigned them.

Reflect *Step 13:* Provide the students with a tool to use for reflecting about what they learned in the unit and how they learned.

Background for Teaching This Content with These Methods

In addition to finding information about the pedagogical approach used in this guide, you will also find background information on these and other topics at *smp.org/LivinginChrist*:

- "The Early Leaders of Israel" (Document #: TX001031)
- "The Book of Exodus" (Document #: TX001030)
- "The Cycle of Redemption" (Document #: TX001032)
- "The Sinai Covenant and the Ten Commandments" (Document #: TX001034)

The Web site also has background information on the following teaching methods:

- "Using Quotations" (Document #: TX001038)
- "Using Google Earth" (Document #: TX001037)
- "Using the Barometer Method" (Document #: TX001021)
- "Using the Take-a-Stand Method" (Document #: TX001035)

Student Book Articles

The articles covered in unit 4 are from "Section 3: Revelation in the Old Testament" of the student book. If you believe the students would do the reading more successfully with additional structure, see the handout "Student Notes for Unit 4" (Document #: TX001164) at *smp.org/LivinginChrist.*

- "Abraham" (article 33)
- "Isaac, Jacob, and Joseph" (article 34)
- "A People Enslaved" (article 35)
- "The Exodus" (article 36)
- "Building Trust in God" (article 37)
- "The Ten Commandments" (article 38)

Scripture Passages

- Genesis 12:1–8 (the call of Abraham)
- Genesis 16:1–15 (the birth of Ishmael)
- Genesis 17:3–7 (the Covenant with Abram)
- Genesis 21:1–8 (the birth of Isaac)
- Genesis 22:1–19 (the testing of Abraham)
- Genesis, chapter 24 (Isaac and Rebekah)
- Genesis, chapter 25 (the birth of Esau and Jacob)
- Genesis 27:1–45 (Jacob's deception)

- Genesis 28:10–22 (Jacob's dream at Bethel)
- Genesis 29:14–30 (Jacob's marriage to Leah and Rachel)
- Genesis 30:1–24 (Jacob's children)
- Genesis 30:22–24 (the birth of Joseph)
- Genesis 32:23–32 (the struggle with the angel)
- Genesis, chapter 33 (Jacob and Esau meet)
- Genesis 35:9–15 (Bethel revisited)
- Genesis, chapter 37 (Joseph sold into Egypt)
- Genesis, chapter 39 (Joseph's temptation)
- Genesis, chapter 40 (the dreams interpreted)
- Genesis, chapter 41 (Pharaoh's dream)
- Genesis 42:1—45:20 (the testing of Joseph's brothers)
- Genesis 46:1–7 (the migration to Egypt)
- Exodus, chapter 1 (oppression of the Israelites in Egypt)
- Exodus 2:1–10 (the birth and adoption of Moses)
- Exodus 2:11–22 (Moses' flight to Midian)
- Exodus 2:23—4:17 (the burning bush and Moses' commission)
- Exodus, chapters 7–11 (the ten plagues)
- Exodus, chapter 12 (the Passover ritual prescribed)
- Exodus, chapter 20 (the Ten Commandments, the fear of God)

Vocabulary

If you choose to provide a vocabulary list for material covered in both the student book and the teacher guide, download and print the handout "Vocabulary for Unit 4" (Document #: TX001112), one for each student.

Exile	Pentateuch
Exodus	pharaoh
genealogy	redemption
idolatry	repentance
Israel	ritual
manna	sacrifice
monotheism	Sinai Covenant
Passover	Ten Commandments
patriarch	theophany

Learning Experiences

Optional Step

Hook the students' interest with a question.

This unit emphasizes the leadership that significant biblical figures in the Penta-teuch embraced after God called them. The students will gain experience con-necting the leadership qualities of these early leaders of Israel to our nation's leader's today.

1. Ask the following question:

    ➤ When a person becomes the president of the United States, what responsibilities does this leader have toward the people? What actions might violate the relationship between the leader and the people? How does this relationship resemble a covenant?

2. Note some of the points the students raise that you might weave into later presentations or activities. Let the students know that learning the unit con-tent and skills will give them greater insight into this question.

Step 1

Preassess what the students already know about the first leaders of Israel.

Explore what the students already know about the first leaders of Israel. The learning experiences help the students to unpack and explore these concepts with increasing depth. There are several different options for assessing what your students know and understand before beginning this unit. Note that each option requires preparing different materials.

Option 1: Mind Map

This learning experience will allow the students to put on paper all their ideas and thoughts about the early leaders of Israel. It will also provide you with a preassessment of what the students know and associate with the key events of the Pentateuch. From this you can determine how much you need to present about the early leaders.

1. Prepare by downloading and printing the handout "Mind Map" (Document #: TX001160), one for each student. Distribute the handout and pens or pencils.

2. Write the prompt phrase "first Israelite leaders" on the board in a large cir-cle. Ask the students to write the same phrase in the center circle on their

copies of the handout. In the connecting circles, have them write words or phrases they immediately think of when they see the prompt phrase. Allow 5 to 10 minutes for the students to work independently.

3. When time is up, invite the students to share with the large group what they have written down. Write their suggestions on the board.

4. Once a list is created, ask the students what all the suggestions have in common. Common perceptions of the early leaders will naturally surface through their suggestions.

5. After writing the students' suggestions on the board, use colored markers to circle words that can be categorized. These categories will help to address the question "Who were the first leaders of Israel and what was their role in early Israel?"

Option 2: Leadership Scavenger Hunt

The focus questions in this learning experience invite the students to think critically about what they know, or what they would like to know, about the early leaders of Israel. From this you can determine how much you need to present about covenant and the early leaders of Israel.

1. Prepare by choosing a variety of men and women from the Pentateuch, or Torah, who played a role in founding the Jewish People. Download and print the handout "Leadership Scavenger Hunt" (Document #: TX001113), one for each small group of four. Make sure each student has a copy of the Bible or the stories you are covering for this learning experience.

2. Divide the class into groups of no more than four. Distribute pens or pencils and copies of the handout to the groups. Ask all group members to put their names on it.

3. Review how the students will complete the handout. It requires the students to use the knowledge they have gained about biblical scholarship and navigation to investigate the leaders of Israel as they appear in the Torah.

4. Allow about 15 to 20 minutes for the groups to complete the handout. When time is up, invite the students back into the large group.

5. Lead a discussion about the information on the handout.

6. After the discussion collect the handouts for your reference and review.

Option 3: Ungraded Association Quiz

This learning experience allows the students to test the knowledge they already have about covenant and the early leaders of Israel. From this you can determine how much to present about the concepts.

1. Prepare by downloading and printing the handout "The Early Leaders of Israel Quiz" (Document #: TX001114), one for each student.

2. Distribute pens or pencils and the copies of the handout. Explain that the quiz will not be graded but rather used as a tool about exercises and information to best help the students to learn about the early leaders of Israel. Allow 10 to 15 minutes for the students to complete the quiz.

3. When time is up, collect the quizzes. Redistribute them for grading. Be sure no students are grading their own quizzes.

4. Grade the quiz with the students, paying special attention to those questions that many students missed or answered incompletely.

5. Review and reinforce those concepts the students continue to struggle with.

6. Collect the quizzes.

Step 2

Follow this assessment by presenting to the students the handouts "Final Performance Task Options for Unit 4" (Document #: TX001110) and "Rubric for Final Performance Tasks for Unit 4" (Document #: TX001111).

This unit provides you with two ways to assess that the students have a deep understanding of the most important concepts in the unit: researching a key biblical figure or researching a woman who shaped Judeo-Christian history. Refer to "Using Final Performance Tasks to Assess Understanding" (Document #: TX001011) and "Using Rubrics to Assess Work" (Document #: TX001012) at *smp.org/LivinginChrist* for background information.

1. Prepare by downloading and printing the handouts "Final Performance Task Options for Unit 4" (Document #: TX001110) and "Rubric for Final Performance Tasks for Unit 4" (Document #: TX001111), one for each student.

2. Distribute the handouts. Give the students a choice as to which performance task they choose and add additional options if you so choose. Review the directions, expectations, and rubric in class, allowing the students to ask questions.

3. Explain the types of tools and knowledge the students will gain throughout the unit so they can successfully complete the final performance task.

4. Answer questions to clarify the end point toward which the unit is headed. Remind the students as the unit progresses that each learning experience builds the knowledge and

---

Teacher Note

You will want to assign due dates for the performance tasks.

If you have done these performance tasks, or very similar ones, with students before, place examples of this work in the classroom. During this introduction explain how each is a good example of what you are looking for, for different reasons. This allows the students to concretely understand what you are looking for and to understand that there is not only one way to succeed.

Unit 4

skills they will need to show you they understand how God called the early leaders of Israel and about the cycle of redemption.

Explain

Step 3

Familiarize the students with the early leaders of Israel, using comic book–style short stories.

Although the stories of the early leaders of Israel are not all comical, their intriguing plots are good for creating visual stories in the genre of the graphic novel or comic strips. In this learning experience, the students gain an overview of the stories in Genesis and Exodus.

1. Prepare by providing white copy paper or cardstock, several sheets for each student. Also provide colored markers and pencils or ask the students to bring their own. Write or post the readings on the board. You may also want to bring several examples of graphic novels and comic strips. One suggested breakdown of these readings follows:

Group 1
- Genesis 16:1–15 (the birth of Ishmael)
- Genesis 21:1–8 (the birth of Isaac)

Group 2
- Genesis 22:1–19 (the testing of Abraham)
- Genesis, chapter 24 (Isaac and Rebekah)

Group 3
- Genesis, chapter 25 (the birth of Esau and Jacob)
- Genesis 27:1–45 (Jacob's deception)

Group 4
- Genesis 28:10–22 (Jacob's dream at Bethel)
- Genesis 29:14–30 (Jacob's marriage to Leah and Rachel)
- Genesis 30:1–24 (Jacob's children)
- Genesis 30:22–24 (the birth of Joseph)

Group 5
- Genesis 32:23–32 (the struggle with the angel)
- Genesis, chapter 33 (Jacob and Esau meet)
- Genesis 35:9–15 (Bethel revisited)

Group 6
- Genesis, chapter 37 (Joseph sold into Egypt)
- Genesis, chapter 39 (Joseph's temptation)
- Genesis, chapter 40 (the dreams interpreted)
- Genesis, chapter 41 (Pharaoh's dream)

Group 7
- Genesis 42:1—45:20 (the testing of Joseph's brothers)
- Genesis 46:1–7 (the migration to Egypt)

Group 8
- Exodus, chapter 1 (oppression of the Israelites in Egypt)
- Exodus 2:1–10 (the birth and adoption of Moses)
- Exodus 2:11–22 (Moses' flight to Midian)

Group 9
- Exodus 2:23—4:17 (the burning bush and Moses' commission)
- Exodus, chapters 7–11 (the ten plagues)

Group 10
- Exodus, chapter 12 (the Passover ritual prescribed)
- Exodus, chapter 20 (the Ten Commandments, the fear of God)

2. On the day of the learning experience, ask the students to count off by ten to form ten small groups. Point out the students' readings on the board. Have the students work on their comic strips individually but alongside others who have the same Bible passages. Distribute the copy paper and markers and pencils. Give the following instructions:

> **Teacher Note**
>
> Suggest that students divide their papers into four or six comic panels by folding.

➤ Read your passages. Using the copy paper and colored markers or pencils, create a comic strip story of these passages. Cover the major events and add basic dialogue as needed. Somewhere on the front of the paper, write your name and the passages you read. Your ability to retell these stories through pictures and words will assist you in reviewing or learning about the early leaders of the Old Testament.

3. This learning experience may take the rest of the period or may need to be completed as homework. When the students have completed their comic strip stories, ask the small groups of students with the same passages to present the stories to the class. Post the comic strip stories around the room.

(This learning experience is adapted from *Leader Guide for "The Catholic Youth Bible®,"* third edition, p. 70.)

Step 4

Present material about the relationship between covenant and the early leaders of Israel.

Consider what you have learned from the preassessment learning experiences to best prepare for the students' needs in your presentation.

- This step utilizes the following student book articles:
  - Abraham" (article 33)
  - "Isaac, Jacob, and Joseph" (article 34)

You may want to have the students read these articles as homework either before or after your presentation.

Teacher Notes

If some students understand the material well enough, you might ask volunteers to share it with the class. If desired, present this content to the students, using as a tool the PowerPoint "The Early Leaders of Israel" (Document #: TX001075) from *smp.org/LivinginChrist.*

Present the Early Leaders of Israel from Genesis, Highlighting Their Calls from God

1. Prepare by making sure the students have their Bibles, because you will stop and read important passages with them.

2. Share the following material, from student book article 33, "Abraham":

   ➤ The Book of Genesis tells us that despite humanity's sin, God chose to stay in relationship with humanity and chose a group of people to call his own, namely the Hebrew people. They would later be called the Israelites.

   ➤ Remind the students that in Genesis, chapter 12, God calls Abram (later renamed Abraham). Abram and his wife, Sarai, are **Semitic** nomads wandering the highlands of the **Near East.**

   Ask a student to read aloud Genesis 12:1–8.

   ➤ God asks Abram to leave everything behind and set out for an unknown territory. God makes a promise to Abram. What exactly does God promise?

   ➤ Abram takes Sarai, his nephew Lot, and all of their possessions and leaves for a strange land, Canaan, not knowing where God is leading them. How would you describe this decision?

   ➤ Sarai and Abram find their faith tested and strengthened. How does the pregnancy of Hagar and the birth of Ishmael show that Sarai and Abram's faith had been tested?

   ➤ When Abram is ninety-nine years old, God again speaks with him and establishes his **Covenant** with Abram and his descendants. A covenant is a solemn agreement between human beings or between God and a human being in which mutual commitments are made.

Ask a student to read aloud Genesis 17:3–7.

➤ Sarai becomes known as Sarah and Abram becomes known as Abraham. Sarah bears Abraham a son, named Isaac.

➤ Through Abraham God chooses to make his Covenant, through which he forms his People. Through this Covenant God later reveals his law to his People through Moses.

➤ God's command that Abraham sacrifice his only son, Isaac, also tests Abraham's faith.

Have a student read Genesis 22:1–19 aloud.

How would you have felt if you were Abraham? if you were Isaac?

➤ Because of his faithfulness and complete trust in God, Abraham and Sarah are blessed with countless descendants.

3. Share the following material, from student book article 34, "Isaac, Jacob, and Joseph":

➤ What is a patriarch?

• A **patriarch** is the father or leader of a tribe, clan, or tradition. Abraham, Isaac, and Jacob were the patriarchs of the Israelite people. In the Christian tradition, the Twelve Apostles, the Church Fathers, and certain bishops in the Eastern Catholic Churches are considered patriarchs.

➤ Isaac was the son of Abraham and Sarah. His father almost sacrificed him, but at the last minute, God saved him. Abraham's servant found Isaac a wife from among Abraham's people and asked for God's help in discerning who she was.

➤ Isaac and Rebekah had twin sons, Jacob and Esau. Esau was born first. Jacob ended up getting his brother's birthright and their father's blessing.

Ask two students to read aloud Genesis 25:19–34 and Genesis 27:1–45.

➤ Through a dream God renewed his covenant with Jacob.

Ask a student to read aloud Genesis 28:10–22.

➤ A patriarch was a natural leader of God's Chosen People. The patriarchs had the following qualities:

• **They obeyed God.** In the Old Testament, the Hebrew word for *obedience* meant primarily "listening" or "hearing." An obedient person heard God's Word and followed it (see Exodus 15:26). To be obedient was simply to align oneself with God's will.

- **They knew God wanted his People to treat all people with justice.** They understood the need for and purpose of divine justice. The Hebrew and Greek words translated as "justice" are also translated as "righteousness" and "judgment." Divine justice calls for the fair and equitable distribution of life's necessities. The scriptural idea of justice is based on the truth that all humans have dignity and worth and are children of God. God's love for all creation is shown in his emphasis on justice, which is love in action.

- **They lived good, moral lives.** They committed themselves to ethical responsibility. The commandments of God are the fundamental rules of conduct for the Chosen People. The Ten Commandments are about the love of God and love of neighbor.

- **They understood that God wanted his People to come back to him with their whole selves.** The patriarchs needed to be able to ask the Jews and Israelites to return to the Covenant in body, mind, and spirit. At this time the Abrahamic and Mosaic Covenants had long been entered into and adhered to by the people. Therefore God no longer looked only for sacrifice to appease him. He sought more. Specifically, God was interested in a full return to the Covenant by his People in body, mind, and spirit. Yet the Israelites were unsure of how to accomplish this goal. The leaders God chose were men and women who committed themselves to a relationship with God and to be his voice. They spoke on God's behalf to the people.

➤ Although at this time, the Sinai Covenant had not yet been entered into, the early patriarchs still held themselves to a specific ethical standard of complete devotion and sacrifice to God. It was the same standard the people near Mesopotamia held around the year 1700 BC, when Abraham and Sarah lived. The predominant focus of this worship was sacrifice.

➤ Sacrifice is making holy. It is a rite offered to God on behalf of the people, presided over by a priest who leads and represents the community in adoration, repentance, gratitude, and honor (see Hebrews 2:17). In the Old Testament, a sacrifice was needed as an atonement, as a healing rite to restore holiness and cleanse the people from infractions against the Law, and as reconciliation in their covenant relationship with God (see Psalm 51:1–17).

➤ God came to men and women and invited them to share in his will. This invitation, or calling (see unit 2), can be seen in nearly any biblical story about the early leaders of the Judeo-Christian people.

4. In the large group, ask the students to consider the following questions as they apply to Abraham, Isaac, Jacob, and Joseph. Rebecca was also called to become Isaac's wife.

➤ How did these calls fit into the pattern?

> ➤ How did God call this person?
> ➤ What did God call the person to?
> ➤ How did the person respond?
> ➤ How did the person continue to respond to God through his or her life?

Step 5

Present information about Moses and the Exodus.

Gauge your presentation by how familiar the students are with the Exodus story from their previous study and the comic book–story learning experience. Discuss the Exodus story in greater depth without retelling it if possible. Use the PowerPoint "Moses and the Exodus" (Document #: TX001076) at *smp. org/LivinginChrist.* See also the articles "The Book of Exodus" (Document #: TX001030), "Moses" (Document #: TX001033), and "The Sinai Covenant and the Ten Commandments" (Document #: TX001034) at *smp.org/LivinginChrist.*

- This step utilizes the following student book articles:
  - ○ "A People Enslaved" (article 35)
  - ○ "The Exodus" (article 36)
  - ○ "Building Trust in God" (article 37)
  - ○ "The Ten Commandments" (article 38)

You may want to have the students read these articles as homework either before or after your presentation.

1. Prepare by downloading and printing the handout "The Ten Command- ments" (Document #: TX001115), one for each student.

Moses' Early Life

2. Share the following material about Moses' early life, some of which comes from student book article 35, "A People Enslaved":

> ➤ The Book of Exodus begins by listing Joseph's descendants and those of his brothers, who came to Egypt to live with him. Together, they were the sons of Israel. "Then a new king, who knew nothing of Joseph, came to power in Egypt" (1:8). This is Pharaoh Ramses II, who lived from 1290 to 1224 BC.
> ➤ Pharaoh feels threatened by the many Israelites, so he enslaves them.
> ➤ Miriam the prophetess is the sister of Moses and Aaron. She plays an important role in the Exodus, saving her infant brother Moses from Pharaoh's plan to kill all Israelite boys at birth. She floats Moses on the

Nile River in a basket, where Pharaoh's daughter finds him. Further, Miriam provides her mother the opportunity to remain in her son's life by suggesting her mother as a nurse for the princess's newly adopted son, Moses.

➤ Even though Moses is brought up as Egyptian royalty, this contact with his family gives him exposure to and sympathy for the Israelites.

➤ After Moses reaches adulthood, he sees an Egyptian striking an Israelite slave. In defense of the slave, Moses kills the Egyptian and hides the body in the sand. When it becomes known what Moses has done, he fears for his life and flees to the land of Midian. There he encounters the daughters of Reuel, a priest of Midian. Moses stays with Reuel and marries his daughter Zipporah.

God Calls Moses

3. Share the following material about God's call to Moses, some of which comes from student book article 36, "The Exodus":

➤ Many years later, God reveals himself to Moses and calls him to a key role in the salvation of his People.

➤ Moses experiences a theophany through a burning bush. A **theophany** is God's manifestation of himself in a visible form to enrich human understanding of him.

➤ God hears the cries of his children enslaved in Egypt.

Have a student read aloud Exodus 3:4–17.

How did Moses' encounter with God in the burning bush begin to change his community's understanding of God?

➤ God identifies himself as "I am who am" (Exodus 3:14) and calls Moses to be his voice of truth and arm of justice.

➤ When Pharaoh does not relent after signs and wonders, God unleashes ten plagues on Pharaoh and Egypt.

➤ In the tenth plague, the lives of all firstborn males, human and animal—including the firstborn son of Pharaoh—are taken.

4. Share the following material about God's saving the Israelites from the Egyptians:

➤ This particular event is known as the **Passover,** during which the Lord passes over all houses marked with the blood of the sacrificial lamb but enters the houses not marked with this sign of faith to kill the firstborn children and animals.

Have a student read Exodus, chapter 12, aloud.

➤ Pharaoh lets the people of Israel go. On the shores of the Red Sea, the Israelites become fearful again as the Egyptians change their minds and pursue the Israelites. God, however, defeats the Egyptians.

5. Share the following material about the Israelites' wandering in the desert, from student book article 37, "Building Trust in God":

➤ On the way to the Promised Land, the Israelites have to cross a vast wilderness.

➤ Encountering these less-than-ideal conditions, the Israelites immediately forget God's liberating action as demonstrated in their Exodus from slavery, and they also forget his promise to protect them even in the darkest times.

➤ Disgruntled by the harsh conditions of the desert and disillusioned by the leadership of Moses, the people question, "Is the Lord in our midst or not?" (Exodus 17:7).

➤ When the people are hungry, God rains down **manna,** little flakes that the people collect and then boil or bake into a breadlike substance. When the people are thirsty, God draws water from a rock. When they are afraid, God protects them. Still they question the presence of God.

6. Share the following material about the Covenant at Sinai and the Ten Commandments, which comes from student book article 38, "The Ten Commandments":

➤ Mount Sinai is the sacred ground where God forms a Covenant with his Chosen People. Contained within this Covenant are laws and obligations, known as the **Ten Commandments.** They will govern the people religiously, morally, and civically.

Ask a student to read Exodus, chapter 20.

➤ Moses returns to the people and shares the Lord's offer of his Covenant. Within the framework of this **Sinai Covenant,** God declares himself to be their God, a God of fidelity, love, and justice. Harking back to the Covenant between God and Abraham, God promises that the Israelites will be his "special possession, dearer to [him] than all other people" (Exodus 19:5).

What Are the Ten Commandments?

I am the LORD your God: you shall not have strange Gods before me.

You shall not take the name of the LORD your God in vain.

Remember to keep holy the LORD's Day.

Honor your father and your mother.

You shall not kill.

You shall not commit adultery.

You shall not steal.

You shall not bear false witness against your neighbor.

You shall not covet your neighbor's wife.

You shall not covet your neighbor's goods.

(CCC, pp. 496–497)

7. Distribute the copies of the handout "The Ten Commandments" (Document #: TX001115). Review the handout's chart with the students. One way to have the students consider the Commandments positively and more deeply is to assign several students per Commandment to create a bumper sticker. On it, they will use each of the ten positively expressed versions of the Ten Commandments (under the column "Meaning"). They should use color, symbols, or images. You can then post these around the room or even around the school.

Step 6

Explore Moses' leadership qualities.

Have the students uncover what quotations say about leadership.

1. Prepare by making sure the students have Bibles, both in class and at home. Download and print the handout "Leadership Quotations" (Document #: TX001116), one for each student. Substitute your own four quotations if desired. These quotations do not have to be biblical but should come from highly regarded leaders throughout history. Download and print the handout "What Kind of Leader Is Moses?" (Document #: TX001117), one for each student.

2. On the day of the learning experience, place the students in groups of no more than four with their desks facing one another. Distribute the copies of the handout "Leadership Quotations" (Document #: TX001116).

3. Instruct the group members to read and consider each quotation carefully. Ask them to write their responses in their notebooks. Have each group choose a reporter. (Every student must write answers on the handout, but only one will share the group's opinions.) Allow about 15 minutes to complete the handout.

Teacher Note

In Christian versions of the Bible, the First Commandment is seen as one Commandment. In the Jewish tradition, this Commandment is divided into two different Commandments—this one and "You shall not carve idols for yourselves. . . . " To maintain the balance of the number ten, the Jewish tradition combines Commandments nine and ten into one rule about not coveting. The Christian tradition maintains there are two commandments about coveting.

Teacher Note

See the article "Using Quotations" (Document #: TX001038) at *smp.org/LivinginChrist* for further explanation of this learning experience.

4. When time is up, have the students rearrange their desks to your original seating chart. Lead a large-group discussion of the characteristics of an effective leader and how the patriarchs display these characteristics.

5. After the discussion distribute the copies of the handout "What Kind of Leader Is Moses?" (Document #: TX001117). Explain that the students will read the passages from Exodus on it and will use the four quotations from the handout "Leadership Quotations" (Document #: TX001116) to analyze Moses' abilities as a leader.

Step 7

Present the cycle of redemption.

From the Exodus until the birth of Jesus, the history of Israel was characterized by the cycle of redemption. We can recognize this cycle in our own lives as we move away from and toward God again by his grace.

1. Prepare by downloading and printing the handout "The Cycle of Redemption" (Document #: TX00118), one for each student. Use the PowerPoint "The Cycle of Redemption" (Document #: TX001077) to accompany your presentation if you wish. See *smp.org/LivinginChrist.*

2. On the day of this learning experience, discuss the religious meaning of the terms *redemption* and *repentance.*

   • **Redemption** comes from the Latin *redemptio,* meaning "a buying back," referring, in the Old Testament, to Yahweh's deliverance of Israel and, in the New Testament, to Christ's deliverance of all Christians from the forces of sin.

   • **Repentance** comes from the Latin *poenitire,* meaning "to make sorry", referring to the recognition and rejection of personal sin.

3. Distribute the copies of the handout. Tell the students they will see a pattern in the Old Testament that resembles the doubts the Israelites displayed as they wandered in the desert. Though God had just saved them from the Egyptians, they quickly lost faith in him. Review the handout with the students.

4. Conclude by noting that the patriarchs and other early Israelite leaders were committed to the principles that kept the people close to the covenantal relationship with God.

Step 8

Use the Middle East as a model for the ups and downs of faith.

Use Google Earth to encourage the students to reflect on their own faith lives. Using a projected image, a large screen, or networked computers, have the students look at the part of the world where the Israelites traveled from captivity to the Promised Land.

1. Prepare by arranging for all the students to view Google Earth at the same time. This may mean reserving a computer lab or other equipment. Take a quick tutorial on this application. See "Using Google Earth" (Document #: TX001037) at *smp.org/LivinginChrist*. No doubt the students can assist you. You will need to find specific parts of Egypt: the pyramids and the Red Sea. Outside Egypt, you will also need to find the Sinai Wilderness, Mount Sinai, and Jericho. Print out several copies of the map of this area for the last part of this step if students choose to label a map rather than write a reflection.

2. Begin by sharing the following thoughts in your own words:

   ➤ It is easy to say the Israelites should have had unfailing faith in God after the Exodus, but our experience tells us we are just as likely to mimic the cycle of redemption in our own lives, having ups and downs, moving toward and away from God.

3. Start Google Earth and begin your "travel" by looking at your own town and school. Ask the students to comment on the geography, terrain, and so on. Then move away from where you live to see the globe and to move to Egypt and the Nile River. As you zoom in on the Nile, ask the students to comment on the terrain and population of this area.

4. As you move from place to place, make the following observations, asking the students to provide examples of different times in a person's faith life. (Let some students move the class along on the Google Earth journey if they know how.)

   ➤ This is the Nile River. Whose story began at the Nile River? *(Answer: Moses!)* In some ways the Nile represents Baptism and the faith of a small child. Many children, though not all, are baptized as infants, and parents and godparents speak on their behalf, pledging to raise the children in a faith-filled way. What adjectives could describe a child's faith in God?

   ➤ These are the pyramids, the burial places of people like Ramses II. Many slaves, such as the Israelites, were involved in creating these wonders of the world.

➤ Here is the Red Sea, where the Israelites had to choose whether to trust God. It was risky to trust God, but the other option was certain slavery or death. We can become slaves to sin. God offers us freedom from sin. This choice can feel risky at times, like any leap of faith.

➤ This is the desert wilderness where the Israelites spent so much time wandering. Many people perceive that their faith lives have long periods of wandering, where the future is unclear and they wonder where God is. Many people feel their spiritual lives are dry for long periods.

➤ Here is Mount Sinai, where Moses received the Ten Commandments. This event was a peak moment in the lives of the Israelites, when they could feel God's presence and were ready to commit themselves to the Covenant. Mountains inspire awe. We all have special moments in our faith lives when we feel more connected to God or see reality with greater clarity, much as we can see a distance from a mountain.

➤ Here is the Promised Land, which God had promised the Israelites. At first the Israelites triumphed under Joshua and had an easy victory at Jericho. The Promised Land symbolizes the times in our lives when everything is going great.

➤ This area is also the site of battles that did not go the Israelites' way. These events remind us of times when everything seems to go wrong.

5. Ask the students to write a reflection about their own faith lives, using the different steps of the Israelite journey to help illustrate it. They can either do this fully in writing or label a printout of the Google map with their reflections. Ask the students to complete this reflection as homework. Conclude by discussing the students' feelings and experiences about this process. Make the following parallels between the Exodus story and their own.

   • God desires that we be free from anything that enslaves us.
   • God is never on the side of people or situations that oppress us.
   • God is always with us, even if we cannot feel his presence.
   • Giving false gods the attention that only God deserves leads to unhappiness.

Step 9

Have the students uncover the relevance of the leaders of the Pentateuch in their own lives.

Provide the students with an opportunity to reflect on and form opinions about the ideas they have learned. Assess the students' understanding and ask for their knowledge and questions. See also the article "Using the Take-a-Stand Method" (Document #: TX001035) at *smp.org/LivinginChrist*.

1. Prepare by looking at the handout "Leadership Statements" (Document #: TX001121). It lists fifteen statements of both popular and actual truths about the role of leaders throughout history. If you choose to find your own statements, include both leaders of the Pentateuch and nonbiblical leaders. Create the following seven signs:

   - Strongly Agree
   - Agree
   - Somewhat Agree
   - Undecided
   - Somewhat Disagree
   - Disagree
   - Strongly Disagree

   Post the signs in a continuum along the walls of your classroom.

> **Teacher Note**
>
> You may want to give the students a few minutes to journal about their response to these statements before discussing them in the large group.

2. Ask the students to stand around the perimeter of the classroom and wait for you to read a leadership statement. Then ask the students to stand underneath the sign that most accurately reflects their feelings about it.

3. When the students have chosen a sign, invite one student from each sign to explain why he or she chose it. Repeat the procedure for all your statements.

4. Finally, lead a discussion about how a person becomes a leader and about the roles leaders play in shaping society.

Step 10

Give a quiz to assess student understanding.

1. Prepare by downloading and printing the handout "Unit 4 Quiz" (Document #: TX001119), one for each student. Note that the quiz is fairly comprehensive, in part because both you and the students want to learn what they do not now know in preparation for a test or the final performance tasks.

2. On the day of the quiz, provide 5 to 10 minutes for the students to review their books and notes. Distribute the quiz and provide sufficient time for the students to work on it. If time remains when the students are done, collect the quizzes and then redistribute them so everyone has someone else's. Go through the quiz, allowing the

> **Teacher Note**
>
> To save paper, use the electronic copy of the quiz from *smp.org/LivinginChrist* and put it up in a visual place via projector, overhead, monitor, and so on. If these options are unavailable, read the quiz to the students slowly. In both cases, have the students record their answers on loose-leaf paper.
>
> To save time, ask the students to choose ten out of the twenty true-or-false questions to complete.

students to correct one another's work and also giving them an opportunity to affirm or change their understanding of concepts. Collect the quizzes and further your analysis about topics that may need more coverage.

Step 11

Encourage the students to think independently by considering a modern patriarch from the Jewish faith.

1. Prepare by downloading and printing the handout "Barometer: Modern Contracts" (Document #: TX001120), one for each student. If you wish, make copies, one for each student, of the story of a different familiar person who has entered into a contract with another person (either someone from the Bible or a famous person from history). An important element of this approach is to keep the person in the story anonymous until the students have discussed the situation.

   Also create the following two signs:

   - Did live up to contract
   - Did not live up to contract

   Display these signs on opposite walls of your classroom.

2. On the day of the learning experience, distribute the copies of the handout "Barometer: Modern Contracts" (Document #: TX001120). Allow about 5 minutes for the students to silently read the story in class.

3. When time is up, tell the students they will show whether they thought the person lived up to his or her part of the contract by standing nearer the sign reading "Did live up to contract" or the sign reading "Did not live up to contract," or anywhere in the middle.

> **Teacher Note**
>
> For further instructions on using this exercise, see "Using the Barometer Method" (Document #: TX001021) at *smp.org/LivinginChrist.*

4. Ask volunteers to share the logic behind why they are standing where they are.

5. Conclude by revealing the identity of the mystery person. Lead a discussion about the characteristics necessary to fulfill an agreement and each party's responsibility when entering into a covenant-like relationship.

Step 12

Now that the students are closer to the end of the unit, make sure they are all on track with their final performance tasks, if you have assigned them.

If possible, devote 50 to 60 minutes for the students to ask questions about the tasks and to work individually.

1. Remind the students to bring to class any work they have already prepared so that they can work on it during the class period. If necessary, reserve the library or media center so the students can do any book or online research. Download and print extra copies of the handouts "Final Performance Task Options for Unit 4" (Document #: TX001110) and "Rubric for Final Performance Tasks for Unit 4" (Document #: TX001111). Review the final performance task options, answer questions, and ask the students to choose one if they have not already done so.

2. Provide some class time for the students to work on their performance tasks. This then allows you to work with the students who need additional guidance with the project.

Step 13

Provide the students with a tool to use for reflecting about what they learned in the unit and how they learned.

This learning experience provides the students with an excellent opportunity to reflect on how their understandings of the early leaders of Israel have developed throughout the unit.

1. Prepare by downloading and printing the handout "Learning about Learning" (Document #: TX001159; see Appendix), one for each student.

2. Distribute the handout and give the students about 15 minutes to answer the questions quietly. Invite them to share any reflections they have about the content they learned as well as their insights into the way they learned.

Final Performance Task Options for Unit 4

The following are the main ideas you are to understand from this unit. They should appear in this final performance task so your teacher can assess whether you learned the most essential content. You will not need to demonstrate understanding of the fourth bulleted point if you are working with a person from before the Exodus.

- The first leaders of Israel had a unique calling from God.
- The people of Israel became who they were through significant events such as the call of Abraham and the other patriarchs, the Exodus, and the Covenant at Mount Sinai.
- We can look to the early leaders of Israel for inspiration in our lives today.
- From the beginning of their covenant relationship with God, the people of Israel had a specific pattern. This was the cycle of redemption, in which they sinned and moved away from the covenant but were able to return to God because of God's faithfulness and love.

Option 1: Group Research on a Key Biblical Figure

This paper will help you to display your understanding of the concept of covenant and the leaders of the Pentateuch.

- Choose one of the following biblical figures. (Your teacher may assign one.)
  - o Abraham
  - o Sarah
  - o Isaac
  - o Jacob
  - o Leah
  - o Rachel
  - o Joseph
  - o Moses
  - o Miriam

- Analyze your figure using the following questions as a guide:
  - o Who is your figure?
  - o List three major characteristics the person displayed.
  - o What obstacles did your figure face?
  - o Did the figure overcome these obstacles? If so, how?
  - o What role did your figure play in salvation history?
  - o How could we learn from this figure today?

- Put your group's answers in presentation form to share with the other students. (Be creative. For example, make an interview with this person on a talk show or present it as a news story.) Follow the rubric for this assignment carefully.
- After you make your presentation, the other students will have time to ask you questions.

Document #:TX001110

Option 2: Research a Woman Who Shaped Judeo-Christian History

Research a woman who shaped Judeo-Christian history by reflecting on the interconnected meanings of *covenant* and *biblical leadership.*

- Choose one of the following biblical figures. (Your teacher may assign one.)
  - Sarah
  - Rebekah
  - Leah
  - Rachel
  - Hagar
  - Miriam
  - Judith
  - Esther
  - Deborah
  - Salome
  - Mary (mother of Jesus)
  - Elizabeth
  - Mary Magdalene
  - Bathsheba
  - Eve
  - Hannah
  - Rahab
  - Jael
  - Joanna
  - Martha (sister of Lazarus)
  - Mary (sister of Lazarus)
  - Naomi
  - Ruth
  - Zipporah

- Write a two-paragraph description of your figure and create a visual depiction of the woman and her story. This could be done through a collage, diagram, painting, or drawing. The two-paragraph description must answer the following questions:
  - Where does this woman appear in the Bible, and what is her story?
  - Why does the Bible mention her? Why is she important to the Judeo-Christian tradition? How did she earn her place in salvation history?
  - How does she fit into her time period? For example, was she a typical woman for her time or was she a trailblazer?
  - What can we learn from her?

- Create a visual depiction of your figure and her story. Attach the two-paragraph explanation to the back of the visual depiction.

Rubric for Final Performance Tasks for Unit 4

Criteria	4	3	2	1
Assignment includes all items requested in the instructions.	Assignment includes all items requested, and they are completed above expectations.	Assignment includes all items requested.	Assignment includes over half of the items requested.	Assignment includes less than half of the items requested.
Assignment shows understanding of the concept *the first leaders of Israel had a unique calling from God.*	Assignment shows unusually insightful understanding of this concept.	Assignment shows good understanding of this concept.	Assignment shows adequate understanding of this concept.	Assignment shows little understanding of this concept.
Assignment shows understanding of the concept *the people of Israel became who they were through significant events such as the call of Abraham and the other patriarchs, the Exodus, and the Covenant at Mount Sinai.*	Assignment shows unusually insightful understanding of this concept.	Assignment shows good understanding of this concept.	Assignment shows adequate understanding of this concept.	Assignment shows little understanding of this concept.
Assignment shows understanding of the concept *we can look to the early leaders of Israel for inspiration in our lives today.*	Assignment shows unusually insightful understanding of this concept.	Assignment shows good understanding of this concept.	Assignment shows adequate understanding of this concept.	Assignment shows little understanding of this concept.
Assignment shows understanding of the concept *from the beginning of their covenant relationship with God, the people of Israel had a specific pattern. This was the cycle of redemption, in which they sinned and moved away from the covenant but were able to return to God because of God's faithfulness and love.*	Assignment shows unusually insightful understanding of this concept.	Assignment shows good understanding of this concept.	Assignment shows adequate understanding of this concept.	Assignment shows little understanding of this concept.
The method of presentation is effective in teaching the class about the person researched because main points are presented clearly.	The method of presentation is extremely effective because main points are presented very clearly.	The method of presentation is effective because main points are presented clearly.	The method of presentation is somewhat effective because main points are presented somewhat clearly.	The method of presentation is not effective because main points are not presented clearly.
Assignment uses proper grammar and spelling.	Assignment has no grammar or spelling errors.	Assignment has one grammar or spelling error.	Assignment has two grammar or spelling errors.	Assignment has more than two grammar or spelling errors.

© 2010 by Saint Mary's Press
Living in Christ Series

Document #: TX001111

Vocabulary for Unit 4

Babylonian Exile: In 587 BC, the Babylonians pillaged Judah, destroyed the Temple and the city of Jerusalem, and banished the people in chains to serve as slaves in Babylon. The Exile lasted until 539 BC.

Exodus: A Greek word meaning "to go out." The Exodus was one of the pivotal events in the Old Testament. God's power was revealed when the nation of Israel was freed from the bondage of Egypt in awe-inspiring and wondrous ways.

genealogy: A type of family tree. More than a bloodline, a genealogy was a literary form used as a proclamation to make connections with important ancestors.

idolatry: The worship of false gods or the love of anything more than the one, true God.

Israel: At the ancient site of Bethel, God affirmed the promises of the Covenant and gave Jacob a new name: Israel (see Genesis 35:9–15). Jacob, or Israel, became the symbol for the struggles of the Hebrew peoples across the millennia. His Hebrew descendants became known as Israelites.

manna: Little flakes the Israelites collected and boiled or baked into a breadlike substance, symbolizing God as the sole sustainer of life.

monotheism: The belief in and worship of one, true God.

Passover: The night the Lord passed over the houses of the Israelites marked by the blood of the lamb, and spared the firstborn sons from death. It also is the feast that celebrates the deliverance of the Chosen People from bondage in Egypt and the Exodus from Egypt to the Promised Land.

patriarch: The father or leader of a tribe, clan, or tradition. Abraham, Isaac, and Jacob were the patriarchs of the Israelite people.

Pentateuch: A Greek word meaning "five books," referring to the first five books of the Old Testament.

pharaoh: A ruler of ancient Egypt.

redemption: From the Latin *redemptio,* meaning "a buying back," referring, in the Old Testament, to Yahweh's deliverance of Israel and, in the New Testament, to Christ's deliverance of all Christians from the forces of sin.

repentance: A word from the Latin *poenitire,* meaning "to make sorry," referring to the recognition and rejection of personal sin.

ritual: A specific ceremony such as the ritual of the Mass, or a book that contains the texts that are to be recited during such ceremonies.

sacrifice: To make holy; a rite offered to God on behalf of the people, presided over by a priest who leads and represents the community in adoration, repentance, gratitude, and honor (see Hebrews 2:17). In the Old

Testament, a sacrifice was needed as an atonement, a healing rite to restore holiness, cleanse people from infractions of the Law, and reconcile their covenant relationship with God (see Psalm 51:1–17).

Sinai Covenant: The Covenant established with the Israelites at Mount Sinai that renewed the Covenant with Abraham's descendants. It establishes the Israelites as God's Chosen People.

Ten Commandments: Sometimes called the Decalogue, the list of ten norms, or rules of moral behavior, that God gave Moses and that are the basis of ethical conduct.

theophany: God's manifestation of himself in a visible form to enrich human understanding of him. An example is God's appearance to Moses in the form of a burning bush.

Document #: TX001112

Leadership Scavenger Hunt

Name: _____

Person Researched	Location of Person (Chapter and Verse)	Role of Person in Book	Summary of Person's Story	Why the Person Is Important in the Story

Document #: TX001113

The Early leaders of Israel Quiz

Name: _____

Write *true* or *false* in the space next to each statement.

_____ God does *not* fulfill his covenant with Hagar for Ishmael to be the father of a large nation.

_____ Abraham's servant prays to God to point out the woman who will become Isaac's wife, with the sign that she offer him and his camels a drink of water.

_____ Isaac's wife must be from Abraham's extended family.

_____ Rebekah receives a blessing similar to Abraham's.

_____ The Lord's blessing "The elder shall serve the younger" comes true in the case of Jacob and Esau.

_____ Of all the patriarch's wives, only Leah is able to have a child without help from the Lord.

_____ Jacob's name is officially changed to Israel because he visited that country many times.

_____ The Twelve Tribes of Israel are named after the many children of Abraham.

_____ The name of Moses' sister is Erin.

_____ Laban tricks Jacob into working for him for many years.

_____ The outward sign of the covenant God makes with Abraham is the yarmulke.

_____ As he is about to be sacrificed, Isaac argues desperately with Abraham.

_____ The covenant God makes with Abraham is mentioned only once and is never renewed.

_____ Bilhah and Zilpah are two of Jacob's wives.

_____ Isaac knows he is giving the birthright to Jacob instead of Esau.

_____ The Promised Land is the land of Ur of the Chaldeans.

_____ The names of biblical figures are changed because God does not like the names they have.

_____ A covenant is a legal agreement that all parties involved sign.

_____ God appears as a loving and compassionate being throughout the Book of Genesis.

_____ Before talking with God, Abraham was a polytheist.

Document #: TX001114

The Ten Commandments

Commandment	Meaning	Reference
I am the LORD your God . . . you shall have no other gods before me.	Love and obey God before all else and let nothing have greater importance in your life.	Ex 20:2–6, Deut 5:6–10
You shall not make wrongful use of the name of the LORD your God.	Honor the name of God. Be reverent in speech.	Ex 20:7, Deut 5:11
Observe the Sabbath day and keep it holy.	Honor the Lord's Day with worship, prayer, and rest. The Sabbath is marked as a day of remembrance.	Ex 20:8–11, Deut 5:12–15
Honor your father and your mother.	Honor your parents, listen to them, and care for them when they are elderly.	Ex 20:12, Deut 5:16
You shall not murder.	Choose life and do not murder.	Ex 20:13, Deut 5:17
Neither shall you commit adultery.	Choose chastity and loyalty. Honor marriage vows to protect the family.	Ex 20:14, Deut 5:18
Neither shall you steal.	Choose justice. Don't steal. Build security and confidence in one another.	Ex 20:15, Deut 5:19
Neither shall you bear false witness against your neighbor.	Choose honesty. Do not lie. Build trust and faith among people. Make your word and witness honorable.	Ex 20:16, Deut 5:20
Neither shall you covet your neighbor's wife. Neither shall you desire your neighbor's house.	Don't covet or entertain fantasies of being with another's spouse. Choose purity of mind. Reject jealousy.	Ex 20:17, Deut 5:21
Neither shall you desire your neighbor's . . . male or female slave, or ox, or donkey, or anything that belongs to your neighbor.	Choose freedom from greed. Don't envy another's property or good fortune. Prevent sin by not entertaining jealous thoughts that might lead to stealing another's property.	Ex 20:17, Deut 5:21

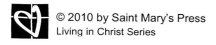

Leadership Quotations

On a separate sheet of paper, for each quotation below, answer the three questions that follow.

Quotation 1: "A leader is a dealer in hope." —Napoleon Bonaparte

Quotation 2: "I suppose leadership at one time meant muscles; but today it means getting along with people." —Mahatma Gandhi

Quotation 3: "A leader takes people where they want to go. A great leader takes people where they don't necessarily want to go, but ought to be." —Rosalynn Carter, wife of former U.S. President Jimmy Carter

Quotation 4: "Cautious, careful people, always casting about to preserve their reputation and social standing, never can bring about reform. Those who are really in earnest must be willing to be anything or nothing in the world's estimation, and publicly and privately, in season and out, avow their sympathy with despised and persecuted ideas and their advocates, and bear the consequences." — Susan B. Anthony, suffragist

1. What does this quotation mean?

2. What are the characteristics of a leader that this quotation claims are desirable?

3. Do you agree or disagree with what this quotation claims? Explain.

What Kind of Leader Is Moses?

Using the quotations from the handout, "Leadership Quotations" (Document #: TX001116), read or review the passages below and note how the speakers of the quotations would assess Moses' leadership in each passage from the Book of Exodus.

Exodus, chapter 1 (oppression of the Israelites in Egypt)

Exodus 2:1–10 (the birth and adoption of Moses)

Exodus 2:11–22 (Moses' flight to Midian)

Exodus 2:23—4:17 (the burning bush and Moses' commission)

Exodus, chapters 7–11 (the ten plagues)

Exodus, chapter 12 (the Passover ritual prescribed)

Exodus, chapter 20 (the Ten Commandments, the fear of God)

The Cycle of Redemption

Throughout salvation history, the Judeo-Christian people have been caught in the cycle of redemption, a theme that runs throughout the Old Testament.

> As the priests and scribes wrote, they saw a pattern that described their history. . . .
> This pattern occurs [as follows:]
> - God creates or enters into a covenant, and it is good.
> - Humanity falls into idolatry, resulting in disease, war, and grief.
> - God sends teachers, kings, prophets, and others who lead the people to repentance.
> - The people return to following the covenant.
> - Peace and God's healing return to the people.

(From *Saint Mary's Press® Essential Bible Dictionary*, by Sheila O'Connell-Roussell

[Winona, MN: Saint Mary's Press, 2005], pages 40–41. © 2005 by Saint Mary's Press. All rights reserved.)

In agreeing to follow the Ten Commandments and accept God's love and protection, the Israelites chose to enter into a covenant with God.

Because of the Ten Commandments, the Israelites are responsible for maintaining the following:
- **Obedience.** In the Old Testament, the Hebrew word for *obedience* meant primarily "listening" or "hearing." An obedient person heard God's Word and followed it (see Exodus 15:26). To be obedient was simply to align oneself with God's will.
- **Respect for divine justice.** The Hebrew and Greek words translated as "justice" are also translated as "righteousness" and "judgment." Divine justice calls for the fair and equitable distribution of life's necessities. The scriptural idea of justice is based on the truth that all humans have dignity and worth and are children of God. God's love for all creation is shown in his emphasis on justice, which is love in action.
- **Openness to Divine Revelation.** Revelation is the act or process by which God reveals himself and the divine plan to humanity. It is a gift, a mystery of the Divine Presence breaking into human history.
- **Commitment to ethical responsibility.** The commandments of God are the fundamental rules of conduct for the Chosen People. The Ten Commandments are about the love of God and love of neighbor.
- **Commitment to the Covenant / Commandments.** The covenants between God and Israel are central to the Old Testament, where God promised to be faithful to the Chosen People, who in turn were expected to observe God's commandments.

The Bible: The Living Word of God

Unit 4 Quiz

Name: _____

Part I: True or False
Write *true* or *false* in the space next to each statement.

_____ God does *not* fulfill his covenant with Hagar for Ishmael to be the father of a large nation.

_____ Abraham's servant prays to God to point out the woman who will become Isaac's wife, with the sign that she offer him and his camels a drink of water.

_____ Isaac's wife must be from Abraham's extended family.

_____ Rebekah receives a blessing similar to Abraham's.

_____ The Lord's blessing "The elder shall serve the younger" comes true in the case of Jacob and Esau.

_____ Of all the patriarchs' wives, only Leah is able to have a child without help from the Lord.

_____ Jacob's name is officially changed to Israel because he visited that country many times.

_____ The Twelve Tribes of Israel are named after the many children of Abraham.

_____ The name of Moses' sister is Erin.

_____ Laban tricks Jacob into working for him for many years.

_____ The outward sign of the covenant God makes with Abraham is the yarmulke.

_____ As he is about to be sacrificed, Isaac argues desperately with Abraham.

_____ The covenant God makes with Abraham is mentioned only once and is never renewed.

_____ Bilhah and Zilpah are two of Jacob's wives.

_____ Isaac knows he is giving the birthright to Jacob instead of Esau.

_____ The Promised Land is the land of Ur of the Chaldeans.

_____ The names of biblical figures are changed because God does not like the names they have.

_____ A covenant is a legal agreement that all parties involved sign.

_____ God appears as a loving and compassionate being throughout the Book of Genesis.

_____ Before talking with God, Abraham was a polytheist.

Document #: TX001119

Part II: Short Answer
Answer the following questions in paragraph form. Use examples, without summarizing (just cite the chapter and verse—for example, Genesis 23:4).

1. Explain how Abraham develops the Covenant and proves his loyalty to God.

2. Four women in the first thirty-five chapters of Genesis play remarkable roles in the futures of their husbands and children. Name these four women, whom they are related to, and how they affect the future of the Israelite people.

3. Citing examples, explain how Jacob's story illustrates divine justice.

Document #: TX001119

Barometer: Modern Contracts

Rabbi Aaron Soloveitchik agreed at a young age to serve his Jewish brothers and sisters. After facing many obstacles along the way, has he lived up to the commitment he made? Read the following article, and then you decide.

Rabbi Endures Pain to Teach Talmud

Every week, Rabbi Aaron Soloveitchik leaves his home in Chicago and boards a plane for New York. There, though a stroke three years ago has left him in constant pain and barely able to walk, he slowly makes his way from an apartment to a classroom building at the Elchanan Theological Seminary, where 70 rabbinical students fill a classroom and listen attentively to the man they call Rav Aaron.

Seated behind a desk cluttered with Jewish texts, the 69-year-old rabbi—considered one of the world's foremost Talmudic scholars and authorities on Jewish law—begins the two-hour *shiur,* or class, slowly articulating complex laws of betrothal and numerous opinions of rabbinic sages recorded throughout the ages.

"It's as if he has the entire Talmud before his very eyes," said a second-year rabbinical student from Pascagoula, Miss., Fivel Smiles. Torah, the oral and written law, "is his life, his therapy."

A Study in Human Character

After suffering his stroke, Rav Aaron continued his teaching in Chicago. And this year, when the Elchanan seminary asked him to come teach a twice-weekly class, the rabbi accepted without hesitation, despite the hardships involved.

"I don't know how people can retire," said the rabbi. "It's sadistic. One's mind begins to rot." To his students and colleagues at the seminary, which is affiliated with Yeshiva University, Rav Aaron is a study in human character as profound as the centuries-old Talmudic texts he has taught for 40 years.

"It's a wonder how such a frail shell can possess a power and enthusiasm that mesmerizes his audiences," said the seminary's director, Rabbi Zevulun Charlop. "You're so taken by his spirit and dynamism, that you don't notice the physical ailment after a while."

"His courage and determination to teach the Torah cannot be stopped," said a postgraduate student, Rabbi Joshua Hoffman, who has studied with Rav Aaron for the last seven years.

A Difficult Task

But after rehabilitation, including, most recently, regular treatments of acupuncture, effects of the stroke on the rabbi's body remain. The daily walk from his apartment on Yeshiva's campus on Amsterdam Avenue and 185th Street to an adjacent classroom building takes nearly a half hour.

"Do you know what it's like to tie my shoes or to put the tefilin on my hand?" he asked, holding out his shaking left hand and pointing to where he binds the traditional phylacteries each morning. "It's as difficult as parting the Red Sea."

"I try to elevate myself through my suffering," said the rabbi. "I'm in constant pain. But when I give a *shiur,* I don't feel it as much."

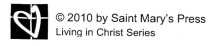

Document #: TX001120

For the rabbi, the opportunity to return to the seminary—where at least one member of the Soloveitchik family has taught since 1929 and where he himself taught for six years in the 1960s—is of special significance.

"It's an invigorating feeling to teach at the school where my brother and father have taught," said the rabbi, who has six children, four of whom are rabbis, and 22 grandchildren. "I have feelings of trepidation and excitement."

His father, Rabbi Moshe Soloveitchik, was a noted scholar in several Eastern European communities before joining the Seminary in 1929. After Rabbi Moshe's death, Rav Aaron's older brother, Dr. Joseph Ber Soloveitchik, became the Seminary's pre-eminent scholar, remaining there 46 years until 1985 when poor health forced him to give up his classes.

Rav Aaron, a graduate of Yeshiva College in 1940 with a Bachelor of Arts degree, earned a law degree from New York University in 1946. In Chicago, where he has lived since 1966, he founded the Yeshiva of Brisk in 1974 to honor his family.

The challenge for stroke victims, the rabbi wrote in an essay from his hospital bed in 1983, "is to galvanize one's moral and spiritual potential."

"I've never allowed myself to become victimized and frustrated by the stroke," he said. "With God's help, I have been strengthened."

(This story is from the *New York Times*, January 4, 1987, at *http://query.nytimes.com/gst/fullpage .html?res=9B0DE0DF1338F937A35752C0A961948260&sec=health&spon=&pagewanted=1*. Used with permission of the *New York Times*.)

© 2010 by Saint Mary's Press
Living in Christ Series

Document #: TX001120

Leadership Statements

Following is a possible list of statements to be used in the step 9 learning experience:

- To be a leader is to be a ruler of a group of people.

- If you are in charge of a group of people, you can control their actions and opinions.

- Good leaders listen to their people and try to do what is best for those people.

- Leaders know exactly where they are leading their followers at all times.

- Leadership can be learned.

- You are born with leadership characteristics.

- God is omniscient and therefore knows who will make a good leader.

- God always chooses people who are obviously going to be great leaders.

- God sometimes chooses leaders from the most unlikely places.

- You must be popular to be a good leader.

- God always calls the gifted.

- God always gifts the called.

- Jacob was an ideal choice to lead Israel.

- Moses was an obvious choice to lead the Israelites out of Egypt.

- The characteristics of leaders should change based on the situations they find themselves in.

Unit 4 Test

Part 1: Multiple Choice

Write your answers in the blank spaces at the left.

1. _____ The number of Apostles parallels the _____.
   - **A.** number of Sacraments
   - **B.** Ten Commandments
   - **C.** Twelve Tribes of Israel
   - **D.** ten Gifts of the Holy Spirit

2. _____ In the Book of Exodus, God is spoken of as all of the following except _____.
   - **A.** as a God who saves
   - **B.** as a God who persecutes
   - **C.** as a compassionate God
   - **D.** as a God who longs to be in a conventional relationship

3. _____ The patriarch who represents God's plan to create a people more numerous than the "stars of the sky" is _____.
   - **A.** Joseph
   - **B.** Abraham
   - **C.** Isaac
   - **D.** Jacob

4. _____ What caused the pharaoh to order the enslavement of the Israelites?
   - **A.** He realized that Moses had been chosen as the Israelite leader.
   - **B.** His military leaders could not control the Israelites.
   - **C.** He saw the growing number of Israelites as a threat.
   - **D.** He discovered that Moses had killed an Egyptian.

5. _____ How did God respond to the enslavement of his People?
   - **A.** He sent an angel to destroy the house of Pharaoh.
   - **B.** He sent Aaron to talk to Pharaoh's daughter.
   - **C.** He convinced Pharaoh's army to turn against the government.
   - **D.** He called Moses to be his voice of truth and arm of justice.

6. _____ The story of the Israelites' crossing the Red Sea from the Book of Exodus is read every year _____.

    A. during the Easter Vigil
    B. on Ash Wednesday
    C. on Palm Sunday
    D. on Christmas

7. _____ Which of the following does not describe Passover?

    A. The night the Lord passed over the houses of Egypt marked by lamb's blood.
    B. The night the firstborn children and animals were killed in houses not marked by lamb's blood.
    C. The feast that celebrates the entrance of Jesus into Jerusalem.
    D. The feast that celebrates the deliverance of the Chosen People from bondage in Egypt.

8. _____ The tenth plague convinced Pharaoh to release the Israelites because _____.

    A. he was grief-stricken when his firstborn son was killed
    B. Moses had left Egypt
    C. there were not enough burial places in Egypt
    D. he was afraid of the Israelites' god

9. _____ Jesus is called the new Paschal Lamb because _____.

    A. his sacrifice saves us from eternal death, or separation from God
    B. he was risen from the dead
    C. his sacrifice saves us from ever having to suffer
    D. he gave us the Sacrament of the Eucharist at the Last Supper

10. _____ The Ten Commandments are sometimes called _____.

    A. the Torah
    B. the Decalogue
    C. the Pentateuch
    D. the New Commandment

Document #: TX001300

Part 2: Matching

Match each statement in column 1 with a term from column 2. Write the letter that corresponds to your choice in the space provided. (*Note:* There are two extra items in column 2).

Column 1

1. _____ Jacob's new name after renewing the covenant promise God made with Abraham.

2. _____ The son of Isaac who symbolizes those descendants of Abraham who will not live directly under the Covenant.

3. _____ The place that God said the children of Abraham would inhabit.

4. _____ The account of the enslaved Israelites, their liberation, and trust.

5. _____ Occurrences meant to upset the authoritative patterns of the Egyptian Empire and lead to the freedom of the Israelites.

6. _____ The sacred ground where God forms a covenant with his Chosen People.

7. _____ Little flakes the Israelites collected and boiled or baked into a breadlike substance.

8. _____ The form in which God identified himself to Moses as "I am who am."

9. _____ The list of norms, or rules of moral behavior, that God gave to Moses and that are the basis of ethical conduct.

10. _____ The brother of Moses whom God asked to assist Moses in confronting Pharaoh.

Column 2

A. Book of Exodus

B. Ten Commandments

C. Mount Sinai

D. Israel

E. Book of Genesis

F. Aaron

G. Esau

H. manna

I. Promised Land

J. tongues of fire

K. ten plagues

L. burning bush

Document #: TX001300

Part 3: Short Answer

Answer each of the following questions in paragraph form on a separate sheet of paper.

1. Who were the first leaders of Israel that God called? What did he ask them to do and how did they respond?

2. How did the Sinai Covenant establish the Israelites as God's Chosen People?

3. What can we learn from the early leaders of Israel for inspiration in our lives today?

4. What was the "pattern" of the relationship between the Israelites and God from the beginning of their covenant with him?

Document #: TX001300

Unit 4 Test Answer Key

Part 1: Multiple Choice

1.	C	6.	A
2.	B	7.	C
3.	D	8.	D
4.	C	9.	A
5.	D	10.	B

Part 2: Matching

1.	D	6.	C
2.	G	7.	H
3.	I	8.	L
4.	A	9.	B
5.	K	10.	F

Part 3: Short Answer

1. The first leaders of Israel, called patriarchs, were Abraham, Isaac, Jacob, and Joseph. Abraham, the first of the patriarchs, makes a covenant with God wherein Abraham will be the father of God's Chosen People. This covenant is passed on to his son, Isaac, whose two sons, Jacob and Esau, feud over the birthright to continue their father's role. Jacob achieves the birthright and produces twelve sons, who will each lead a tribe, becoming the Twelve Tribes of Israel. The youngest of his sons, Joseph, when sold into slavery in Egypt by his brothers, becomes powerful and represents how God's Chosen People will go out into the world outside Israel.

2. Through the Exodus, God guides the people from slavery to the Promised Land. The Sinai Covenant renewed the covenant God made with Abraham and his descendants. In it God promises the Israelites they will be his Chosen People, a kingdom of priests, a holy nation, if they live according to his Law by being righteous and moral; if the Israelites agree to the covenant, they will dwell in the Promised Land and will know God, who is merciful.

3. From Abraham and Sarah, his wife, we can learn trust in God and faith in his promises and his goodness; God asked Abraham to move, to be a leader of God's People, and to sacrifice his son, Isaac; Sarah believed in God's Word that she would bear a son and waited with patience. Jacob, although a schemer, is a repentant brother, a good father, and a successful herder, giving us an example in our families and in our work. Joseph forgave his brothers and used his knowledge for good purposes, just as we should forgive others and use our abilities for good.

4. The pattern was the cycle of redemption, in which the Israelites sinned and moved away from the covenant, but were able to return to God because of God's faithfulness and love. *(Refer to examples during the Exodus when the Israelites doubted God's protection and concern, only to be shown his mercy and acceptance.)*

Unit 5   Israel's Response to the Covenant under the Judges and Kings

Overview

This fifth unit examines Israel's covenant relationship with God under different leaders. The Israelites were in a cycle in which they moved away from God and then needed a servant leader to bring them back to the Covenant. The students become familiar with the various judges and kings and reflect on the personal qualities that were in line with what God wanted.

Key Questions and Understandings

At the end of this unit, the students will possess a deeper understanding of the following important concepts:

- The covenant relationship between the Israelites and God required specific responsibilities from the people of Israel and their leaders.
- God wanted the judges and the kings to rule in a way that was faithful to the Covenant.
- The judges and kings were tempted by other gods and pleasures and sometimes turned away from the Covenant.
- Servant leadership was the model of governance that ensured fidelity to the Covenant with God.

At the end of this unit, the students will have answered these questions:

- What was the Covenant between God and the Israelites after they entered the Promised Land?
- What temptations led the people of Israel and their leaders—judges and kings—away from the Covenant?
- What was the relationship between the people of Israel and their leaders?
- What characteristics made it possible for judges or kings to rule the way God wanted them to?
- What can the failures and successes of the Israelite judges and kings teach us about leadership today?

How Will You Know the Students Understand?

These tools will help you to assess the students' understanding of the main concepts:

- handout "Final Performance Task Options for Unit 5" (Document #: TX001122)
- handout "Rubric for Final Performance Tasks for Unit 5" (Document #: TX001123)
- handout "Unit 5 Test" (Document #: TX001275)

The Suggested Path to Understanding

This teacher guide provides you with one path to take with the students, enabling them to examine leadership and become familiar with the leadership of the judges and kings of Israel. It is not necessary to use all the learning experiences, but if you substitute other material from this course or your own material for some of the material offered here, check to see that you have covered all relevant facets of understanding and that you have not missed knowledge or skills required in later units.

| Explain | **Step 1:** Preassess what the students already know about the judges and kings. |

| Empathize | **Step 2:** Follow this assessment by presenting to the students the handouts "Final Performance Task Options for Unit 5" (Document #: TX001122) and "Rubric for Final Performance Tasks for Unit 5" (Document #: TX001123). |

| Perceive | **Step 3:** Lead the students in defining *heroism*. |

| Apply | **Step 4:** Use the jigsaw method to establish the qualities of a covenant hero and servant leader. |

| Interpret | **Step 5:** Have the students reflect on the role of a judge. |

| Explain | **Step 6:** Present information about Joshua and the judges. |

| Interpret | **Step 7:** Invite the students to get to know the judges. |

| Empathize | **Step 8:** Give a quiz to assess student understanding. |

| Explain | **Step 9:** Have the students "meet and interview" the kings of Israel. |

| Interpret | **Step 10:** Have the students create Jesus' family tree from David to Jesus. |

> **Teacher Note**
>
> Step 9 may require two or more class periods for the project and two or more days for the final presentation.

| Explain | **Step 11:** Have the students prepare for critical analysis of selected Scripture passages. |

| Empathize | **Step 12:** Lead a discussion of the essay. |

| Empathize | **Step 13:** Now that the students are closer to the end of the unit, make sure they are all on track with their final performance tasks, if you have assigned them. |

Step 14: Provide the students with a tool to use for reflecting about what they learned in the unit and how they learned.

Background for Teaching This Content with These Methods

In addition to finding information about the pedagogical approach used in this guide, you will also find background information on these and other topics at *smp.org/LivinginChrist:*

- "The Book of Joshua" (Document #: TX001044)
- "King Solomon and the Divided Monarchy: The Book of Kings" (Document #: TX001042)
- "Introduction to the Historical Books" (Document #: TX001041)
- "Kings Saul and David: The Books of Samuel" (Document #: TX001043)
- "The Book of Judges" (Document #: TX001045)

The Web site also has background information on the following teaching methods:

- "Using the Think-Pair-Share Method" (Document #: TX001019)
- "How to Lead a Socratic Seminar" (Document #: TX001006)

Student Book Articles

The articles covered in unit 5 are from "Section 3: Revelation in the Old Testament" of the student book. If you believe the students would do the reading more successfully with additional structure, see the handout "Student Notes for Unit 5" (Document #: TX001046) at *smp.org/LivinginChrist.*

- "Joshua: God Is on Our Side" (article 39)
- "Judges: The Book of Deliverers" (article 40)
- "From Saul to Solomon: The Desire for Unity" (article 41)
- "David: Recognizing a Servant" (article 42)

Scripture Passages

- Exodus 3:11–22 (Moses)
- Joshua, chapters 1–2 (God promises to assist the Transjordan tribes)
- Joshua 1:1–11 (divine promise of assistance)
- Joshua, chapter 5 (rites at Gilgal)
- Joshua 21:43—22:9 (God fulfills his promise to Joshua and the Israelites)
- Joshua 23:1—24:28 (final plea and Joshua's farewell)
- Joshua 24:1–14 (reminder of the divine goodness)
- Judges 3:7–11 (Othniel)

- Judges 3:12–30 (Ehud)
- Judges, chapter 4 (Deborah and Barak)
- Judges, chapters 6–8 (the story of Gideon)
- Judges 6:1–24 (the call of Gideon)
- Judges 11:1—12:7 (Jepthah and the Shibboleth incident)
- Judges 13:1—16:31 (the story of Samson)
- Judges 16:4–22 (Samson and Delilah)
- Judges 21:25 (explanation for lawlessness during the period of judges)
- 1 Samuel 2:12–17 (wickedness of Eli's sons)
- 1 Samuel 2:22–25 (Eli's futile rebuke)
- 1 Samuel 2:27–36 (doom of Eli's house)
- 1 Samuel 7:2–6 (religious reform)
- 1 Samuel 8:1–5 (request for a king)
- 1 Samuel 8:6–22 (God grants the request)
- 1 Samuel 12:1–18 (Samuel warns the people about a king)
- 1 Samuel 13:1–14 (Saul offers sacrifice and is reproved)
- 1 Samuel 17:32–51 (David defeats Goliath)
- 2 Samuel 5:1–5 (David, king of Israel)
- 2 Samuel, chapter 7 (David's Covenant with God)
- 2 Samuel 7:8–29 (the Lord's promises and David's prayer)
- 2 Samuel, chapter 11 (David's sin)
- 2 Samuel 12:7–25 (David's punishment and repentance)
- Matthew 1:1–17 (the genealogy of Jesus)
- Matthew 4:18–22 (the call of the first disciples)
- Acts 13:16–43 (Paul's address in the synagogue)

Vocabulary

If you choose to provide a vocabulary list for material covered in both the student book and the teacher guide, download and print the handout "Vocabulary for Unit 5" (Document #: TX001124), one for each student.

Ark of the Covenant	First and Second Kings	judges
Baal . . . Asherah	First and Second Samuel	king
Canaan	genealogy	servant leadership

Learning Experiences

 Explain

Step 1

Preassess what the students already know about the judges and kings.

Explore what the students already know about the judges and the kings to determine their prior knowledge about this subject.

Option 1: What Makes a Good Leader?

Teacher Note

Identifying good and poor leadership qualities requires the students to recall examples of God's interaction with humanity. Be sure to present the good and poor qualities only as they relate to following the Covenant. Avoid characterizing certain leaders as good or bad people. Be sure the students have Bibles to look up Bible passages.

This learning experience provides the students the opportunity to recall their understanding of *covenant* and to analyze its role in the relationship between God and humanity during the period of the judges and kings in salvation history.

1. Prepare by downloading and printing the handout "Biblical Passages about Leadership" (Document #: TX001125), one for each student. Choose two to four of the excerpts from Joshua, Judges, and First and Second Samuel, depending on their length.

2. On the day of the learning experience, encourage the students to individually brainstorm examples of when they have been good leaders. Allow 1 to 2 minutes for this task.

3. They should further explore it by writing answers to the following questions:

   - What was the situation?
   - Who was involved?
   - Did I have any obstacles to overcome or problems to solve? What did I accomplish?
   - What did I learn from this situation?

   Distribute pens or pencils and allow about 5 to 7 minutes for the students to write.

4. When time is up, discuss the characteristics the students demonstrated as good leaders. Ask volunteers to write the students' suggestions on the board.

5. Ask the students to identify similarities among the suggestions. Ask:

   ➤ What characteristics does a good leader have? Why are they important?

6. Next, explain that the students will analyze examples of leadership from the books of Joshua, Judges, and First and Second Samuel. Distribute copies of the handout "Biblical Passages about Leadership" (Document #: TX001125). Identify the passages you have chosen and ask the students to locate them in their Bibles. Explain that the students should choose one example of good leadership and one of poor leadership. Allow the students about 10 minutes to read.

7. When time is up, invite the students to summarize for the large group the passages they read. From their own reading and after hearing from their classmates, ask the students to choose one character they most associate themselves with. Have them write a brief journal paragraph to explain why.

8. Ask:

> ➤ If you were in this character's situation, what might you have done and why?

9. Collect the students' journal entries or ask them to keep their reflections in their class notebooks for later use.

Option 2: Think-Pair-Share

In this learning experience, the students will work together to assess good and poor leadership qualities.

1. Prepare by downloading and printing the handout "Biblical Passages about Leadership" (Document #: TX001125), one for each student. From the handout, choose enough passages from each book of the Bible to accommodate pairs or groups of three. The passages should highlight good and poor leadership qualities. Download and print the handout "Graph for Evaluating Leadership Qualities" (Document #: TX001126), one for each student.

2. On the day of the learning activity, distribute pens or pencils and ask the students to individually write in their notebooks the characteristics of a good leader. They may include individuals they think embody these characteristics and explain why. Allow 3 to 5 minutes for writing. When time is up, ask the students to write down characteristics of a poor leader.

3. Next, place the students into groups of two or three. Ask the groups to compare definitions or examples of good and poor leaders. Tell them to combine their lists onto one page with combined definitions, which they will hand in at the end of the learning experience. The groups should identify the top three characteristics they think describe good and poor leaders.

4. Distribute copies of the handout "Biblical Passages about Leadership" (Document #: TX001125). Assign each small group a passage from the handout. Ask the groups to read the passages and identify the qualities of the leader portrayed. The group members will decide whether the leader is good or poor

based on their definitions. The students should discuss whether they would want this person to lead them. Allow about 10 minutes for discussion.

5. When time is up, ask the small-group members to introduce to the class the leader they studied, identify the person's leadership characteristics, and explain whether they would want the person to lead them and why.

6. While the groups present, ask the other students to use the handout "Graph for Evaluating Leadership Qualities" (Document #: TX001126) to take notes on the leaders and their characteristics.

7. When the presentations are finished, collect the handouts or the students' notes to assess the students' level of understanding. This will help you to determine how much review needs to occur before moving on.

Option 3: Rule of the Day

This option provides the students the chance to evaluate classroom rules that directly affect them.

1. Prepare by having available plain copy paper and markers or colored pencils. On sheets of newsprint or on the board, create two lists of rules. In the first column or list, write seven rules you use in your classroom every day. In the other column or list, write seven rules that are the complete opposite.

2. On the day of the learning experience, point out the lists to the students. Tell the students they will creatively write or draw pictures of the class for each list.

3. Distribute the markers or colored pencils and paper. Then read the second list first. Tell the students that these could be new rules of the class. Ask the students to describe or portray one classroom scene that might result from adopting the new rules. Tell them they should include positive and negative results of the rules. Allow 10 to 15 minutes for the students to write or draw.

4. Next, read the list of standard classroom rules and ask the students to describe or portray a second classroom scene that might result from these rules. Ask them to include positives and negatives for such rules. Allow 10 to 15 minutes for the students to write or draw.

5. When time is up, invite the students to share their creations. You may choose to have the students post their work around the classroom for the other students to observe, or you may choose to have the students present their writings or drawings.

6. To conclude, ask the students to explain how this learning experience illustrates salvation history, thinking especially of the Ten Commandments (see Exodus 20:1–17). Ask the students to draw parallels between the trouble the Israelites get themselves into when they don't trust in God and their success when they are faithful to God and "the rules."

7. Ask the students to make connections among covenant, rules, faithfulness to and consequences of laws or commandments, and the leadership of Israel.

Step 2

Follow this assessment by presenting to the students the handouts "Final Performance Task Options for Unit 5" (Document #: TX001122) and "Rubric for Final Performance Tasks for Unit 5" (Document #: TX001123).

This unit provides you with two ways to assess whether the students have a deep understanding of the most important concepts in the unit: comparing and contrasting a biblical servant leader with a contemporary leader or creating a critical analysis essay. Refer to "Using Final Performance Tasks to Assess Understanding" (Document #: TX001011) and "Using Rubrics to Assess Work" (Document #: TX001012) at *smp.org/LivinginChrist* for background information.

1. Prepare by downloading and printing the handouts "Final Performance Task Options for Unit 5" (Document #: TX001122) and "Rubric for Final Performance Tasks for Unit 5" (Document #: TX001123), one for each student.

2. Distribute the handouts. Give the students a choice as to which performance task they select and add additional options if you so choose. Review the directions, expectations, and rubric in class, allowing the students to ask questions.

3. Explain the types of tools and knowledge the students will gain throughout the unit so they can successfully complete the final performance task.

4. Answer questions to clarify the end point toward which the unit is headed. Remind the students as the unit progresses that each learning experience builds the knowledge and skills they will need to show you they understand how people responded to the Covenant in the Books of Joshua, Judges, First and Second Samuel, and First and Second Kings.

Teacher Note

Think ahead of time how to use the final performance tasks. Will you have the students complete option 1, "Heroes Today," on their own and then write the critical analysis essay during the unit study? Note that the directions for option 2, "Critical Analysis Essay," are also found later in step 11 if you would like to use both final performance task options.

You will want to assign due dates for the performance tasks.

If you have done these performance tasks, or very similar ones, with students before, place examples of this work in the classroom. During this introduction explain how each is a good example of what you are looking for, for different reasons. This allows the students to concretely understand what you are looking for and to understand that there is not only one way to succeed.

Step 3

Lead the students in defining heroism.

This learning experience defines *heroism*. In combination with step 4, it will help the students to identify how modern-day heroes compare to the heroes who upheld the Covenant.

1. Ask the students to name heroes from literature, movies, television, or public life. Encourage the students to select heroes with personal meaning.

2. Next, ask the students to select two of the heroes they named and to write their characteristics in their notebooks. Allow 5 minutes for the students to work.

3. When time is up, create a class list of characteristics that define a hero. Write the students' suggestions on the board.

4. After writing suggestions give the students a list of five to seven people from unit 5 who may or may not exemplify heroism. For example, you may choose from among Joshua, Deborah, Gideon, Samson, Samuel, Saul, David, or Solomon.

5. Place the students into small groups of four or five. Assign the groups one of the Scripture passages covered in this unit (see Overview at the beginning of the unit). Explain that the students will read and analyze their passages to determine whether the person is heroic based on the class definition. They will write down heroic qualities of their person. Ask the students to list any unheroic qualities as well. Allow the students 5 to 7 minutes to complete the task.

Teacher Note

The Collaborative International Dictionary of English defines *hero* as a person "of distinguished valor or enterprise in danger, or fortitude in suffering; a prominent or central personage in any remarkable action or event; hence, a great or illustrious person" (found at *define.com*).

6. When time is up, hold a large-group discussion. Ask the question "What is a hero?" and write the students' responses on the board.

7. Ask the students about the situation in which the biblical individual thrived as a hero or about others in the story whose behavior magnified someone else's heroism.

8. To conclude ask the students what a covenant hero is. List their suggestions on the board and create a group definition. Ask the students to copy the definition into their notebooks.

Apply

Step 4

Use the jigsaw method to establish the qualities of a covenant hero and servant leader.

Having a definition of what a hero is, the students will use the jigsaw method to establish the qualities of covenant heroes and servant leaders.

1. Prepare by downloading and printing the handout "Jigsaw Process" (Document #: TX001161; see Appendix), one for each small group of four.

2. As homework, assign the students to read one of four different stories from the Bible that show servant leadership. Tell the students they will write a two-paragraph theme. The first paragraph will summarize their stories. The second paragraph will analyze how the stories show servant leadership. You may choose other stories, but the following work well:

   > **Teacher Note**
   >
   > As background see "Using the Jigsaw Process" (Document #: TX001020) at *smp.org/LivinginChrist* for an explanation of this learning process.

   - Exodus 3:11–22 (Moses)
   - Joshua 1:1–11 (divine promise of assistance)
   - 1 Samuel 12:1–18 (Samuel warns the people about a king)
   - 2 Samuel 5:1–5 (David, king of Israel)
   - Acts 13:16–43 (Paul's address in the synagogue)

   Tell the students to bring their completed themes with them to class.

3. During the next class period, allow 1 to 2 minutes for the students to review their themes.

4. Next, place the students into small groups of four. Each student in the group should read a different passage.

5. Provide each group with a copy of the handout "Jigsaw Process" (Document #: TX001161; see Appendix) and ask the groups to answer the questions on it. The students will think critically not only about the stories each has read but also about the connections and similarities that exist throughout the Bible. Allow about 10 minutes for the small groups to complete the questions.

6. When time is up, call the students back into the large group to discuss the questions and how each illustrates the concept of servant leadership.

7. After the discussion ask the students to identify the qualities of a servant leader and to note similarities and differences of the characters in their stories. Write the students' final definition on the board.

8. Next, ask the students to find a connection between the qualities of a hero, defined in step 3, and servant leadership. Allow about 2 minutes for the students to review their notes from step 3.

9. To conclude, ask the students to choose from among one of the heroes from step 3 and one of the examples of servant leaders from step 4 to decide what *heroism* truly means in the context of the covenant relationship. Ask the students to share their reflections with the large group.

10. Finally, have the students read aloud together Joshua 24:1–28 to show Joshua's good leadership of the Israelites found in his dedication to the Covenant.

Step 5

Have the students reflect on the role of a judge.

As you introduce the transition of leadership from Moses and Joshua to the judges, compare and contrast the role of modern-day judges with judges in the Scriptures.

1. Ask the students to write in their notebooks about a time others judged them. Allow 5 to 10 minutes for them to respond to the following prompt and questions:

   • Think of a time when you believed you were being judged.
   • What was the situation?
   • Who was involved? (Tell students not to use names but rather "friend," "best friend," "mom," "dad," "brother," "sister," "coach," and so on.)
   • What were you "accused" of?
   • How did you feel in the situation?
   • How was it resolved?

2. When time is up, ask the students to brainstorm again on a new page. This time they will answer the same questions for the same situation as if they were the judge. Allow 5 to 10 minutes for brainstorming.

3. After the students have taken notes on judging, ask them to take out their copies of the handout "Sprint Through Salvation History" (Document #: TX001107). Ask them to review the section "Taking Over the Promised Land" on the handout. Ask:

   ➤ How does this part of salvation history reflect the Chosen People's commitment to the Covenant?

   If the students need help, encourage them to look back at their notes for details of the Covenant or reread Genesis 15:1–16 and Exodus 20:1–17.

Teacher Note

The students should recognize the contrast between modern-day judging and the function of the biblical judges. We often see judging today as ruling on someone's behavior. The role of the biblical judges was to help bring the people back to God by obeying the laws and Covenant. The exercise asks the students to reflect on actions that separate us from God and how we can avoid them.

4. Remind the students of God's covenant promise for the descendants of Abraham: "To your descendants I give this land" (Genesis 15:18). Also remind them how Moses fulfilled his part of the Covenant to "send men to reconnoiter the land of Canaan, which I am giving the Israelites" (Numbers 13:1) and how the judges further fulfilled their part of the Covenant.

5. You may want to use the PowerPoint "Joshua and the Judges" (Document #: TX001078) found at *smp.org/LivinginChrist.* It will assist you in explaining the following material to the students:

   - The Books of Joshua and Judges recount the battles and conquests of the Israelites in occupying the land of Canaan.

   - These books include successes and failures resulting from the Israelites' obedience or disobedience to the Covenant in each event.

   - The Book of Judges contains a pattern, called the Judges cycle, as follows:

     1. The Israelites worshipped other gods.
     2. God becomes angry and gives the Israelites over to the power of their enemies.
     3. The Israelites cry out to God.
     4. God raises a judge to deliver the Israelites.
     5. The judge frees the Israelites from their enemies.
     6. The land has peace while the judge lives.
     7. The judge dies and the cycle begins again.

     (*Saint Mary's Press*® *College Study Bible,* p. 306)

Explain

Step 6

Present information about Joshua and the judges.

1. Prepare by asking the students to read articles 39, 40, 41, and 42 about Joshua, the judges, the kings, and King David, in the student book.

2. During the next class period, have the students keep their student books open to these articles as you present the following information. You may want to use the PowerPoint "Kings" (Document #: TX001079) at *smp.org/LivinginChrist.* It will assist you with this presentation.

Joshua

➤ Joshua, the successor to Moses, leads the Israelites into Canaan. After the death of Moses, the Israelites need a strong leader to guide their path toward the Promised Land. God commissions the heroic and faithful Joshua.

➤ The land of Canaan was the land God promised to Abraham and his descendants.

➤ There are two reasons the Israelites find Canaan to be hostile:

 • There are the **polytheistic beliefs** of the Canaanites, including the worship of the god **Baal** and his consort, the goddess **Asherah.** Polytheistic beliefs are beliefs in many gods and goddesses.
 • The native peoples refuse to hand over their land.

➤ Joshua and the Israelite army swiftly conquer the land of Canaan. One of the pivotal moments in their conquest is the fall of a small town on the West Bank known as Jericho.

➤ In the accounts of battles and conquest in the Book of Joshua, God is presented as a warrior waging a holy war. How can a God of love wage such a savage and brutal war? Can the image of warrior be reconciled with the image of a compassionate and merciful God? It is important to remember that the words in the Sacred Scriptures are conditioned by the language and culture of the Israelites. The Israelites believed God was on their side.

➤ Joshua not only serves as a strong military leader for the Israelites but also models a true commitment to the Covenant with God.

The Judges

➤ Israelite history from 1200 to 1000 BC is marked by the leadership of twelve heroic, yet flawed, individuals known as the **judges.**

➤ These leaders settled disputes within their tribes or between tribes. The judges also led the military defense against outside invaders. Most important, they challenged Israel to remain faithful to God.

➤ The Book of Judges is a series of short accounts about human leaders accomplishing God's will.

➤ After the death of Joshua, the Israelites fall into a cycle of sin. This cycle includes sin, calamity, repentance, and deliverance. The judges emerge when the Israelites begin to fall away from their core religious identity by worshipping false gods. Two of the main gods that the Israelites were worshipping were Baal and Asherah.

➤ The judges act as a conscience for the Israelites, continually calling and reminding them to be faithful to their Covenant with God.

The Kings

➤ Following the time of the judges, the Israelites demanded a centralized form of leadership under a king, a form known as a **monarchy.** They were concerned about the growing divisions among the Twelve Tribes and the increased power of other nations.

➤ Samuel is the last of the judges and the first prophet of Israel.

➤ From the Tribe of Benjamin and anointed king by Samuel, Saul commits his reign to freeing the Israelites from their enemies. However, after Saul is anointed king, he twice disobeys God's Law.

➤ King David (1000–961 BC) is a successful military leader, savvy politician, gifted musician, and lover of God. David struggles with his humanity and lust for power. But he accomplishes what he sets out to do when he follows the will of God.

➤ Solomon is the third king of Israel. He is noted for building the Temple of the Lord in honor of his father, for strengthening and modernizing the Isra-elite army, and for creating trade alliances with other nations.

➤ He is a man of great wisdom and judgment, as well as an ambitious ruler who imposes steep taxes and forced labor on the Israelites.

King David

➤ King David unites the northern and southern kingdoms.

➤ David's sinful ways sometimes hinder him in seeing or promoting the will of God.

➤ Unique about David is that he always returns to the Lord begging for mercy and promising to change.

➤ David models **servant leadership.** Despite all his sins and faults, he beckons to God to raise him from the abyss of despair so he may rule with a just heart and serving hand. Servant leaders recognize their need for forgiveness and reconciliation. In return they can extend mercy and com-passion to all in need.

➤ Many people of Jesus' time did not acknowledge him as a fulfillment of the Old Testament prophecy that the Messiah would come from David's descendants because he did not fit the traditional image of a king. He denounced the trappings of royal leadership and wealth by taking on the humility of a man, eventually resulting in his death on a cross.

Step 7

Invite the students to get to know the judges.

The students examine passages about successful and unsuccessful judges and the reasons for their success or failure.

1. Prepare by downloading and printing the handout "The Role of a Judge in Ancient Israel" (Document #: TX001127), one for each student. The students will need their Bibles.

2. During the next class period, place the students in six small groups. Each group will read a passage from the handout that shows the role of the judges in Israel. Distribute the copies of the handout and ask the students to fill it in as they read. Allow 10 to 15 minutes for the students to complete the handout.

3. When time is up, ask representatives from each small group to introduce their judge to the other students and briefly describe the judge's situation or obstacle.

4. Ask the students to define what a biblical judge is. Write their suggestions on the board to create a group definition. Eventually, you will want to share the expanded definition below with them. You may want to write this expanded definition of *judge* on the board as shorter points:

> One of the men and women who served the Hebrew people as tribal leaders and military commanders. The judges settled disputes and proclaimed the will of God. They were not judges as we understand that role today, presiding over legal cases. Instead, they were charismatic leaders whom the Holy Spirit inspired to lead the Israelites when they were a loosely knit federation of tribes (1200–1000 BC). The judge was a clan hero who empowered the faith of the people in times of crisis and focused their attention on the promises of the Covenant.
>
> Twelve judges of Israel were called to lead the Twelve Tribes by uniting them to God and the Law. . . .
>
> Some judges were very faithful to the Covenant, some were not. God's will was accomplished through them or in spite of them.
>
> (*Saint Mary's Press® Essential Bible Dictionary,* p. 94)

5. After *judge* has been defined, discuss the difference between the students' experience of being judged or judging others and the role of the biblical judges.

Empathize

Step 8

Give a quiz to assess student understanding.

1. In preparation for this assessment, download and print the handout "Unit 5 Quiz" (Document #: TX001128), one for each student. Note that the quiz is fairly comprehensive, in part because both you and the students want to learn what they do not now know in preparation for a test or the final performance tasks.

2. On the day of the quiz, provide 5 to 10 minutes for the students to review their books and notes. Distribute the quiz and provide sufficient time for the students to work on it. If time remains when the students are done, collect the quizzes and then redistribute them so everyone has someone else's. Go through the quiz, allowing the students to correct one another's work and also giving them an opportunity to affirm or change their understanding of concepts. Collect the quizzes and further your analysis about topics that may need more coverage.

> **Teacher Note**
>
> To save paper, use the electronic copy of the quiz at *smp.org/LivinginChrist* and put it up in a visual place via projector, overhead, monitor, and so on. If these options are unavailable, read the quiz to the students slowly. In both cases, have the students record their answers on loose-leaf paper.
>
> To save time, ask the students to choose two of the six Scripture passages in the short-answer section.

Explain

Step 9

Have the students "meet and interview" the kings of Israel.

The students create "interviews" with the kings of Israel and present their findings to the other students. The students vote on the "best king of Israel," drawing from earlier criteria of a successful leader.

1. Prepare by reserving a computer lab or time in a library for students' research on their kings. Also collect magazine and newspaper interviews with world leaders and media clips to illustrate the goal of this learning experience. (See *smp.org/LivinginChrist* for some examples.) Download and print the handout "The Best King of Israel" (Document #: TX001129), one for each student.

2. During the next class period, ask the students to review the handout "Sprint Through Salvation History" (Document #: TX001107). Ask them to reread the sections "The Nation and the Temple" and "The Kings and the Prophets."

3. Point out the following passages. Tell the students you will place them in six small groups. Each small group will read and summarize one passage to present to the class:

   • Judges 21:25 (explanation for lawlessness during the period of judges)
   • 1 Samuel 2:12–17 (wickedness of Eli's sons)

- 1 Samuel 2:22–25 (Eli's futile rebuke)
- 1 Samuel 2:27–36 (doom of Eli's House)
- 1 Samuel 7:2–6 (religious reform)
- 1 Samuel 8:6–22 (God grants the request)

These passages illustrate why the people of Israel wanted a new leader. Provide the following background for the students:

➤ Following the period of the judges, Israel fell into poor leadership, characterized by lawlessness and disregard for God's Covenant and Commandments.

➤ God raised a righteous leader, Samuel, to help Israel return to the Covenant.

Recall for the students the connection between "righteous" and "servant leadership."

➤ The people demanded a king. God told Samuel to honor their request and find a king, but also to warn against kings.

➤ The Books of First and Second Samuel are concerned with the creation of the monarchy. The Books of First and Second Kings continue to question the monarchy's value. These books present the history of the monarchy until the destruction of the northern kingdom in 701 BC and of the southern kingdom and Jerusalem in 587 BC.

4. Explain that the students will evaluate the period of kings by identifying strong and weak leaders. The students will also characterize these kings' leadership under the Covenant. This learning experience will help the students' to better understand salvation history.

5. Tell the students that each small group will research an assigned king and then create an interview with that king. Each group will decide on a format for conducting the interview, such as a skit, a newspaper article, a blog, or another form of media. The interview will take place as if the king were a candidate for "best king of Israel." The students should act as impartially as possible in their interviews so the students afterward can elect one as best king of Israel. The students' final product will include a written and a visual component.

Teacher Note

If possible, show a clip of an interview news show or ask the students to locate and watch one independently.

6. Distribute the copies of the handout "The Best King of Israel" (Document #: TX001129). Review the handout directions with the students. Answer any student questions.

7. Place the students in six small groups. Assign one king to each group to read about and research. Possible choices include Saul, David, Solomon, Rehoboam, Asa, and Josiah.

8. To begin, instruct the small groups to find passages about their assigned king. They will need three to five passages about his successes and three

to five about obstacles he faced. These passages should be used in the interview. The interviews will be based on these examples.

9. Next, take the students to the computer lab or library for research. If the Internet is not available, bring reference books to the classroom or take the students to the school library to find reference material on their own. Remind the students to use only reliable resources and to cite their sources appropriately. Direct the students to start working.

10. After the projects are finished, allow one or two class periods for the students to present their interviews. After the presentations ask the students to vote for the best king of Israel.

11. Following the vote, discuss the results as follows:

   ➤ Why was the winner chosen?

   ➤ What characteristics did he possess? What obstacles did he overcome?

   ➤ How did he uphold the Covenant?

12. Read First Samuel 8:6–22. After reading, ask the class to answer the following questions:

   ➤ Did the winner ignore the warnings from God delivered through Samuel?

   ➤ How did this king understand his role?

   ➤ How did the other kings understand their roles?

13. To conclude, read the following definition of *king:*

   The rule of Israel was to follow the vision of justice and monotheism called for by their primal Covenant relationship with God. The true king of Israel was forever to be the Lord God, King of Kings (1 Samuel 2:1–2).

   (*Saint Mary's Press® Essential Bible Dictionary*, p. 96)

Interpret

Step 10

Have the students create Jesus' family tree from David to Jesus.

The students broaden their understanding of salvation history beyond the Old Testament.

1. Ask the students to form pairs. The students will look up scriptural passages about David, using a biblical concordance if possible. Ask them to write down the passages in their notebooks. Encourage the students to begin with their notes from the interviews with the kings and then to build on their understanding of David with scriptural passages. Allow the pairs 10 minutes for the work.

2. When time is up, ask a few volunteers to list three or four passages on the board that show various elements of David's personality. Have them write bullet-point notes next to each passage to briefly introduce it.

3. After the lists are finished, ask the students to explain one or two of their passages. Have them answer the following:

   - What was David doing?
   - How is he described?
   - Has his relationship with God changed? Explain.

4. After reviewing the passages on David from the board and discussing his portrayal, ask the students to quietly read Matthew 1:1–17. Allow 2 minutes for reading.

5. When time is up, ask them the following questions:

   ➤ Why do you think the Gospel of Matthew begins with a genealogy (or family tree) that traces David to Jesus?

   ➤ How does David act as a servant leader?

   ➤ How does David understand his role in the Covenant?

   Allow about 5 to 10 minutes for discussion.

6. If no student makes the point that God fulfills the promises he made to David in Second Samuel 7:8–16, ask the class to read this passage and comment on its relevance to the learning experience.

7. To conclude, ask the students to open their notebooks. Either as homework or in the last minutes of class, ask the students to write an answer to the question "How does seeing the direct connection from David to Jesus further your understanding of salvation history?"

Explain

Step 11

Have the students prepare for critical analysis of selected Scripture passages.

The students read and analyze several passages and write a thematic essay. This learning experience is recommended as a final unit performance task.

1. As homework, assign the students to read the following passages:

   - Joshua 23:1—24:28 (final plea and Joshua's farewell)
   - 2 Samuel, chapter 7 (David's Covenant with God)
   - Matthew 4:18–22 (the call of the first disciples)

Explain that this learning experience will prepare the students to write a critical analysis essay. Make available different biblical tools such as a biblical dictionary, a comparison of translations, or a concordance.

2. Ask the students to take notes on the readings, as well as write down any questions about them to bring to the next class period. This will form the basis of future discussion.

3. During the next class period, divide the board into three sections, designating one column for each assigned reading. Ask the students what they understand each passage to mean. Ask the following questions:

   - What happened?
   - Who was involved?
   - What lessons did we learn from it?

   Allow 10 to 15 minutes for discussion. Ask a student to record the main points of the discussion on the board.

4. When time is up, ask if the students have any questions. If so, have them ask the other students to answer the questions. Use the biblical tools as necessary. Allow about 10 minutes for discussion.

5. Write the following question on the board:

   - What theme can you identify among these three passages?

   Ask the students to write a multiparagraph response to the question. Discuss your expectations of the paper, including appropriate citation of passages. Answer any questions the students have about the assignment.

6. Ask the students to begin to draft their essays and to bring their analyses to the next class period.

7. You may use these follow-up opportunities:

   - If you follow this writing exercise with a Socratic seminar, the students will organize and discuss their themes as a group. The written responses will be the students' ticket into the seminar. (Continue with step 12, option 1.)
   - If you do not follow up with a seminar, you may choose to have the students discuss the themes with partners or in small groups. (Continue with step 12, option 2.)

> **Teacher Note**
>
> See "How to Lead a Socratic Seminar" (Document #: TX001006) at *smp.org/ LivinginChrist* for background information.

Step 12

Lead a discussion of the essay.

The students have opportunities to test and support their writing skills through two options: a Socratic seminar or the critical essay from step 11.

Option 1: Lead a Socratic Seminar

This class seminar gives the students the opportunity to test their analytical skills through oral debate. They must support the thematic connection they have identified with direct support or evidence from the Scriptures. See "How to Lead a Socratic Seminar" (Document #: TX001006) at *smp.org/LivinginChrist*.

Option 2: Follow Up the Critical Analysis with Group Discussion

1. The students should bring their written responses from step 11 and their Bibles. Both are necessary to participate in the discussion.

2. Ask the students to find a partner to discuss their written responses. Explain that one partner will explain the theme to the other partner and then reverse the process. Together they will create a master list of their themes with three excerpts (one from each reading in step 11) that support their conclusion. Allow 5 to 10 minutes for discussion.

3. When time is up, invite one member of each pair to write on the board one theme and one passage from each reading.

4. Finally, hold a large-group discussion to identify the characteristics of each theme, the relationship each individual illustrates with God, and the covenant relationship between Judaism and Christianity.

Empathize

Step 13

Now that the students are closer to the end of the unit, make sure they are all on track with their final performance tasks, if you have assigned them.

If possible, devote 50 to 60 minutes for the students to ask questions about the tasks and to work individually or in their small groups.

1. Remind the students to bring to class any work they have already prepared so that they can work on it during the class period. If necessary, reserve the library or media center so the students can do any book or online research. Make extra copies of the handouts "Final Performance Task Options for Unit 5" (Document #: TX001122) and "Rubric for Final Performance Tasks for Unit 5" (Document #: TX001123). Review the final performance task options, answer questions, and ask the students to choose one if they have not already done so.

2. Provide some class time for the students to work on their performance tasks. This then allows you to work with the students who need additional guidance with the project.

Reflect

Step 14

Provide the students with a tool to use for reflecting about what they learned in the unit and how they learned.

This learning experience provides the students with an excellent opportunity to reflect on how their understandings of the judges and kings have developed throughout the unit.

1. Prepare by downloading and printing the handout "Learning about Learning" (Document #: TX001159; see Appendix), one for each student.

2. Distribute the handout and give the students about 15 minutes to answer the questions quietly. Invite them to share any reflections they have about the content they learned as well as their insights into the way they learned.

Final Performance Task Options for Unit 5

Important Information for Both Options

The following are the main ideas you are to understand from this unit. They should appear in this final performance task so your teacher can assess whether you learned the most essential content.

- The covenant relationship between the Israelites and God required specific responsibilities from the people of Israel and their leaders.
- God wanted the judges and the kings to rule in a way that was faithful to the covenant.
- The judges and kings were tempted by other gods and pleasures and sometimes turned away from the covenant.
- Servant leadership was the model of governance that ensured fidelity to the covenant with God.

Option 1: "Heroes Today"

Your assignment is to compare and contrast biblical servant leaders with a more contemporary leader who is also a person of faith.

The context of this paper is a contrast and comparison of a modern leader with a biblical servant leader. Consider a modern person who is or has been an exceptional leader and who is also a person of faith. Choose a leader you will be able to find information on with relative ease.

- If you have chosen a global figure, look up three to five articles online, in print, or elsewhere to learn more about the person and his or her work.
- Gather three scriptural passages that explain how one servant leader is similar to the modern leader or choose passages with the characteristics of biblical servant leaders who are similar to your chosen leader.
- Within your report address the following questions:
  - Does the contemporary leader live out a covenant relationship with the people he or she leads or led?
  - Is this a person of faith? Does she or he keep a covenant relationship with her or his religious beliefs?
  - Does this person lead or govern in a manner faithful to religious values?
  - What temptations to turn away from religious values has this person faced?

- Finally, with support from the scriptural passages, state how the leader you have chosen either reflects the characteristics of one biblical servant leader or the combined characteristics of several servant leaders. Give specific examples from your leader's accomplishments and works.
- Take careful notes during your research. If you are researching, be sure to cite all your sources carefully and properly.
- After writing, proofread your work for spelling, grammar, and punctuation errors. Be sure to include the proper heading at the top of the first page, including your name.
- Create a visual component to connect to the theme of your paper. You could use a collage, a drawing, or another visual representation. (*Note:* Your project will be displayed in the classroom.)
- Turn in both the completed, proofread paper and the visual component.

© 2010 by Saint Mary's Press
Living in Christ Series

Option 2: Critical Analysis Essay

Your assignment is to closely examine a passage from the Scriptures and the way God's covenant with the people was treated.

- Choose one of the following passages. You will prepare for a critical analysis essay.
    - Joshua 23:1—24:28 (final plea and Joshua's farewell)
    - 2 Samuel, chapter 7 (David's covenant with God)
    - Matthew 4:18–22 (the call of the first disciples)

- Take notes on the chosen reading and write down questions you have about it to bring to the next class period. Be sure to answer the following:
    - What happened?
    - Who was involved?
    - How was the covenant respected or broken in this passage?
    - What temptations did the biblical figures face?
    - What qualities or characteristics did the biblical characters possess that enabled them to remain faithful to the covenant? Use the Scriptures to back yourself up.
    - What can the chosen passage teach you about the nature of God's covenantal relationship with us and your role in that relationship?

- Write a three- to four-page report in which you identify a theme in the passage and incorporate the answers to the questions above. Be sure to properly cite any sources used and turn in your final draft when it is complete.

Rubric for Final Performance Tasks for Unit 5

Criteria	4	3	2	1
Assignment includes all items requested in the directions.	Assignment includes not only all items requested but they are completed above expectations.	Assignment includes all items requested.	Assignment includes over half of the items requested.	Assignment includes less than half of the items requested.
Assignment shows understanding of the concept *the covenant relationship between the Israelites and God required specific responsibilities from the people of Israel and their leaders.*	Assignment shows unusually insightful understanding of this concept.	Assignment shows good understanding of this concept.	Assignment shows adequate understanding of this concept.	Assignment shows little understanding of this concept.
Assignment shows understanding of the concept *God wanted the judges and the kings to rule in a way that was faithful to the covenant.*	Assignment shows unusually insightful understanding of this concept.	Assignment shows good understanding of this concept.	Assignment shows adequate understanding of this concept.	Assignment shows little understanding of this concept.
Assignment shows understanding of the concept *the judges and kings were tempted by other gods and pleasures and sometimes turned away from the covenant.*	Assignment shows unusually insightful understanding of this concept.	Assignment shows good understanding of this concept.	Assignment shows adequate understanding of this concept.	Assignment shows little understanding of this concept.
Assignment shows understanding of the concept *servant leadership was the model of governance that ensured fidelity to the covenant with God.*	Assignment shows unusually insightful understanding of this concept.	Assignment shows good understanding of this concept.	Assignment shows adequate understanding of this concept.	Assignment shows little understanding of this concept.
Assignment uses proper grammar and spelling.	Assignment has no grammar or spelling errors.	Assignment has one grammar or spelling errors.	Assignment has two grammar or spelling errors.	Assignment has more than two grammar or spelling errors.

Document #:TX001123

Vocabulary for Unit 5

Ark of the Covenant: A sacred chest that housed the tablets of the Ten Commandments. It was placed within the sanctuary where God would come and dwell.

Baal . . . Asherah: Two Canaanite gods of earth and fertility that the Israelites worshipped when they fell away from the one true God.

Canaan: The land God promised to Abraham and his descendants.

First and Second Kings: These books present the history of the monarchy until the destruction of the northern kingdom in 701 BC and of the southern kingdom and Jerusalem in 587 BC.

First and Second Samuel: These books are concerned with the creation of the monarchy.

genealogy: A type of family tree. More than a bloodline, a genealogy was a literary form used during biblical times as a proclamation to make connections with important ancestors.

judges: The eleven men and one woman who served the Hebrew people as tribal leaders, military commanders, arbiters of disputes, and enliveners of faith.

king: The ruler of Israel was to follow the vision of justice and monotheism called for by the Israelites' primal Covenant relationship with God. The true king of Israel was forever to be the Lord God, King of Kings (1 Samuel 2:1–2).

servant leadership: A type of leadership based on humble service to all God's people.

© 2010 by Saint Mary's Press
Living in Christ Series

Document #: TX001124

Biblical Passages about Leadership

Book of Joshua (examples of good leadership)
- Joshua, chapters 1–2 (God promises to assist the Transjordan tribes)
- Joshua, chapter 5 (rites at Gilgal)
- Joshua 21:43—22:9 (God fulfills his promise to Joshua and the Israelites)
- Joshua, chapter 24 (the tribes settle Canaan, a warning to follow commandments, Joshua's farewell, Israel's success)

Book of Judges (examples of good and questionable leadership)
- Judges 3:7–11 (Othniel—good)
- Judges, chapter 4 (Deborah and Barak—good)
- Judges 6:1–24 (the call of Gideon—good)
- Judges 16:4–22 (Samson and Delilah—questionable)

First and Second Samuel (examples of good and poor leadership)
- 1 Samuel 8:1–5 (request for a king—poor)
- 1 Samuel 8:6–22 (God grants the request—warning of poor leadership)
- 1 Samuel 13:1–14 (Saul offers sacrifice and is reproved—poor)
- 1 Samuel 17:32–51 (David defeats Goliath—good)
- 2 Samuel 5:1–5 (David king of Israel—good)
- 2 Samuel 7:8–29 (the Lord's promises and David's prayer—good)
- 2 Samuel, chapter 11 (David's sin—poor)
- 2 Samuel 12:7–25 (David's punishment and repentance—good)

Graph for Evaluating Leadership Qualities

Name: _____

You will explore the qualities that make a good leader. Fill in the chart below to help you.

Individual	Bible Citation	Qualities	Good or Poor Leader?

The Role of a Judge in Ancient Israel

Name: _____

Look up each judge below and fill in the rest of the chart.

Judge	What situation or obstacle does this judge face?	How does this judge handle the situation?	What law does this judge follow or how does this judge show covenantal commitment?
Othniel (Judges 3:7–11)			
Ehud (Judges 3:12–30)			
Deborah (Judges, chapter 4)			
Gideon (Judges, chapters 6–8)			
Jephthah (Judges 11:1—12:7)			
Samson (Judges, chapters 13–16)			

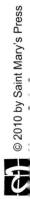

Unit 5 Quiz

Name: _____

Part I: Definitions

According to our class discussion and scriptural analysis, write definitions for the following terms:

- servant leader

- judge

- covenant

Part II: Short Answer

Choose five of the six passages below. In the spaces provided, identify the passage you have chosen and answer the following questions for each choice:

- What event does the passage refer to?

- Briefly describe this event.

- How is the covenant fulfilled or neglected in this passage?

- Why is this event important for salvation history?

Passage

- o Deuteronomy 34:1–5
- o Joshua 1:1–11
- o Joshua 6:20–27
- o Judges 2:1–14
- o Judges, chapters 4–5
- o Judges, chapters 13–16

_____(Passage)

_____

_____

_____

_____

_____(Passage)

_____

_____

_____

_____

_____(Passage)

_____

_____

_____

_____

_____(Passage)

_____

_____

_____

_____

_____(Passage)

_____

_____

_____

_____

Document #: TX001128

The Best King of Israel

Name: _____

Use the Scriptures and reliable print or Internet sources to research your assigned king. You will present your king to the class as a candidate for "the best king of Israel." You will demonstrate that you understand your king and the historical context of his reign. Answer the following questions in your final product:

- Who is your king?
- Was he related to another king? If so, to whom and how were they related?
- When did he live?
- Where did he live?
- What obstacles did he face? (Provide at least two examples.)
- What events was he involved in? (Provide at least two examples.)
- What or who influenced his reign and how? Was it a positive or negative influence?
- How long was he king?
- How did his monarchy end?
- Was he faithful to the covenant?

After researching, compile your findings in an interview-style paper. You may choose to "interview" your king in a modern medium or as if you were interviewing him during his reign. Both offer a unique perspective into the presentation of the king. You must represent your king accurately according to the Scriptures for this learning experience.

You will present your final interview to the class. It should answer all the above questions. The interview should last 2 to 3 minutes.

For the visual component, you may choose to present the interview as a skit using members of your group as the characters; as a news story reporting on the king with media clips to illustrate scenes from his reign; or as a presentation using another visually interesting method. (Get your teacher's permission first.)

Each member of the group will receive both an individual and a group grade, so share the tasks equally among group members.

Document #: TX001129

Unit 5 Test

Part 1: Multiple Choice

Write your answers in the blank spaces at the left.

1. _____ In the battle accounts and conquests in the Book of Joshua, God is presented as a

   _____.

   A. loving peacemaker
   B. creator of the heavens and the earth
   C. warrior waging a holy war
   D. friend to Israel's enemies

2. _____ The authors of the historical books of the Bible intended to write _____.

   A. a sacred history that reveals God's plan of salvation
   B. about the lives of people like Moses and Aaron
   C. about the historical events of their day
   D. a history to impress the Israelites with God's vengeance

3. _____ The two Canaanite gods of earth and fertility that the Israelites worshipped when they fell away from God were _____.

   A. Isis and Osiris
   B. Zeus and Poseidon
   C. Mars and Jupiter
   D. Baal and Asherah

4. _____ One way the worship at the Jerusalem Temple foreshadows our worship of Jesus Christ is

   _____.

   A. the Israelites burned incense to God, and we light candles for Jesus
   B. the Israelites had animal sacrifices, while we worship Christ and his saving sacrifice
   C. the Israelites had the golden calf, and we have statues of Jesus
   D. the Israelites had the Ark of the Covenant, and we have the cross

5. _____ All of the following can be said about the historical books except that _____.

   A. they focus on the settlement of the Promised Land and the unification of the kingdom under David
   B. they discuss the eventual division of the united kingdom into northern and southern kingdoms
   C. they portray the destruction of the two kingdoms and the rebuilding of a nation after exile
   D. they cover the journey of the Israelites from Egypt

Document #: TX001302

6. _____ God tells _____ to cross the River Jordan into Canaan.
   A. Joshua
   B. Jacob
   C. Aaron
   D. Isaac

7. _____ Gideon makes it his mission to destroy the altars of false gods in which he used to believe when he was a(n) _____ man.
   A. unfaithful
   B. lustful
   C. idolatrous
   D. unforgiving

8. _____ The _____ is the promise of a royal dynasty, a line of descendants that will last forever and be fulfilled in the birth of Jesus Christ.
   A. Mosaic line
   B. Davidic Covenant
   C. Magisterium
   D. papal line

9. _____ The _____ place God at the center of human experience, giving meaning to the struggles of everyday life.
   A. Acts of the Apostles
   B. wisdom books
   C. historical books
   D. Books of Job and Ruth

10. _____ The harlot Rahab, who helps the Israelites in the Book of Joshua, can be seen as an example of _____.
   A. how God can work through anyone to bring salvation to his people
   B. the power of prayer and penance
   C. how someone who is evil can do good
   D. the power of the Pharisees to convert bad people

Document #: TX001302

Part 2: Fill-in-the-Blank

Use the word bank to fill in the blanks in the following sentences. (*Note:* There are two extra terms in the word bank.)

WORD BANK

polytheistic beliefs	Ruth	Yahweh
Book of Judges	Law of Moses	Ark of the Covenant
Samson	monarchy	Solomon
Joshua	Rahab	theocracy

1. A _____ is a centralized form of leadership under one person.

2. The first three kings of Israel are Saul, David, and _____.

3. Samuel wanted a _____, a nation ruled by God.

4. The _____ is a series of short accounts about human leaders accomplishing God's will.

5. The Canaanites and other peoples held to _____, worshipping many gods.

6. _____ accomplishes amazing feats for God, including tearing a lion apart with his bare hands.

7. The _____ was a sacred chest that housed the tablets of the Ten Commandments.

8. The _____ refers to the first five books of the Old Testament, which are also called the Torah.

9. _____ was the name God revealed to Moses within the burning bush, meaning "I am who am."

10. The name that means "lover of God" is _____.

Document #: TX001302

Part 3: Short Answer

Answer each of the following questions in paragraph form on a separate sheet of paper.

1. What specific responsibilities did God require of the people of Israel and their leaders in fulfilling the covenant he made with them?

2. How did the judges and kings rule in ways that were faithful to God's covenant?

3. How did some of the judges and kings sometimes turn from the covenant?

4. What is servant leadership? How did it ensure fidelity to the covenant with God?

Unit 5 Test Answer Key

Part 1: Multiple Choice

1. C
2. A
3. D
4. B
5. D

6. A
7. C
8. B
9. C
10. A

Part 2: Fill-in-the-Blank

1. monarchy
2. Solomon
3. theocracy
4. Book of Judges
5. polytheistic beliefs

6. Samson
7. Ark of the Covenant
8. Law of Moses
9. Yahweh
10. Joshua

Part 3: Short Answer

1. As part of the covenant made between God and the Israelites through Moses, the Israelites came to Canaan, the Promised Land. In conquering this hostile land, bravery and determination were needed. Joshua, with God's help, provided this leadership, and the Israelites fought bravely. After a time, when the Israelites fell into pagan ways, it was up to the judges, such as Deborah, Gideon, and Samson, to lead the Israelites back to being faithful to the covenant. Once the kingdom was secure, the kings Saul, David, Samuel, and Solomon ruled the Israelites.

2. The judges were faithful to the covenant, especially after the Israelites fell into pagan worship, by settling disputes within their own tribes or between tribes, leading military defenses against outside invaders, and challenging Israel to remain faithful to God. The kings bring unity to the tribes; David will unite the northern and southern kingdoms. Each king stresses the unity of worship of God and respect for Mosaic Law.

3. Among the judges, Gideon was, at one time, a worshipper of false idols before his conversion. Periodically, his faith weakens, and he leads the Israelites back into idolatry. Samson has trouble keeping his religious commitments. Among the kings, when each man remains true to God's plan, he is able to accomplish great things and create a unifying bond among the Israelites; when ego and self-interest get in the way, then he stands in the way of what is good and holy. King David especially lets his lust for women blind him, for a time, to his commitment to be a role model of faithfulness to the covenant.

4. Servant leadership is a type of leadership based on humble service to all God's people. King David models servant leadership so that he might rule with a just heart and serving hand. Servant leaders recognize the need for forgiveness and reconciliation. In return, they can extend mercy and compassion to all in need. Thus, David both models and directs fidelity to the covenant.

 © 2010 by Saint Mary's Press
Living in Christ Series

Document #: TX001303

Unit 6

The Prophets: Bearers of Challenge and Hope

Overview

This sixth unit introduces the prophets who participated in the cycle of redemption by calling the kings back to the covenant relationship with God. The students consider how God calls them to be prophetic today.

Key Understandings and Questions

At the end of this unit, the students will possess a deeper understanding of the following important concepts:

- Prophets were individuals God called to speak to the people on his behalf.
- The prophets reinforced that God wanted a close relationship with his People, which meant the people must be faithful to him alone and treat one another with justice.
- The prophets gave the people hope when they had strayed from God and were in trouble.
- God calls us today to hear the words of the prophets, apply them to our lives, and be prophetic ourselves.

At the end of this unit, the students will have answered these questions:

- What was the role of the prophets in salvation history?
- Who were the prophets and what messages did they deliver to Israel and why?
- What was the prophets' effect on Israel?
- What difference can the Old Testament prophets make for us today?

How Will You Know the Students Understand?

These tools will help you to assess the students' understanding of the main concepts:

- handout "Final Performance Task Options for Unit 6" (Document #: TX001130)
- handout "Rubric for Final Performance Tasks for Unit 6" (Document #: TX001131)
- handout "Research for Unit 6 Final Performance Tasks" (Document #: TX001133)
- handout "Rubric for Research for Unit 6 Final Performance Tasks" (Document #: TX001134)
- handout "Unit 6 Test" (Document #: TX001304)

The Suggested Path to Understanding

This teacher guide provides you with one path to take with the students, enabling them to begin their study of the prophets. It is not necessary to use all the learning experiences, but if you substitute other material from this course or your own material for some of the material offered here, check to see that you have covered all relevant facets of understanding and that you have not missed knowledge or skills required in later units.

Explain **Step 1:** Preassess what the students already know about the biblical prophets.

Empathize **Step 2:** Follow this assessment by presenting to the students the handouts "Final Performance Task Options for Unit 6" (Document #: TX001130) and "Rubric for Final Performance Tasks for Unit 6" (Document #: TX001131).

Interpret **Step 3:** Discover commonly shared prophetic characteristics, using Elijah as an example.

Explain **Step 4:** Emphasize the characteristics that distinguish the prophets.

Explain **Step 5:** Introduce the major prophets and review the lives of other prophets.

Empathize **Step 6:** Give a quiz to assess student understanding.

Apply **Step 7:** Have the students consider their own prophetic roles.

Interpret **Step 8:** Examine the role of the prophets in relation to the Messiah.

Interpret *Optional Learning Experience: From Jesus to Christ:* Reinforce and deepen the students' understanding about the prophets and the Messiah by showing "The First Christians," a segment of the PBS documentary *From Jesus to Christ* (2004, 240 minutes, not rated).

Empathize **Step 9:** Now that the students are closer to the end of the unit, make sure they are all on track with their final performance tasks, if you have assigned them.

Reflect **Step 10:** Provide the students with a tool to use for reflecting about what they learned in the unit and how they learned.

Empathize **Step 11:** Have the students review and respond to the other students' final performance tasks.

Background for Teaching This Content with These Methods

In addition to finding information about the pedagogical approach used in this guide, you will also find background information on these and other topics at *smp.org/LivinginChrist:*

- "The Prophets" (Document #: TX001051)
- "Messianism and Zionism" (Document #: TX001047)
- "The Book of Ezekiel" (Document #: TX001048)
- "The Book of Isaiah" (Document #: TX001049)
- "The Book of Jeremiah" (Document #: TX001050)

The Web site also has background information on the following teaching methods:

- "Setting Up a Blog" (Document #: TX001052)
- "Blogging and Beyond" (Document #: TX001053)

Student Book Articles

The articles covered in unit 6 are from "Section 3: Revelation in the Old Testament" of the student book.

- "The Prophets: A Radical Redemption" (article 43)
- "Major and Minor Prophets" (article 44)
- "Ezekiel: Challenging Idolatry and Injustice" (article 45)
- "Jeremiah: Success in the Lord" (article 46)
- "Isaiah: The Long-Awaited One" (article 47)

Scripture Passages

- 1 Kings 17:1–6 (drought predicted by Elijah)
- 1 Kings 17:7–24 (Elijah and the widow)
- 1 Kings, chapter 18 (Elijah and the prophets of Baal)
- 1 Kings 19:1–18 (flight to Horeb)
- 1 Kings 19:19–21 (call of Elisha)
- 1 Kings, chapter 21 (seizure of Naboth's vineyard)
- 2 Kings 2:1–18 (Elisha succeeds Elijah)
- 2 Kings 4:1–37 (the widow's oil)
- 2 Kings, chapter 5 (cure of Naaman)
- Isaiah 2:1–4 (Zion, the messianic capital)
- Isaiah 5:1–7 (the vineyard song)

- Isaiah, chapter 6 (call of Isaiah)
- Isaiah 10:1–4 (social injustice)
- Isaiah 30:19–21 (Isaiah comforts the people)
- Jeremiah 1:4–10 (call of Jeremiah)
- Jeremiah 4:1–2 (God asks his People to return)
- Jeremiah 10:23–25 (prayer of Jeremiah)
- Jeremiah 15:10–21 (Jeremiah's complaint)
- Jeremiah 20:7–13 (Jeremiah's interior crisis)
- Jeremiah 23:5–6 (Jeremiah predicts a messianic king)
- Jeremiah 31:31–34 (the New Covenant)
- Jeremiah 51:1–5 (the second prophecy against Babylon)
- Ezekiel, chapter 1 (the vision: God on the cherubim)
- Ezekiel 2:1–10 (eating of the scroll)
- Ezekiel 4:1–8 (acts symbolic of siege and the Exile)
- Ezekiel, chapter 8 (vision of abominations in the Temple)
- Ezekiel 12:1–6 (acts symbolic of the Exile)
- Ezekiel 37:1–14 (vision of the dry bones)
- Various messianic prophecies

Optional: Review from unit 5: 1 Samuel, chapters 1–5, 8, 10, 13–18, 24, 28, 31 (the prophet Samuel)

Vocabulary

If you choose to provide a vocabulary list for material covered in both the student book and the teacher guide, download and print the handout "Vocabulary for Unit 6" (Document #: TX001132), one for each student.

Babylonian Exile	messiahship
cycle of redemption	northern kingdom
fidelity	prophecy
herald	prophesy
House	prophet
Immanuel	remnant
justice	salvation
Messiah	southern kingdom

Learning Experiences

Step 1

Preassess what the students already know about the biblical prophets.

Explore what the students already know about the prophets.

Option 1: Prophet Association

Reflect with the students on what they know about the prophets. This exercise will also help you determine how much to present about them.

1. Prepare by reminding the students they will need their own Bibles.

2. On the day of the learning experience, distribute pens or pencils, write the word *prophet* on the board, and ask the students to define it in their notebooks. Next, instruct the students to write down the names of all the biblical prophets they can think of. Allow about 5 minutes for this task.

3. When time is up, instruct the students to find passages in the Bible that refer to prophets or that have been written by prophets. Allow about 5 to 10 minutes for this work.

4. When time is up, ask the large group to define *prophet,* writing the definition on the board.

5. Next, write the following three questions on the board and ask the students to write answers in their notebooks:

   • Who are the prophets?

   • How did you discover this information?

   • Did you use any resources other than the books of the Bible to get your information? If so, list them.

Option 2: Ungraded Association Quiz

Teacher Note

For further information about this type of quiz, see the article "Using an Ungraded Association Quiz" (Document #: TX001010) at *smp.org/LivinginChrist.*

This exercise allows the students to test the knowledge they already have about the prophets and which ones they can identify. From this you will be able to determine how much to present about the prophets and the Messiah in salvation history.

1. Prepare by downloading and printing the handout "Unit 6 Ungraded Association Quiz" (Document #: TX001136), one for each student.

2. Explain that this is an ungraded quiz to find out what the students already know about the prophets. Ask the students to respond honestly and not to worry about material they may not be familiar with.

3. Distribute the quiz and pens or pencils and provide sufficient time for the students to work. Collect the quizzes and redistribute them so everyone has someone else's. Go through the quiz, allowing the students to correct one another's work and also giving them an opportunity to affirm or change their understanding of concepts. Collect the quizzes for your reference and review.

Option 3: Text to Text / Text to Self / Text to World

This exercise provides the students the opportunity to think critically about how they understand the prophets. It will also help you to determine how much you need to present about the prophets.

1. Prepare by gathering three sheets of newsprint, a marker, and a roll of masking tape. Write the following titles on the sheets: "Text to Text," "Text to Self," and "Text to World." Post the sheets on different classroom walls. For each student you also will need three different-colored sticky notes.

2. On the day of the learning experience, distribute the sticky notes and pens or pencils to the students. Each student should have three different colors of notes.

3. Write the following definition of *prophet* on the board:

> A person God chooses to speak his message of salvation. In the Bible, primarily a communicator of a divine message of repentance to the Chosen People, not necessarily a person who predicted the future.

Next to the definition, write the following questions:

- *Text to Text:* Does the definition remind me of a book I have read, a movie I have seen, or a song I have heard?
- *Text to Self:* What does this definition have to do with me? What is my relationship to the prophets?
- *Text to World:* How does this definition fit my understanding of the world? What do I know about the world that makes this definition relevant?

4. Ask the students to use a particular color of sticky note to answer one question. For example, if you are using red, blue, and green notes, all responses to "Text to Text" should be on the red note, "Text to Self" on the blue note, and "Text to World" on the green note.

5. After the students have written their answers, ask them to place the sticky notes on the appropriate sheets of newsprint around the room. Invite the students to walk around the room to read the responses quietly.

6. Call the students back into the large group. Discuss the definition of *prophet.* Collect the sheets of newsprint for later review.

Empathize

Step 2

Follow this assessment by presenting to the students the handouts "Final Performance Task Options for Unit 6" (Document #: TX001130) and "Rubric for Final Performance Tasks for Unit 6" (Document #: TX001131).

This unit provides you with two ways to assess that the students have a deep understanding of the most important concepts in the unit: doing a collaborative research project or writing a prophetic letter. Refer to "Using Final Performance Tasks to Assess Understanding" (Document #: TX001011) and "Using Rubrics to Assess Work" (Document #: TX001012) at *smp.org/LivinginChrist* for background information.

Teacher Note

The rubric handouts will guide the students in their work and let you evaluate how they are doing before they complete their final projects. If you feel your students do not need this step, exclude these two handouts and the related information.

1. Prepare by downloading and printing the handouts "Final Performance Task Options for Unit 6" (Document #: TX001130), "Rubric for Final Performance Tasks for Unit 6" (Document #: TX00131), "Research for Unit 6 Final Performance Tasks" (Document #: TX001133), and "Rubric for Research for Unit 6 Final Performance Tasks" (Document #: TX001134), one for each student.

2. Distribute the handouts. Give the students a choice as to which performance task they choose and add more options if you so choose. Review the directions, expectations, and rubric in class, allowing the students to ask questions. Say something similar to the following:

➤ In this unit you will learn about the prophets in the Old Testament, why the people of Israel and Judah needed prophets, and what God asked the prophets to do. You will learn how the prophets are similar and different. You will also learn about different prophets. You will apply what you have learned to prophets who are new to you.

Explain the performance task steps, as follows:

➤ First, decide whether to work by yourself or with others. If you want to work with others, you must choose option 1 and work with no more than two other people. If you want to work on your own, you may choose either option 1 or option 2.

➤ You or your group must answer the questions on the handout "Research for Unit 6 Final Performance Tasks" (Document #: TX001133) accurately and thoroughly. Once I have met with you about your research, you may continue to prepare either the multimedia presentation or the letter.

3. Explain the types of tools and knowledge the students will gain throughout the unit so they can successfully complete the final performance task.

4. Answer questions to clarify the end point toward which the unit is headed. Remind the students as the unit progresses that each learning experience builds the knowledge and skills they will need to show you that they understand who the prophets are and what their role is in salvation history.

 Interpret

Step 3

Discover commonly shared prophetic characteristics, using Elijah as an example.

Build on the students' understanding of the prophets to create understanding of salvation history. Showing the prophets' relationship to the kings provides a foundation for the students. Introduce the handout "The Prophetic Checklist" (Document #: TX001135) and apply it to the prophet Elijah.

- In preparation for this step, have the students read the following student book article:
  - "The Prophets: A Radical Redemption" (article 43)

1. Prepare by downloading and printing the handouts "Kings and Prophets" (Document #: TX001137) and "Kings and Prophets Worksheet" (Document #: TX001138), one for each student.

2. On the day of the learning experience, distribute the copies of the handouts and explain that you want the students to see how the prophets and the kings they have studied interact in salvation history.

3. Place the students in groups of three with their desks facing one another. Instruct the students to read through the handout "Kings and Prophets" (Document #: TX001137) carefully and to answer the questions on the handout "Kings and Prophets Worksheet" (Document #: TX001138) with their group members. Allow about 10 minutes for the small groups to work.

4. When time is up, have the small groups choose a reporter. Invite the reporters to share with the large group their answers from the worksheet.

5. When the discussion is done, have the students rearrange their desks to your original seating chart.

Introduce the Prophets and Their Common Characteristics

Present the PowerPoint "Prophets" (Document #: TX001080) at *smp.org/ LivinginChrist,* if desired. For more background on the prophets, see the article "The Prophets" (Document #: TX001051) at *smp.org/LivinginChrist.*

1. Prepare by downloading and printing the handouts "Vocabulary for Unit 6" (Document #: TX001132) and "The Prophetic Checklist" (Document #: TX001135), one for each student. You may also want your students to use the handout "Student Notes for Unit 6" (Document #: TX001055). Adjust the checklist handout, omitting material you will not be using or inserting additional material.

2. Distribute the copies of the handouts. Present the following information:

   ➤ Who is a prophet? A biblical prophet was not necessarily someone who could tell the future, although you can find that definition in many dictionaries.

   ➤ A biblical prophet was a person chosen by God to communicate a message of salvation.

   ➤ A prophecy is a message communicated by prophets on behalf of God, usually a message of divine direction or consolation for the prophet's own time. Because some prophetic messages include divine direction, their fulfillment may be in the future.

   ➤ When the Israelites or Jewish people strayed from their covenant relationship with God, God sent leaders to encourage them to return to the Covenant.

   ➤ When the Israelites lose their way, they need someone to call them back to the source of all life and hope, God. They need a prophet.

   ➤ Prophets play an important role in the cycle of redemption. (Ask the students to supply you with the steps in this cycle from unit 5.)

      1. God creates or enters into a covenant, and it is good.
      2. Humanity falls into idolatry, resulting in disease, war, and grief.
      3. God sends teachers, kings, prophets, or others who lead the people to repentance.
      4. The people return to following the Covenant.
      5. Peace and God's healing return to the people.

      (*Saint Mary's Press® Essential Bible Dictionary,* pp. 40–41)

   ➤ God chose prophets who shared the following characteristics:

      • **They obeyed God.** In the Old Testament, the Hebrew word for *obedience* meant mainly "listening" or "hearing." An obedient person heard God's Word and followed it (see Exodus 15:26). To be obedient was simply to align oneself with God's will.

- **They knew that God wanted his People to treat all people with justice.** They understood the need for and purpose of divine justice. The Hebrew and Greek words translated as "justice" are also translated as "righteousness" and "judgment." Divine justice calls for the fair and equitable distribution of life's necessities. The scriptural idea of justice is based in the truth that all humans have dignity and worth and are children of God. God's love for all creation is shown in his emphasis on justice, which is love in action.

- **They lived good, moral lives themselves.** They committed themselves to ethical responsibility. The commandments of God are the fundamental rules of conduct for the Chosen People. The Ten Commandments are about loving God and neighbor.

- **They understood that God wanted his People to come back to him with their whole selves.** They needed to be able to ask the Jews and Israelites to return to the Covenant in body, mind, and spirit. At this time the Abrahamic and Mosaic Covenants had been entered into and long adhered to by the people. Therefore God no longer looked only for sacrifice to appease him. He sought more. Specifically, God was interested in a full return to the Covenant by his People in body, mind, and spirit. Yet the Israelites were unsure of how to accomplish this goal.

- The leaders God chose were men and women who committed themselves to a relationship with God and to be his voice among the people. They spoke on God's behalf to the people.

➤ Who else had these characteristics?

Reinforce the Prophets' Common Characteristics with the Story of Elijah

If the students have not yet studied Elijah, assign them to read his story and assess his characteristics as a prophet.

1. Prepare by downloading and printing the handout "The Prophetic Checklist" (Document #: TX001135), one for each student. Review the account of Elijah for yourself and work through the checklist so you can help to guide the students. Emphasize that the characteristics listed are from your presentation and that Elijah will be a prophet with whom the students will test the characteristics.

2. On the day of the exercise, have the students read the following accounts about Elijah. They may work in pairs, or you might like to have students take turns reading the passages aloud. Answer any questions about the accounts:

- 1 Kings 17:1–6 (drought predicted by Elijah)
- 1 Kings 17:7–24 (Elijah and the widow)
- 1 Kings, chapter 18 (Elijah and the prophets of Baal)
- 1 Kings 19:1–18 (flight to Horeb)
- 1 Kings 19:19–21 (call of Elisha)
- 1 Kings, chapter 21 (seizure of Naboth's vineyard)
- 2 Kings 2:1–18 (Elisha succeeds Elijah)

3. Distribute the handout "Kings and Prophets Worksheet" (Document #: TX001138). Using the accounts listed in part 2, discuss how Elijah's role as prophet has the characteristics listed on the handout.

Step 4

Emphasize the characteristics that distinguish the prophets.

After teaching the students to categorize the prophets, have them examine the writing styles that distinguish the nonwriting prophets from the writing prophets.

- In preparation for this step, have the students read the following student book article:
    - "Major and Minor Prophets" (article 44)

Present Ways to Group the Prophets

You may want to use the PowerPoint "Prophets" (Document #: TX001080) at *smp.org/LivinginChrist.*

1. Share the following information with the students:

    ➤ Old Testament prophets are grouped in different ways because there are so many of them.

    ➤ The prophets in First and Second Samuel and First and Second Kings (Samuel, Nathan, Gad, Elijah, and Elisha) are sometimes known as nonwriting prophets because they left no written record of their own outside of these two biblical books.

    ➤ The writing prophets have biblical books named after them that contain their writings.

    Have the students open their Bibles and identify the other nine minor prophets.

➤ Having studied the judges and kings, you have already seen some nonwriting prophets, such as Samuel. Some people consider Moses and his sister, Miriam, to be prophets.

➤ Prophets are called former and latter prophets because of how, not when, each book was written.

- Former prophets wrote in prose. They include Samuel, Nathan, Gad, Elijah, and Elisha.

- Latter prophets wrote in poetry. This group is further divided into major prophets (Isaiah, Jeremiah, and Ezekiel) and minor prophets (Hosea, Joel, Amos, Obadiah, Jonah, Micah, Nahum, Habakkuk, Zephaniah, Haggai, Zechariah, and Malachi).

Explore Former and Latter and Writing and Nonwriting Prophets

1. Discuss the differences between prose and poetry. Read aloud the story of Elisha and the widow's oil from 2 Kings 4:1–7. Then tell about the prophet Ezekiel (see student book article 45, "Ezekiel: Challenging Idolatry and Injustice") and read aloud Ezekiel 1:1–28.

2. Ask half the students to translate Elisha's speech from Second Kings into poetry. Have the other half choose two or three verses from Ezekiel to translate into prose. Allow 5 to 10 minutes for the task.

3. When time is up, invite volunteers to share their translation efforts. Ask the following questions:

➤ What do you expect when you read or hear poetry? when you read or hear prose?

➤ Why do you think most of the prophets' speech is recorded as poetry?

Explain

Step 5

Introduce the major prophets and review the lives of other prophets.

Give the students a taste of the major prophets while learning about the lives of the other prophets. The students will use the jigsaw method to share with one another what they have learned.

1. Prepare by having the students read as homework student book articles 45, 46, and 47, "Ezekiel: Challenging Idolatry and Injustice," "Jeremiah: Success in the Lord," and "Isaiah: the Long-Awaited One." Download and print

the handouts "Evaluating the Prophet Isaiah" (Document #: TX001140), "The Inner Life of the Prophet Jeremiah" (Document #: TX001141), and "Ezekiel: Symbolic Prophecy and Visions" (Document #: TX001142), one for each student.

2. On the day of the learning experience, distribute the copies of the handouts. Review the main points about Isaiah, Jeremiah, and Ezekiel from the corresponding student book articles.

> **Teacher Note**
>
> If needed for review, refer students to the handout "Kings and Prophets" (Document #: TX001137).

3. Place the students into three small groups, one for each prophet. Then subdivide these small groups into pairs or threesomes. In their smaller groups, have the students follow the directions on their handouts and read aloud to one another the passages, filling out the handout as they go. Allow about 20 minutes for the task. If you run out of class time, have the students complete the handouts as homework.

4. When time is up, place the students in new small groups of three through the jigsaw method. Each small group needs one representative from the Isaiah, Jeremiah, and Ezekiel groups. Ask the group members to share what they learned about their prophet. The other students will fill out the corresponding handouts. Allow about 15 minutes for this part of the learning experience.

5. When time is up, call the students back into the large group. Review and discuss the handouts with the students.

Step 6

Give a quiz to assess student understanding.

> **Teacher Note**
>
> To save paper, use the electronic copy of the quiz from *smp.org/LivinginChrist* and put it up in a visual place via projector, overhead, monitor, and so on. If these options are unavailable, read the quiz to the students slowly. In both cases, have the students record their answers on loose-leaf paper.
>
> To save time, ask the students to choose two of the four questions to answer.

1. In preparation for this assessment, download and print the handout "Unit 6 Quiz" (Document #: TX001139), one for each student. Note that the quiz is fairly comprehensive, in part because both you and the students want to learn what they do not now know in preparation for a test or the final performance tasks.

2. On the day of the quiz, provide 5 to 10 minutes for the students to review their books and notes. Distribute the quiz and provide sufficient time for the students to work on it. If time remains when the students are done, collect the quizzes and then redistribute them so everyone has someone else's. Go through the quiz, allowing the students to correct one another's work and also giving them an opportunity to affirm or change their understanding of

concepts. Collect the quizzes and further your analysis about topics that may need more coverage.

Step 7

Apply

Have the students consider their own prophetic roles.

In his song "Something to Say," contemporary Christian singer Matthew West challenges his listeners to realize that everyone has something to say, because God's light shines through us all and our lives are gifts from God.

1. Prepare by inexpensively downloading "Something to Say" from iTunes or another Web site, or obtain a copy of the music CD *Something to Say* (Sparrow Records, January 2008). Download and print the handout "'Something to Say,'" (Document #: TX001143), one for each student. Obtain a device for playing the song in class.

2. Distribute the copies of the handout. Ask the students to take out their notebooks. Play the song as the students look at the lyrics. Invite the students to write down what they think the artist is saying. Ask them to write down anything in the song that invites them to think about themselves and their roles as prophets in a new way.

3. Play the song once or twice more. Invite the students to think of ways God might want to speak to others through them. Remind them that prophets challenge their audiences to behave better, comfort their audiences, and call them back to God. Then have the students write down some messages God might want them to give others.

4. Ask the students to share what they have written or their thoughts about their own prophetic roles. Ask the following questions:

   ➤ Do you have role models of people who really speak to others with God's voice?

   ➤ How might God call people to speak in prophetic ways today?

Step 8

Examine the role of the prophets in relation to the Messiah.

Familiarize students with the messianic prophecies.

1. Prepare by downloading and printing the handouts "Messianic Prophecies" (Document #: TX001144) and "Messianic Prophecies Worksheet" (Document #: TX001145), one for each student.

2. On the day of the learning experience, ask:

   ➤ What is a messiah?

      After the students have offered some ideas, distribute the copies of the handouts.

3. Instruct the students to read through the handout "Messianic Prophecies" (Document #: TX001144), paying special attention to the purpose and content of each column in the chart. Place the students in pairs to fill out the handout "Messianic Prophecies Worksheet" (Document #: TX001145). Allow about 10 minutes for the task.

4. When time is up, lead a presentation about messianic prophecies.

5. Redefine the word *Messiah.* It comes from a Hebrew word meaning "God's anointed one." It is translated in Greek as "Christ." The position of the Messiah can also be called a **messiahship.** Note that in unit 7, which is about Jesus, the students will examine whether Jesus resembles the Messiah the Jews were looking for.

Optional Learning Experience: From Jesus to Christ

Reinforce and deepen the students' understanding about the prophets and the Messiah by showing "The First Christians," a segment of the PBS documentary *From Jesus to Christ* (2004, 240 minutes, not rated).

At *smp.org/LivinginChrist* you will find a link to this documentary. The video segment has a scholar discussing how Jesus often quoted the Jewish Scriptures (the Christian Old Testament) and how, after his death, his followers turned to them for clues to the meaning of his life and message. Use the video segment as the basis for a class discussion or assignment on how the prophet's message prepared the Jewish people for the coming of Jesus Christ, the Mesiah.

Step 9

Now that the students are closer to the end of the unit, make sure they are all on track with their final performance tasks, if you have assigned them.

If possible, devote 50 to 60 minutes for the students to ask questions about the tasks and to work individually or in their small groups.

1. Remind the students to bring to class any work they have already prepared so that they can work on it during the class period. If necessary, reserve the library or media center so the students can do any book or online research. Download and print extra copies of the handouts "Final Performance Task Options for Unit 6" (Document #: TX001130) and "Rubric for Final Performance Tasks for Unit 6" (Document #: TX001131). Also print copies of the handouts "Research for Unit 6 Final Performance Tasks" (Document #: TX001133) and "Rubric for Research for Unit 6 Final Performance Tasks" (Document #: TX001134). Review the handouts, answer questions, and ask the students to choose one if they have not already done so.

2. Provide some class time for the students to work on their performance tasks. This then allows you to work with the students who need additional guidance with the project.

Step 10

Provide the students with a tool to use for reflecting about what they learned in the unit and how they learned.

This learning experience provides the students with an excellent opportunity to reflect on how their understandings of Divine Revelation have developed throughout the unit.

1. To prepare for this learning experience, download and print the handout "Learning about Learning" (Document #: TX001159; see Appendix), one for each student.

2. Distribute the handout and give the students about 15 minutes to answer the questions quietly. Invite them to share any reflections they have about the content they learned as well as their insights into the way they learned.

Step 11

Have the students review and respond to the other students' final performance tasks.

In class or through blogging, have the students respond to one another's multimedia prophet presentations or prophetic letters.

1. Depending on time, class size, and so on, have the students share their final projects about the prophets with one another. They can do so in several ways:

   - They can project their PowerPoint presentations. Students can either read their letters aloud to, or record and play them back for, the other students.

   - If your room has several computer monitors or if the students have laptops, enable the students to access the projects digitally. Small groups of students can read and view other students' projects.

   - Set up a blog system and assign the students to view certain projects on their own time. Ask them to write responses to the projects they view. If you need guidance, see the article "Setting Up a Blog" (Document #: TX001052) at *smp.org/LivinginChrist.* Set up guidelines for the students to use in their blog evaluations—ideas can be found in the same article.

   - Take this blogging a step further by finding another teacher in the school, area, or country who is doing the same assignment. Have that teacher give your students access to a blog about his or her students' work. Do the same for his or her students. See the article "Blogging and Beyond" (Document #: TX001053) at *smp.org/LivinginChrist.*

Final Performance Task Options for Unit 6

The following are the main ideas you are to understand from this unit. They should appear in this final performance task so your teacher can assess whether you learned the most essential content:

- Prophets were individuals God called to speak to the people on his behalf.
- The prophets reinforced that God wanted a close relationship with his people, which meant the people must be faithful to him alone and treat one another with justice.
- The prophets gave the people hope when they had strayed from God and were in trouble.
- God calls us today to hear the words of the prophets, apply them to our lives, and be prophetic ourselves.

Option 1: Collaborative Research

You will display your understanding of the role of biblical prophets through a PowerPoint presentation about one of them. With the students in your group, research your prophet, completing the handout "Messianic Prophecies" (Document #: TX001144) before putting together your PowerPoint presentation. The presentation should cover the following elements:

- an introduction to the prophet (Who was he? When did he live?)
- a map showing where he came from (ancient and modern)
- an introduction to the people the prophet wanted to reach and an explanation of what God wanted from these people
- an artistic presentation of the prophet's quotations of warning and hope
- an evaluation of how successful the prophet was
- an illustration of this prophet
- a picture of how this prophet might look in today's world
- some quotations you might attribute to this prophet today
- ideas of how you might bring the community and yourselves closer to God based on what this prophet says

You may choose any of the following prophets:

- Amos
- Elisha
- Habakkuk
- Haggai
- Hosea
- Joel
- Jonah
- Malachi

- Micah
- Nahum
- Nathan
- Obadiah
- Samuel
- Zechariah
- Zephaniah

Option 2: Prophetic Letter

You will display your understanding of the prophet's role in society and compose a letter from a modern-day prophet that shares the message and style of an Old Testament prophet. Follow the steps below to complete the project.

- Read material from the Bible written by the prophet, either prose or poetry. Also read background material about the prophet.
- Fill out the handout "Research for Unit 6 Final Performance Tasks" (Document #: TX001133).
- Write a two-page, typed prophetic letter to a modern audience that resembles the audience the prophet addressed. Use the prophet's speech patterns and express his concerns in a modern context. Follow the format of the prophet researched, as below.
  - Create headings to divide the letter into different types of writing, if needed.
  - Imitate the introduction to the prophetic book.
  - Imitate at least four types of writing in the prophetic book: a narration of events, a prayer, a blessing of God with song, a vision, a challenge to leaders or the people, a prediction of destruction because of poor behavior, comfort, an offer of hope, stories, a description of the prophet's call and his experiences as a prophet.
  - The letter should speak to a modern audience with modern concerns even while using an ancient style.
  - Imitate the conclusion of the prophetic book.

You may choose any of the following prophets:

- Amos
- Elisha
- Habakkuk
- Haggai
- Hosea
- Joel
- Jonah
- Malachi

- Micah
- Nahum
- Nathan
- Obadiah
- Samuel
- Zechariah
- Zephaniah

Rubric for Final Performance Tasks for Unit 6

Criteria	4	3	2	1
Assignment includes all items requested in the instructions.	Assignment not only includes all items requested but they are completed above expectations.	Assignment includes all items requested.	Assignment includes more than half of the items requested.	Assignment includes less than half of the items requested.
Assignment shows understanding of the concept *prophets were individuals God called to speak to the people on his behalf.*	Assignment shows unusually insightful understanding of this concept.	Assignment shows good understanding of this concept.	Assignment shows adequate understanding of this concept.	Assignment shows little understanding of this concept.
Assignment shows understanding of the concept *the prophets reinforced that God wanted a close relationship with his people, which meant the people must be faithful to him alone and treat one another with justice.*	Assignment shows unusually insightful understanding of this concept.	Assignment shows good understanding of this concept.	Assignment shows adequate understanding of this concept.	Assignment shows little understanding of this concept.
Assignment shows understanding of the concept *the prophets gave the people hope when they had strayed from God and were in trouble.*	Assignment shows unusually insightful understanding of this concept.	Assignment shows good understanding of this concept.	Assignment shows adequate understanding of this concept.	Assignment shows little understanding of this concept.
Assignment shows understanding of the concept *God calls us today to hear the words of the prophets, apply them to our lives, and be prophetic ourselves.*	Assignment shows unusually insightful understanding of this concept.	Assignment shows good understanding of this concept.	Assignment shows adequate understanding of this concept.	Assignment shows little understanding of this concept.
Assignment uses method of communication (PowerPoint presentation or letter) in a way that clearly conveys what the assignment requests.	Assignment outstandingly conveys what the assignment requests.	Assignment clearly conveys what the assignment requests.	Assignment at times clearly conveys what the assignment requests.	Assignment does not convey what the assignment requests.
Assignment uses proper grammar and spelling.	Assignment has no grammar or spelling errors.	Assignment has one grammar or spelling error.	Assignment has two grammar or spelling errors.	Assignment has more than two grammar or spelling errors.

Document #: TX001131

Vocabulary for Unit 6

Babylonian Exile: In 587 BC the Babylonians pillaged Judah, destroyed the Temple and the city of Jerusalem, and banished the people in chains to serve as slaves in Babylon. In 586 the Exile began. The Exile lasted until 539 BC.

cycle of redemption: Five-part cycle that occurs throughout the Bible: "[1] God creates or enters into a covenant, and it is good. [2] Humanity falls into idolatry, resulting in disease, war, and grief. [3] God sends teachers, kings, prophets, or others who lead the people to repentance. [4] The people return to following the Covenant. [5] Peace and God's healing return to the people" (*Saint Mary's Press Essential Bible Dictionary,* pages 40–41).

fidelity: Faithfulness to obligation, duty, or commitment.

herald: To proclaim or announce a saving message.

House: A family line.

Immanuel: A Hebrew word meaning "God is with us."

justice: Justice calls for the fair and equitable distribution of life's necessities. The scriptural idea of justice is based on the truth that all humans have dignity and worth and are children of God. God's love for all creation is shown in his emphasis on justice, which is love in action.

Messiah: A Hebrew word meaning "God's anointed one." Translated as "Christ" in Greek.

messiahship: The position of the Messiah.

northern kingdom: A kingdom formed by the ten northernmost Tribes of Israel.

prophecy: A message communicated by prophets on behalf of God, usually a message of divine direction or consolation for the prophet's own time. Because some prophetic messages include divine direction, their fulfillment may be in the future.

prophesy: To foretell or predict; to deliver messages from God.

prophet: A person God chooses to speak his message of salvation. In the Bible, primarily a communicator of a divine message of repentance to the Chosen People, not necessarily a person who predicted the future.

remnant: A prophetic term for the small portion of people who will be saved because of their faithfulness to God.

salvation: From the Latin *salvare,* meaning "to save," referring to the forgiveness of sins and assurance of permanent union with God, attained for us through the Paschal Mystery—Christ's work of redemption accomplished through his Passion, death, Resurrection, and Ascension. Only at the time of judgment can a person be certain of salvation, which is a gift of God.

southern kingdom: The land of Judah. The kingdom that contained Jerusalem.

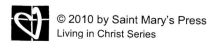

Research for Unit 6 Final Performance Tasks

Name: _____

Fill in the following items in preparation for the final performance task.

Name of Prophet Being Researched _____

1. Who is the prophet?

2. What makes him a prophet?

3. How did he become a prophet?

4. When did he write his book?

5. In which geographic area did he live? What is the ancient and modern name for that region?

6. To whom did he speak?

7. Why did he speak to them? What behavior caused God to send a prophet to these people?

Document #: TX001133

8. What warnings did the prophet give? (If the prophet gave several warnings, focus on two of them. For each warning, cite two scriptural verses that illustrate the warning.)

9. Did this prophet give hope? If so, provide two scriptural verses illustrating this.

10. Did these predictions come true? You will need to research this information outside the Bible.

11. How is the prophet's message important or useful to our society today?

12. What do you think about this prophet? Was he effective? Did his prophecy influence the people of Israel or Judah?

13. What did God want from the people of Israel and Judah?

14. Does God still want the same thing from us today? Explain.

15. How would you translate this prophet's warning into a modern situation?

16. How effective might this prophet be today?

Rubric for Research for Unit 6 Final Performance Tasks

	4	3	2	1	0
Research Handout	Handout answers all questions thoroughly, accurately, and in detail.	Handout answers all questions, most of them thoroughly, accurately, and in detail.	Handout answers most questions in an average way.	Handout answers a few of the questions.	Handout was not turned in.

Document #: TX001134

The Prophetic Checklist

Name: _____

As you read about a prophet, check off the characteristics below that are common to biblical prophets and put the relevant biblical citation next to each characteristic.

Shared Characteristics	Biblical Citations That Illustrate Each Characteristic
They obeyed God. In the Old Testament, the Hebrew word for *obedience* meant primarily "listening" or "hearing." An obedient person heard God's Word and followed it (see Exodus 15:26). To be obedient was simply to align oneself with God's will.	
They knew that God wanted his people to treat all people with justice. They understood the need for and purpose of divine justice. The Hebrew and Greek words translated as "justice" are also translated as "righteousness" and "judgment." Divine justice calls for the fair and equitable distribution of life's necessities. The scriptural idea of justice is based in the truth that all humans have dignity and worth and are children of God. God's love for all creation is shown in his emphasis on justice, which is love in action.	
They lived good, moral lives themselves. They committed themselves to ethical responsibility. The commandments of God are the fundamental rules of conduct for the Chosen People. The Ten Commandments are about loving God and neighbor.	
They understood that God wanted his People to come back to him with their whole selves. They needed to be able to ask the Jews and Israelites to return to the Covenant in body, mind, and spirit. At this time the Abrahamic and Mosaic Covenants had been entered into and long adhered to by the people. Therefore God no longer looked only for sacrifice to appease him. He sought more. Specifically, God was interested in a full return to the Covenant by his People in body, mind, and spirit. Yet the Israelites were unsure of how to accomplish this goal. The leaders God chose were men and women who committed themselves to a relationship with God and to be his voice among the people. They spoke on God's behalf to the people.	

© 2010 by Saint Mary's Press
Living in Christ Series

Document #: TX001135

Unit 6 Ungraded Association Quiz

Name: _____

Part I: Answer the following questions.
- What is a prophet?

- What is prophecy?

- What does it mean to prophesy?

- What did the biblical prophets prophesy about?

- Who is the Messiah?

- What did the prophets say about the Messiah?

Part II: Write down words or phrases you associate with the following prophets. Leave blank those you are unfamiliar with.

Samuel

Isaiah

Elijah

Elisha

Ezra

Nehemiah

Jeremiah

Document #: TX001136

Kings and Prophets

Kings and Prophets of the United Monarchy

Kings	Prophets
Saul 1020–1000	Samuel
David 1000–960	Nathan
Solomon 960–922	

Kings and Prophets of the Divided Monarchy

Kings of Judah	Kings of Israel	Prophets	Ancient Near East
Rehoboam 922–915	Jeroboam I 922–901		Egypt: Shishak Invades Judah 918
Abijah 915–913			
Asa 913–873	Nadab 901–900		
	Baasha 900–877		
	Elah 877–876		Syria: Benhadad I 880–842
	Zimri 876		
	Tibni 876–?		
Jehoshaphat 873–849	Omri 876–869		
	Ahab 869–850	Elijah	
	Ahaziah 850–849	Elisha	
Jehoram/Joram 849–842	Jehoram 849–842		Hazael 842–806
Ahaziah 842			
Athaliah 842–837			
Joash/Jehoash 837–800	Jehu 842–815		
Amaziah 800–783	Jehoahaz 815–801		Rezon 740–732
	Joash 801–786		
Uzziah 783–742			
Jotham 750–735	Jeroboam II 786–746	Amos (ca. 750)	Assyria: Tiglath-Pileser 745–727
	Zechariah 746–745	Hosea (ca. 745)	
Ahaz 735–715	Shallum 745		
	Menahem 745–736	Isaiah (ca. 740)	
Syro-Ephraimitic War 734	Pekahiah 736–735		
	Pekah 735–732		
	Hoshea 732–722	Micah (ca. 730)	Damascus Falls to Assyrians in 732
	Samaria		Shalmaneser V 727–722
	Falls to Assyrians 722		Sargon II 722–705

Document #: TX001137

Kings and Prophets of Judah Alone

Kings of Judah	Prophets	Ancient Near East
Ahaz 735–715 BC	Isaiah	**Assyria:**
Hezekiah 715–687	Isaiah	Sennacherib 705–681
		Siege of Jerusaem 701
Manasseh 687–642	Jeremiah	Esarhaddon 681–669
Amon 642–640	Zephaniah	Ashurbanipal 669–633?
Josiah 640–609	Habakkuk?	Ashuretililani 633–629?
		Sinsharishkun 629–612
		Fall of Nineveth to Babylon 612
Battle of Megiddo 609	Nahum	**Egypt:** Necho 609–593
Jehoahaz 609		
Jehoiakim 609–598	Jeremiah	**Babylon:** Nebuchadnezzar
Jehoiakin 598–597		605–562
(in Jerusalem)		
First Deportation 597	Ezekiel	*Battle of Carchemish 605*
Zedekiah 597–587		
Fall of Jerusalem to Babylon 587		

CHART OF THE TWO NATIONS

	South	**North**
Name of the country	Judah	Israel
Number of tribes	2	10
Capital city	Jerusalem	Samaria (most often)
Location(s) of the national temple(s)	Jerusalem (also referred to as "Zion")	Dan and Bethel
Royal family	Davidides	Various families; the most prominent were the Omrides
Year the nation fell	587	722
To whom it fell	Babylonians	Assyrians

(The charts on this handout are from *Encountering Ancient Voices: A Guide to Reading the Old Testament,* by Corrine L. Carvalho [Winona, MN: Saint Mary's Press, 2006], pages 193–194. Copyright © 2006 by Saint Mary's Press. All rights reserved.)

Document #: TX001137

Kings and Prophets Worksheet

Name: _____

1. Each prophet has been associated with a king. On average, how many kings was one prophet responsible for?

2. Determine the approximate date of the earliest prophet and the latest one by looking at the date connected with the prophet himself or for the rulers of the time. Then look at the "Chart of the Two Nations" on the handout "Kings and Prophets" (Document #: TX001137). Why do you think God needed to send the people prophets during this time?

3. Use your Bible to determine where three of the prophets on the chart on the handout "Kings and Prophets" (Document #: TX001137) did their prophesying: in Israel or Judah.

Unit 6 Quiz

Name: _____

1. What is a biblical prophet? Why did the Hebrew people need prophets?

2. What role do the prophets play in the cycle of redemption? List the stages of this cycle.

3. What are three characteristics all prophets share?

4. What is the difference between a former and a latter prophet?

Document #: TX001139

Evaluating the Prophet Isaiah

Name: _____

Look up and read each passage below from the Book of Isaiah. Then draw a line from the passage to the prophetic characteristic it illustrates. One passage may illustrate more than one characteristic.

Passages from Isaiah   Characteristics Shared by Biblical Prophets

Isaiah 2:1–4   A. They obeyed God.

Isaiah 5:1–7   B. They knew God wanted his People to treat all people with justice.

Isaiah 6:1–13   C. They lived a good, moral life themselves.

Isaiah 10:1–4   D. They understood that God wanted his People to come back to him with their whole selves.

© 2010 by Saint Mary's Press
Living in Christ Series

Document #: TX001140

The Bible: The Living Word of God

The Inner Life of the Prophet Jeremiah

Name: _____

The prophet Jeremiah gives us special insight into the life and difficulties of a prophet. Read the passages below from the Book of Jeremiah and summarize each. When appropriate, write which stage in the cycle of redemption is being described.

Jeremiah 1:4–10

Jeremiah 4:1–2

Jeremiah 10:23–25

Jeremiah 15:10–21

Jeremiah 20:7–13

Jeremiah 23:5–6

Jeremiah 31:31–34

Jeremiah 51:1–5

Document #:TX001141

The Bible: The Living Word of God

Ezekiel: Symbolic Prophecy and Visions

Name: _____

God called the prophet Ezekiel to symbolically act out many of his prophecies. Summarize the passages below.

Dramatic Prophecy

Ezekiel 2:1–10

Ezekiel 4:1–8

Ezekiel 12:1–6

Visions

Ezekiel 1:1–28

Ezekiel 8:1–18

Ezekiel 37:1–14

"Something to Say"
Matthew West

[Unofficial lyrics]
Wake up, 7:32 AM
Can't believe it's time to do it over again
Yesterday, it took all that you had
And you're wonderin' if you'll ever get it back
But the whole wide world is waiting for
Waiting for you to step out that door
Come on and let your life be heard today

You got something to say
If you're livin', if you're breathin'
You got something to say
And you know if your heart is beatin'
You got something to say
And no one can say it like you do
God is love and love speaks through
You got it, you got it
You got something to say

Yeah, yeah
Something to say
Yeah, oh

Listen up, I got a question here
Would anybody miss you if you disappeared?
Well your life is the song that you sing
And the whole wide world is listening
Well the answer to the question is
You were created, your life is a gift and
The lights are shining on you today, 'cause

You got something to say
If you're livin', if you're breathin'
You got something to say
And you know if your heart is beatin'
You got something to say

And no one can say it like you do
God is love and love speaks through
You got it, you got it
You got something to say

Yeah
You got something to say
Come on, come on, yeah

Sing na na na na na na na na
Na na na na na na
Na na na na na, yeah

Listen up, I got a question here
Would anybody miss you if you disappeared?
Well your life is the song that you sing
And the whole wide world is listening

Oh . . .

You got something to say
And no one can say it like you do
God is love and love speaks through
You got it, you got it
You got something to say

Yeah
Something to say
Come on, come on, yeah

And the world is listening now
And the lights are shining down
Shining down on you today, 'cause
You got something to say

So just say it

Messianic Prophecies

Prophecy	Old Testament	New Testament
Descendant of the house of David	The Messiah is heir of the eternal dynasty of the house of David (Ru 4:14–22; 1 Sm 16:1; 2 Sm 7:26; Ps 89:5). David's righteous heir will rule (Jer 23:5).	Jesus is David's descendant, called Lord (Mk 12:35–37); of the house of David (Mt 1:1–17; Lk 1:27,69; 3:23–38); given the throne of David by God (Lk 1:32).
Born in Bethlehem	A shepherd of Israel comes from Bethlehem (Mi 5:1–3).	Jesus, the Good Shepherd, was born in Bethlehem (Mt 2:1–6; Lk 2:1–20; Jn 10:11–18).
Emmanuel (Immanuel) God with us	Born of a virgin girl and named Immanuel (Is 7:14)	Jesus, Emmanuel, was born to the Virgin Mary and called Son of God (Mt 1:18–25; Lk 1:26–38).
One like Moses	The Messiah will be a prophet and teacher like Moses and a son of Israel (Dt 18:15–19). Moses was called by God to lead the Israelites out of Egypt (Ex 3:10). Moses, the great teacher, spoke for God (Ex 4:12).	Like Moses, Jesus was called out of Egypt (Mt 2:15). Jesus was the fulfillment of the promises of Moses and the prophets (Lk 24:26–27; Jn 1:45; 5:46). Jesus honored the teachings of Moses (Mk 7:10). Jesus was called Teacher (Jn 20:16; Eph 2:20).
The Son of Man of the Heavens	The son of man, the Bar Nasa, came on the clouds of heaven, was ministered to by heavenly beings, and was given by God an everlasting kingdom (Dn 7:9–28).	Jesus used the divine title "Son of Man" to refer to himself and his Passion (Mt 8:20; 12:34; Lk 9:58; 18:8; Jn 8:28; 9:31–32); was fully human (Lk 7:34); came from heaven (Jn 3:13) to save the lost (Lk 19:10); was honored as Lord (Acts 2:36); was ministered to and honored by angels (Lk 24:23; Jn 20:12); returned to the heavens (Acts 1:10–11); and will return to earth amid wondrous signs (Mt 24:27–31,37,39,44; Mk 14:62; Lk 7:19–22; 12:40; Jn 6:62).
Miracle worker	On the day of the Lord, the blind will see, the deaf will hear, the mute will sing, and the lame will leap (Is 29:18; 35:5–6).	Jesus heals the deaf and the mute (Mk 7:31–37), the blind (Mt 20:29–34; Mk 8:22–26; 9:32; Jn 9:1–41), and the lame (Jn 5:1–9).
Savior King of the Jews	The savior king enters Jerusalem on a donkey (Zec 9:9) amid palm branches and shouts of joy (1 Mc 13:51–52).	Jesus enters Jerusalem on a donkey amid palms and chants (Mt 21:5–11; Jn 12:12–16).
God's Suffering Servant	God's suffering servant is silent before his accuser (Is 53:7); scorned and despised (Ps 22:7–8); beaten and spit upon (Is 50:6); abandoned (Ps 22:2–4) and his clothing divided (Ps 22:18); thirsts (Ps 22:15–16); given vinegar to drink (Ps 69:21–22); dies among the wicked (Is 53:12); incorruptible and will rise from the dead (Ps 16:9–11).	Jesus remains silent before the chief priests and Pilate (Mt 27:11–14; Mk 15:3–4; Lk 23:1–16); was betrayed and condemned (Mt 20:18; 26:2,14–16; Mk 8:31; 10:33); is beaten and spit upon (Mt 26:67; 27:30; Mk 14:65); is mocked as "King of the Jews" (Mt 27:29–37; Mk 15:9,31–32; Lk 23:38; Jn 18:33–19:3,19–22); thirsts and is given vinegar to drink (Mt 27:34; Mk 15:23; Jn 19:28–30); is mocked as he dies with criminals (Mt 27:38–44; Mk 15:27; Lk 23:35); has his clothes divided (Mt 27:35; Jn 19:23–24); rises from the dead (Mt 28:1–10; Mk 16:1–8; Lk 24:1–12; Jn 20:1–18; Acts 2:22–24).

The Bible: The Living Word of God

Messianic Prophecies Worksheet

Name: _____

Answer the following questions while analyzing the handout "Messianic Prophecies" (Document #: TX001144).

1. According to the handout "Messianic Prophecies" (Document #: TX001144), which prophets played a role in prophesying about the Messiah?

2. Eight prophecies about the Messiah are listed on the handout "Messianic Prophecies." Based on what you know about the Messiah, are any characteristics missing? If nothing is missing, why do you believe this is a complete list?

3. Analyze the New Testament column on the handout "Messianic Prophecies." Do you see the fulfillment of the Old Testament prophecies? If yes, how? If not, why not?

Document #: TX001145

Unit 6 Test

Part 1: Multiple Choice

Write your answers in the blank spaces at the left.

1. _____ The low points in the journey through salvation history are due to all of the following except
that _____.
   A. human beings are weak and forgetful
   B. human beings often lose sight of their covenant relationship with God
   C. human beings become absorbed in the sinful ways of the world
   D. God abandons humanity in their hours of need

2. _____ A prophecy is all of the following except _____.
   A. a message communicated by a prophet on behalf of God
   B. a message of divine direction or consolation for the time of the prophet
   C. a message communicated by a prophet on behalf of the pharaoh
   D. a message including divine direction that may be fulfilled in the future

3. _____ What type of messages did the prophets deliver to the Israelites after the Babylonian Exile?
   A. comfort and hope
   B. thanks and praise
   C. warning
   D. reformation

4. _____ What type of messages did the prophets deliver before the Babylonian Exile?
   A. peace
   B. warning
   C. comfort
   D. hope

5. _____ Readings from the Book of Isaiah are proclaimed at the Mass mainly during the liturgical
season of _____.
   A. Lent
   B. Easter
   C. Advent
   D. Christmas

Document #: TX001304

6. _____ The central theme of Jeremiah's message is for the Israelites to _____.

    A. unite their kingdoms under King David

    B. merge with the Samaritans to strengthen themselves against their enemies

    C. go to the Temple each year during Passover

    D. repent and return to the Lord

7. _____ The truth that all human beings have innate dignity and worth as children of God is based on the biblical idea of _____.

    A. prudence

    B. justice

    C. fortitude

    D. temperance

8. _____ The priest and prophet of the southern kingdom who is often plagued with doubt and fear is _____.

    A. Ezekiel

    B. Daniel

    C. Jeremiah

    D. Isaiah

9. _____ The Book of _____ heralds an event that will change the course of salvation: the arrival of the Word of God Made Flesh.

    A. Isaiah

    B. Ruth

    C. Psalms

    D. Daniel

10. _____ Ezekiel uses _____ to get his message across regarding the need for the Israelites to abandon their idolatrous ways.

    A. parables

    B. fables

    C. symbolic language

    D. poetry

Document #: TX001304

Part 2: Matching

Match each statement in column 1 with a term from column 2. Write the letter that corresponds to your choice in the space provided. (*Note:* There are two extra terms in column 2.)

Column 1

1. _____ Faithfulness to an obligation, duty, or commitment.

2. _____ The northern kingdom after the death of Solomon.

3. _____ The leader in the southern kingdom.

4. _____ A Hebrew word meaning "God is with us."

5. _____ The Jewish belief and expectation that a messiah would come to protect, unite, and lead Israel to freedom.

6. _____ To proclaim or announce a saving message.

7. _____ The _____ banished the Israelites in the southern kingdom in chains to serve as slaves.

8. _____ A phrase taken from Isaiah 11:1 that traces Jesus' lineage to King David.

9. _____ Individual strength and courage to overcome obstacles to a moral life.

10. _____ In Ezekiel, the symbol for the foolish and idolatrous beliefs of the surrounding cultures.

Column 2

A. Immanuel

B. fortitude

C. Yahweh

D. stump of Jesse

E. fidelity

F. messianic hope

G. wild beasts

H. Israel

I. prophet

J. Babylonian Exile

K. Judah

L. herald

Document #: TX001304

Part 3: Short Answer

Answer each of the following questions in paragraph form on a separate sheet of paper.

1.   Who were the prophets and what were their roles?

2.   What relationship did the prophet have with his people?

3.   What messages of hope did Jeremiah and Isaiah give to the Israelites?

4.   What should be our role as prophets today?

Document #: TX001304

Unit 6 Test Answer Key

Part 1: Multiple Choice

1. D
2. C
3. A
4. B
5. C

6. D
7. B
8. C
9. A
10. C

Part 2: Matching

1. E
2. H
3. K
4. A
5. F

6. L
7. J
8. D
9. B
10. G

Part 3: Short Answer

1. Prophets were individuals called by God to speak on his behalf. They reminded the people that God would hold them accountable for their idolatrous and unjust practices. When the people were in crisis, the prophets reminded the people of God's saving love. The prophetic message was essentially threefold: act justly toward one another, return to God with faithful hearts, and have hope in God's deliverance.

2. The prophets reinforced that God wanted a close relationship with his people, which meant the people must be faithful to him alone and treat one another with justice. *(Answers also might include: As heralds of God's salvation, prophets act as the conscience of a people who have become complacent and sinful; they assure people that God has not abandoned them and that they need to repent of their sins in order to find joy again; prophets open their eyes to the many obstacles standing in the way of a meaningful relationship with God and others; they challenge people to reflect and respond in a spirit of hope to the unjust practices of the world; they provide comfort and solace to an oppressed people.)*

3. Jeremiah promised that if the Israelites repented of their ways and returned to God, God would destroy their enemies, they would be safe from God's wrath, and God would make a new Covenant with them, which is a law that would be written on their hearts. Isaiah prophesied that a virgin would bear a son and name him Immanuel, and he would be the messiah. He would establish a kingdom where justice and peace would reign; the savior would lift up the lowly and set them free.

4. The vocation to prophecy never dies. Every generation needs men and women to challenge it to remain faithful to God in good times and in bad. Sin, injustice, and despair affect every time and place. Therefore, a saving message of love must be proclaimed. According to the *Catechism of the Catholic Church,* God raises up holy prophets [today] to "proclaim a radical redemption of the People of God, purification from all their infidelities, a salvation which will include all the nations" (64). Thus God calls us today to hear the words of the prophets, apply them to our lives, and be prophetic ourselves.

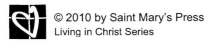 © 2010 by Saint Mary's Press
Living in Christ Series

Document #: TX001305

Unit 7   Jesus Fulfills the Covenant

Overview

This seventh unit connects the Old and New Testaments, paying specific attention to prophecies, servant leadership, and messianic hope. Also, the students recognize Jesus as the unlikely fulfillment of the Covenant and articulate the reasons for the acceptance and rejection of Jesus as he fulfilled the Covenant.

Key Understandings and Questions

At the end of this unit, the students will possess a deeper understanding of the following important concepts:

- Jesus fulfills both the Covenant and salvation history.
- Knowledge of the communities to whom the Gospels were written can help us to understand the Gospels' similarities and differences.
- The Beatitudes interpret the Ten Commandments and carry the Covenant forward.
- We can encounter Jesus today in the Gospels.

At the end of this unit, the students will have answered these questions:

- Why and how does Jesus fulfill the Covenant from the Old Testament?
- Why are there four Gospels, and why are they different from one another?
- How do the Gospel writers show that Jesus is connected to God's Covenant with Abraham, Moses, and David?
- Why are the Gospels important to Christians today?

How Will You Know the Students Understand?

These tools will help you to assess the students' understanding of the main concepts:

- handout "Final Performance Task Options for Unit 7" (Document #: TX001146)
- handout "Rubric for Final Performance Tasks for Unit 7" (Document #: TX001147)
- handout "Unit 7 Test" (Document #: TX001306)

The Suggested Path to Understanding

This teacher guide provides you with one path to take with the students, enabling them to get to know the New Testament and Jesus, the fulfillment of the Covenant, and salvation history. It is not necessary to use all the learning experiences, but if you substitute other material from this course or your own material for some of the material offered here, check to see that you have covered all relevant facets of understanding and that you have not missed knowledge or skills required in the final unit.

Explain | **Step 1:** Preassess the students' understanding of the Gospels and Jesus Christ.

Empathize | **Step 2:** Follow this assessment by presenting to the students the handouts "Final Performance Task Options for Unit 7" (Document #: TX001146) and "Rubric for Final Performance Tasks for Unit 7" (Document #: TX001147).

Apply | **Step 3:** Send the students on a biblical scavenger hunt.

Explain | **Step 4:** Fill in the students' gaps in knowledge of the Gospels.

Empathize | **Step 5:** Give a quiz to assess student understanding.

Interpret | **Step 6:** Ask the students to determine Matthew's interpretation of Jesus' place in salvation history.

Explain | **Step 7:** Introduce the relationship between the Ten Commandments and the Beatitudes.

Interpret | **Step 8:** Instruct the students to creatively interpret Jesus as "the Word."

Interpret | **Step 9:** Challenge the students to compare and contrast the Gospels' Kingdom of God with other kingdoms.

Empathize | **Step 10:** Now that the students are closer to the end of the unit, make sure they are all on track with their final performance tasks, if you have assigned them.

Reflect | **Step 11:** Provide the students with a tool to use for reflecting about what they learned in the unit and how they learned.

Background for Teaching This Content with These Methods

In addition to finding information about the pedagogical approach used in this manual, you will also find background information on these and other topics at *smp.org/LivinginChrist*:

- "The New Testament and Other Early Christian Literature" (Document #: TX001058)
- "Jesus Fulfills the Covenant and Salvation History" (Document #: TX001057)
- "Wonders, Miracles, and Signs in the New Testament" (Document #: TX001060)
- "Gospel Comparison Chart" (Document #: TX001175)

The Web site also has background information on the following teaching methods:

- "Using a Mind Map" (Document #: TX001009)
- "How to Lead a Socratic Seminar" (Document #: TX001006)
- "Using Final Performance Tasks to Assess Understanding" (Document #: TX001011)

Student Book Articles

The articles covered in unit 7 are from "Section 4: Revelation in the New Testament." If you believe the students would do the reading more successfully with additional structure, see the handout "Student Notes for Unit 7" (Document #: TX001059) at *smp.org/LivinginChrist.*

- "The Central Place of the Gospels" (article 53)
- "Three Stages in Gospel Formation" (article 54)
- "Why Four Gospels?" (article 55)
- "The Gospel of Matthew" (article 56)
- "The Gospel of Mark" (article 57)
- "The Gospel of Luke" (article 58)
- "The Central Accounts in the Synoptic Gospels" (article 59)
- "The Parables and Miracles in the Synoptic Gospels" (article 60)
- "The Paschal Mystery in the Synoptic Gospels" (article 61)
- "The Gospel of John: God Incarnate" (article 62)
- "Signs and Miracles" (article 63)
- "The 'I Am' Statements" (article 64)
- "The Bread of Life and Last Supper Discourses" (article 65)
- "The Passion, Death, and Resurrection" (article 66)

Scripture Passages

- Matthew 1:1–17 (the genealogy of Jesus)
- Matthew 1:18—2:7,17–18,23 (Jesus as the fulfillment of prophecy)
- Matthew 2:13–16,19–22 (the flight to Egypt, the return from Egypt)
- Matthew, chapters 5–7 (the Sermon on the Mount)
- Matthew 5:3–12, Luke 6:20–26 (the Beatitudes)
- Matthew 13:31–32, Mark 4:30–32, Luke 13:18–19 (the Parable of the Mustard Seed)
- Matthew 27:1–56, Mark 15:1–41, Luke 23:1–49, John 18:28—19:37 (Jesus' Passion and death)
- John 1:1 (Jesus, the Word)

Vocabulary

If you choose to provide a vocabulary list for material covered in both the student book and the teacher guide, download and print the handout "Vocabulary for Unit 7" (Document #: TX001148), one for each student.

allegory	mysticism
anawim	parables
Essenes	Paraclete
Evangelists	Pharisees
Gentiles	Quelle
Gospels	rabbi
Herodians	Sadducees
Johannine	scribes
Kingdom of God	symbol
Logos	synoptic Gospels
Messiah	Theophilus
messianic hope	Zealots
messianic secret	

Learning Experiences

Step 1

Preassess the students' understanding of the Gospels and Jesus Christ.

The students put on paper all their ideas and thoughts about the Bible in a safe environment and provide you with a preassessment of what they know and associate with the Gospels and Jesus Christ. The students will submit questions about Jesus and the Gospels they would like to be answered.

1. Prepare by downloading and printing the handout "Mind Map" (Document #: TX001160; see Appendix), two for each student, or make double-sided copies, one for each student. (Consider having the students instead mimic the handout by creating a large circle with a series of connected circles in their notebooks.) The students will brainstorm about Jesus Christ on one handout and about the Gospels on the other.

2. Distribute the copies of the handout and pens or pencils. Write the prompt term *Jesus Christ* on the board in a large circle. Ask the students to do the same in the large circle on their handouts. In the connecting circles, have them write words or phrases they think of when they see *Jesus Christ.* Allow about 5 to 10 minutes for the work.

3. When time is up, ask the students to turn to the second mind map handout. Write *Gospel* on the board and ask the students to write *Gospel* in the center circle of the handout. Allow 5 to 10 minutes of similar brainstorming.

4. When time is up, place the students in pairs. Ask the partners to share their mind maps with one another. Allow 10 minutes for sharing.

5. When time is up, invite the students back into the large group. Draw two mind maps or two columns on the board. In them you will list the major terms and ideas the students brainstormed. Ask the students for suggestions for the list.

6. When the list is complete, tell the students the list shows what they know already about these topics. Answer any questions the students have about Jesus or the Gospels. Either ask the students to write these questions in the extra space on their mind maps to be turned in, or have them volunteer questions that you write on the board as a class list. Explain that these will be the guiding questions for the remainder of the unit.

Teacher Note

At this point you may share the essential questions of the unit, found earlier under the section "Key Understandings and Questions."

7. Write the list of questions on a separate sheet of paper for your reference. Answer them at the appropriate time.

8. Collect the mind maps and the students' questions. They will guide you in which material needs introduction, review, or clarification.

Empathize

Step 2

Follow this assessment by presenting to the students the handouts "Final Performance Task Options for Unit 7" (Document #: TX001146) and "Rubric for Final Performance Tasks for Unit 7" (Document #: TX001147).

Teacher Note

You will want to assign due dates for the performance tasks.

The students may have trouble with an Internet search for "Lamb of God" from school. Lamb of God is the name of a heavy-metal group with questionable song lyrics. Even though the students may search for images, some school firewalls may block the searches for this reason. Speak with your Internet administrator about how to deal with this challenge.

If you have done these performance tasks, or very similar ones, with students before, place examples of this work in the classroom. During this introduction explain how each is a good example of what you are looking for, for different reasons. This allows the students to concretely understand what you are looking for and to understand that there is not only one way to succeed.

This unit provides you with two ways to assess that the students have a deep understanding of the most important concepts in the unit: participation in a Socratic seminar or a written reflection on an artistic representation of Jesus, the Lamb of God. Refer to "Using Final Performance Tasks to Assess Understanding" (Document #: TX001011) and "Using Rubrics to Assess Work" (Document #: TX001012) at *smp.org/LivinginChrist* for background information.

1. Prepare by deciding ahead of time whether to have the students work together in a Socratic seminar or work independently to complete a project. Download and print the handouts "Final Performance Task Options for Unit 7" (Document #: TX001146) and "Rubric for Final Performance Tasks for Unit 7" (Document #: TX001147), one for each student.

2. Distribute the handouts. Review the directions, expectations, and rubric in class, allowing the students to ask questions.

3. Explain the types of tools and knowledge the students will gain throughout the unit so they can successfully complete the final performance task.

4. Answer questions to clarify the end point toward which the unit is headed. Remind the students as the unit progresses that each learning experience builds the knowledge and skills they will need to show you they understand how Jesus fulfills the Covenant.

Step 3

Send the students on a biblical scavenger hunt.

Groups of students search the Bible to locate major events in the life of Jesus Christ, illustrating the similarities and differences among the Gospels.

- You may find it useful to assign the students to read the following student book articles before this activity:
  - "The Central Place of the Gospels" (article 53)
  - "Three Stages in Gospel Formation" (article 54)
  - "Why Four Gospels?" (article 55)

Teacher Note

A chart titled "Wonders, Miracles, and Signs in the New Testament" (Document #: TX001060) is available at *smp.org/LivinginChrist*. This chart can be helpful in finding the scriptural references for the scavenger hunt handout.

1. Prepare by downloading and printing the handout "Biblical Scavenger Hunt for Events in the Life of Jesus" (Document #: TX001149), one for each student.

2. On the day of the learning experience, place the students into four small groups, one group for each Gospel. Distribute the copies of the handout. Assign one Gospel to each group. Ask the groups to find the examples from the handout for their assigned Gospel and write down the chapter and verse. Allow 10 to 15 minutes for this work.

3. When time is up, ask the small groups to share with one another what they have found. Have the small groups for Matthew and Mark share with each other while the groups for Luke and John do the same. Then have Matthew share with Luke, John share with Mark, and so on. Allow 10 minutes for each matching.

4. When time is up, call the students back to the large group. Discuss the students' findings. Ask:

   ➤ What did you notice about the events listed on the handout and the way they are placed in the Gospels?

Step 4

Fill in the students' gaps in knowledge of the Gospels.

In this learning experience, the students learn about the differences among the Gospels, influenced greatly by the specific needs of the communities to which they were written.

1. Prepare by downloading and printing the handouts "Vocabulary for Unit 7" (Document #: TX001148) and "Gospel Basics" (Document #: TX001150), one for each student. As homework, assign the students to fill in the handout while reading the following articles from the student book: "The Gospel of Matthew" (article 56), "The Gospel of Mark" (article 57), "The Gospel of Luke" (article 58), and "The Gospel of John: God Incarnate" (article 62). Make an extra copy of the handout "Gospel Basics" (Document #: TX001150) that you can project on the board as the students help you fill it in. You may wish to use the PowerPoint "Introduction to the Gospels" (Document #: TX001081) as you review this information with your students, also found at *smp.org/LivinginChrist.*

   - You may also choose to assign the students to read some or all of the following student book articles for additional insight:
     - "The Central Accounts in the Synoptic Gospels (article 59)
     - "The Parables and Miracles in the Synoptic Gospels" (article 60)
     - "The Paschal Mystery in the Synoptic Gospels" (article 61)
     - "Signs and Miracles" (article 63)
     - "The 'I Am' Statements" (article 64)
     - "The Bread of Life and Last Supper Discourses" (article 65)
     - "The Passion, Death, and Resurrection" (article 66)

2. On the day of the learning experience, distribute the copies of the handouts.
3. Review the following information about the Gospels:

   ➤ God's saving work did not end with the words of the prophets. In fact, the Covenants, the Law, and the prophets of old prepared the way for one of the most important events in salvation history: the Incarnation. The divine Son of God assumed a human nature and became man for the sake of our salvation.

   ➤ The very heart of the Scriptures is the four **Gospels.** The Gospels According to Matthew, Mark, Luke, and John herald the Good News that God came to earth to fulfill the promises made to our ancestors, to form a Covenant with all people, and to overcome the slavery of sin and the darkness of death.

   ➤ Christians use the term *Gospel* to refer to the Good News revealed through Jesus Christ: his life, ministry, teachings, Passion, death, Resurrection, and Ascension.

   ➤ *Gospel* is translated from a Greek word meaning "good news," referring to the four books attributed to Matthew, Mark, Luke, and John, "the principal source for the life and teaching of the Incarnate Word"[1] (*CCC,* 125), Jesus Christ.

   ➤ Each Gospel presents Jesus' life and teachings from a different perspective. Yet in harmony and without error, they announce the truth that Jesus is the one and only way to the Father.

➤ The Gospels are our primary source for information about Jesus Christ, the axis and center of salvation history.

➤ Building on themes from the Old Testament, the four Gospels point to Jesus as the New Covenant.

➤ Matthew, Mark, and Luke are called **synoptic Gospels** (from a Greek word meaning "seeing the whole together"). These Gospels are similar in style and share much of the same content. This is because Luke and Matthew probably used Mark, as well as the **Quelle,** or the Q Source, when compiling their Gospels.

➤ The Quelle, also called the Q Source, is a theoretical collection of ancient documents of the teachings of Jesus shared among the early followers of Christianity. Scholars believe the Evangelists Matthew and Luke used this collection, also called the "Sayings of Jesus," as their source in creating their Gospels.

➤ The Gospel of John was written much later than the synoptic Gospels. It used more symbolic language to express the true identity of Jesus.

4. Ask the students to use the handout "Gospel Basics" (Document #: TX001150) to help you fill in a chart that you project on the board.

Gospel of Matthew

Who: Jewish Christian well versed in the Hebrew Scriptures

When: about AD 85

Community: mixed community of Jewish Christians and **Gentiles**

Community Issues: The **Matthean** community probably experienced rejection and even some persecution by Jewish leaders as a result of their belief in Jesus.

This Gospel's Presentation of Jesus:

• Matthew wanted his Jewish Christian readers to know that believing in Jesus was not a break with their tradition; he wanted them to see it as a continuation of their tradition.

• Matthew highlights Jesus as the fulfillment of many Old Testament hopes and prophecies.

• Matthew validates the community's link to the covenantal promises of the past. At the same time, he justifies these Christians' new devotion to Christ and his mission.

• Jesus' ancestry through Judaism is presented.

• Jesus is presented as a descendant of David and as the Messiah, or "anointed one."

• The Gospel of Matthew presents Jesus as the teacher and Savior of all people.

Gospel of Mark

Who: Gentile Christian who may have been a disciple of Peter

When: about AD 65–70

Community: non-Jewish Christians

Community Issues: The members of the community were being persecuted (even to death) for their beliefs.

This Gospel's Presentation of Jesus:

- The Gospel of Mark carries an aura of secrecy around the identity of Jesus. This atmosphere is known as the **messianic secret.**
- Mark emphasizes the humanity of Jesus.
- Central to Mark's Christology is the image of Jesus as the Suffering Servant.
- Mark presents a Messiah who suffers to do the will of God his Father. Jesus' Passion and death are necessary for God's saving plan to be realized.
- Other people in the Gospel of Mark do identify Jesus as the Messiah.
- At the start of Mark's Gospel, the disciples are lifted up as models. They are the ones who leave everything behind to follow Jesus. As the Gospel continues, Mark sometimes portrays the disciples unfavorably. Mark depicts the disciples as lacking trust and faith. They are unable to comprehend Jesus' teachings and are disloyal in Jesus' darkest hour.
- True discipleship must imitate Jesus in both his ministry and his suffering. The call to be a disciple is the call to remain faithful to Jesus' message even in times of great difficulty and persecution.

Gospel of Luke

Who: Gentile convert to Christianity. The author wrote not only the Gospel of Luke but also another book in the New Testament called the Acts of the Apostles (or simply Acts).

When: about AD 80–90

Community: The audience of both the Gospel of Luke and the Acts of the Apostles is identified by the title Theophilus. This term means "lover of God." It refers to Gentile Christians in Antioch of Syria or Achaia in Greece.

This Gospel's Presentation of Jesus:

- Luke makes it clear that Jesus is the compassionate Savior who welcomes all. In several ways he emphasized that Jesus is a friend to those who are poor and those who are outsiders.
- Much of Jesus' ministry and preaching is directed toward the plight of the *anawim. Anawim* is the Hebrew word for "the poor and marginalized."

- Luke emphasizes the presence of women in the ministry of Jesus.
- The final groups given special attention in the Gospel of Luke are the sick and sinners. During Jesus' time sickness was thought to be a sign of evil or a punishment from God for a sinful life. Dispelling this myth, Jesus travels throughout Galilee healing people possessed by demons, those with leprosy, and those who are paralyzed. He offers forgiveness to sinners.
- His message of salvation is not confined to a particular religious or social group. Rather, it is for all who willingly hear and heed the Good News.
- In the Gospel of Luke, Jesus fulfills the hopes of ancient Israel. At the same time, Jesus demonstrates God's fidelity to all humanity, including the lowly and marginalized. Jesus is the universal Savior, healing, redeeming, and reconciling all creation.

Gospel of John

Who: Many people credit this Gospel to a man named John, "the [disciple] whom Jesus loved" (John 13:23), but the actual author is unknown. Many believe the author was a member of a Christian community founded by the **Beloved Disciple.** Its tradition and teachings represent the whole **Johannine** community rather than just one individual.

When: about AD 90–100

This Gospel's Presentation of Jesus:

This Gospel was written for two main reasons. First, it was composed to evangelize both Gentiles and Jews. Second, the author wanted to strengthen the faith of his local Christian community, as well as Christians everywhere. John's Gospel is divided into two major sections:

- **The Book of Signs (1:19—12:50):** The focus of the Book of Signs is seven miraculous signs Jesus performed. In contrast to the synoptic Gospels, in the Gospel of John, Jesus teaches primarily through signs, not parables. These signs reveal the identity of Jesus as the one sent from the Father in Heaven.
- **The Book of Glory (13:1—20:31):** The Book of Glory centers on the Paschal Mystery. It is called the Book of Glory because John describes the Passion, death, Resurrection, and Ascension as a glorification of Jesus according to the Father's plan. Throughout the Book of Glory, John emphasizes the importance of the Holy Spirit in the life of the Church after Jesus' death.
- While the synoptic Gospels emphasize the humanity of Jesus, the Gospel of John stresses his divinity.
- The central image of Jesus is God Incarnate. In his **Prologue,** John describes Jesus as the preexistent *Logos* (Word), who is God and was

with God at the beginning of Creation and takes on flesh to dwell among us.

- John proclaims that Jesus, the Incarnate Word, is "the light of the human race" (John 1:4). In declaring Jesus as the Light, the Evangelist asserts the divinity of Jesus.

- John concludes his Prologue by saying that Jesus is the fulfillment of the Old Law.

Step 5

Give a quiz to assess student understanding.

1. In preparation for this assessment, download and print the handout "Unit 7 Quiz" (Document #: TX001151), one for each student. Note that the quiz is fairly comprehensive, in part because both you and the students want to learn what they do not now know in preparation for a test or the final performance tasks.

2. On the day of the quiz, provide 5 to 10 minutes for the students to review their books and notes. Distribute the quiz and provide sufficient time for the students to work on it. If time remains when the students are done, collect the quizzes and then redistribute them so everyone has someone else's. Go through the quiz, allowing the students to correct one another's work and also giving them an opportunity to affirm or change their understanding of concepts. Collect the quizzes and further your analysis about topics that may need more coverage.

> **Teacher Note**
>
> To save paper, use the electronic copy of the quiz from *smp.org/LivinginChrist* and put it up in a visual place via projector, overhead, monitor, and so on. If these options are unavailable, read the quiz to the students slowly. In both cases, have the students record their answers on loose-leaf paper.

Step 6

Ask the students to determine Matthew's interpretation of Jesus' place in salvation history.

The students investigate how the Gospel of Matthew presents the theme of this unit: Jesus as the fulfillment of salvation history and the Covenant. This learning experience has two parts. The first part focuses on the connections in the Gospel of Matthew between Jesus and events in salvation history. The second part explores the passages more closely in light of the Covenant in the Old Testament, leading to deeper understanding. You may want to adapt this learning experience based on the needs of your students and your own timeline.

Part I: Jesus Fulfills Salvation History

1. Briefly review salvation history yourself or ask the students to look at their salvation history timelines from unit 3. Remind the students of the definition from the student book: "The pattern of specific events in human history that reveal God's presence and saving actions."

2. Place the students into three small groups. Explain that each small group will be assigned a passage from the Gospel of Matthew. They will read the passage and then answer the question "What is Matthew's interpretation of Jesus' place in salvation history?" Ask the students to copy this question into their notebooks to focus their reading. Ask them to take notes as they read.

3. Assign one of the following readings to each small group. Be careful not to reveal the themes of the readings. Allow 10 minutes for reading and taking notes.

    - Matthew 1:1–17 (the genealogy of Jesus)
    - Matthew 1:17—2:7,17–18,23 (Jesus as the fulfillment of prophecy)
    - Matthew 2:13–16,19–22 (the flight to Egypt, the return from Egypt)

4. When time is up, call the students back into the large group. Ask a volunteer from each small group to write the group's response to the question (in bullet-point form) on the board. These students should cite examples from the Scriptures that support their response. Allow 5 minutes for writing.

5. When time is up, ask another volunteer from each small group to read that group's passage aloud. Following each reading ask the students in that small group who did not read or write notes on the board to explain their responses to the question.

Part II: Jesus Fulfills the Covenant

1. Once each group has read its passage and explained its response to the question, ask:

    ➤ How does Matthew understand Jesus in relation to God's Covenants with Abraham, Moses, and David?

2. Review the order of the Covenants between God and his People throughout salvation history.

    - Genesis, chapters 12 and 15 (the call of Abram and God's Covenant with Abraham)
    - Exodus 20:1–17 (the Ten Commandments)
    - Exodus, chapter 24 (ratification of the Covenant)
    - 2 Samuel 7:8–17 (the Lord's promises)

3. Ask the students to write in their notebooks individual responses to the question about the Covenants of the Old Testament, using the notes and discussion and working in their three small groups before building a large-group response.

4. Discuss the question with the large group. Encourage the students to take notes on the other students' suggestions. Review and emphasize the following points as needed by revisiting the passages from the Old Testament and Matthew. Read these passages aloud or ask the students to do so.

   A. Reread Matthew 1:1–17, the genealogy of Jesus. Ask the following questions:

      ➤ To whom is Jesus related according to this genealogy?

      ➤ What does the author illustrate with this passage?

   B. Reread Genesis, chapters 12 and 15, the Covenant with Abraham.

   C. Reread Second Samuel 7:8–17, the Covenant with David.

   D. Reread Matthew 2:13–16,19–22, the flight to Egypt and the return from Egypt.

      • Remind the students of Exodus 1:15—2:10, Pharaoh's command to kill the Hebrew babies and Moses' deliverance. Also remind them of Exodus 4:18–31, Moses' return to Egypt. Note how Matthew's account alludes to these episodes from Moses' life.

      • Matthew makes another allusion to Moses when he shows Jesus as the giver of the Law. See Matthew 5:17–20 and compare it to Moses' receiving the Ten Commandments at Mount Sinai (see Exodus 20:1–17) and the ratification of the Covenant (see Exodus, chapter 24).

   E. Reread Matthew 1:17—2:7,17–18,23, Jesus as the fulfillment of prophecy. Ask the following question:

      ➤ Why would the author of Matthew want to connect Jesus and David?

5. Conclude by asking the students to share what they thought of the learning experience.

Explain

Step 7

Introduce the relationship between the Ten Commandments and the Beatitudes.

The students review the Ten Commandments (or Decalogue) (see Exodus 20:1–26) and the Beatitudes (see Matthew 5:3–10 and Luke 6:20–26). The students determine

Teacher Note

This learning experience may be used as an individual essay assessment or as a class project in the form of a Socratic seminar.

how the Beatitudes interpret the Commandments and carry forward the Covenant. They either write an analytical essay on this topic or discuss their findings in a Socratic seminar.

Option 1: Individual Essay

1. As homework, assign the students to review the passages containing the Decalogue (see Exodus 20:1–26) and the Beatitudes (see Matthew 5:3–10 and Luke 6:20–26). Ask them to find the relationship between the two and determine how the Beatitudes interpret the Decalogue and carry forward the Covenant.

2. In class ask the students to answer the following questions:

   • How is the Covenant represented in these passages?

   • How do Jesus and Moses embody servant leadership in the ways they present these teachings?

   • How do these passages contribute to salvation history?

3. If you choose to use this learning experience as an individual assessment, ask the students to write a multiparagraph analytical essay on this topic, including secondary resources. For example, the article "The Eight Beatitudes" on the New Advent Web site is an excellent secondary resource.

4. Before the students hand in their essays, ask them to share with the other students a portion of their essays.

Option 2: Socratic Seminar

You may want to have the students discuss this topic during a Socratic seminar. Ask the students to address the same questions as in option 1 but instead to write a two-paragraph essay rather than a longer paper. Prepare for the seminar as described in the article "How to Lead a Socratic Seminar" (Document #: TX001006) at *smp.org/LivinginChrist,* or review the material on the seminar found in unit 1. The appendix contains the handouts "The Socratic Seminar" (Document #: TX001015), "Socratic Seminar Symbol Codes" (Document #: TX001014), "Student Evaluation for the Socratic Seminar" (Document #: TX001013), and "Rubric for an Oral Presentation" (Document #: TX001174), which you will need for the seminar.

Step 8

Instruct the students to creatively interpret Jesus as "the Word."

The Gospel of John refers to Jesus as the Word: "In the beginning was the Word, / and the Word was with God, / and the Word was God" (1:1). The students interpret this passage creatively. They may paint, draw, write a creative scene, write a poem, perform a skit, or create in another medium to address the passage.

1. Prepare by having available art materials for the students or ask them to bring their own to class.

2. On the day of the learning experience, ask the students to brainstorm on John 1:1, focusing on the following questions:

   - What is the Word?
   - How do we hear the Word?
   - How do we understand the Word?

   Allow 5 to 10 minutes for brainstorming.

3. When time is up, present the following information:

   ➤ **Logos:** A Greek word meaning "Word." *Logos* is a title of Jesus Christ found in the Gospel of John that illuminates the relationship between the three Persons of the Holy Trinity. (See John 1:1,14.)

   ➤ Greek and Roman culture directly influenced Jewish culture. We see signs of this in John's Gospel.

   Ask the students to identify some of the signs in John's Gospel and analyze what they reveal about Jesus and God. Have the students identify the events listed in the Book of Glory and analyze what they reveal about Jesus and God. Explain that the Advocate (or Paraclete) is a Johannine name for the Holy Spirit, whom Jesus promised to send the disciples as an advocate and counselor. Ask:

   ➤ What is the connection between the Word and the Paraclete? How can we recognize the presence of the Word with us today? the presence of the Paraclete?

4. Provide time in class for the students to work on their artistic interpretations of the Word. If the students have art supplies at home, have them finish the assignment as homework. If not, make other arrangements with them.

   To further discuss allusions to people and events from the Old Testament, ask the students to present examples and explain their choices. For example, from Matthew, Jesus can be compared to Moses for his focus on teaching and the Law.

Step 9

Challenge the students to compare and contrast the Gospels' Kingdom of God with other kingdoms.

The students critically evaluate each kingdom. They present their analysis of similarities and differences in a PowerPoint presentation or other visual medium and hand in a written explanation.

1. With the students, identify the main characteristics of the Kingdom of God and the passages where the Scriptures portray it. Write the characteristics on the board. Provide the following definition of the Kingdom of God:

   • The reign or rule of God over the hearts of people and, as a consequence, the development of a new social order based on unconditional love. Also called the Reign of God.

2. Next, ask the students to think of or find a worldly, literary, or cinematic kingdom to compare and contrast the characteristics of God's Kingdom. You may wish to place the students in small groups for this learning experience.

3. Tell the students they will complete a project about God's Kingdom. Provide the following instructions:

   ➤ You will prepare a visual, such as a PowerPoint presentation, that shows the similarities and differences between the Kingdom of God and the worldly, literary, or cinematic kingdom you have chosen. The presentation will explain and illustrate major symbols used to explain the Kingdom of God. It will compare and contrast these symbols with those of the other kingdom you identified. The PowerPoint presentation should be 2 to 3 minutes long.

   ➤ You also will create a two-page written analysis of the similarities and differences between the kingdoms. The analysis will cite passages from the Scriptures.

4. When time is up, collect the written analyses. Ask the students to present their visuals. Encourage the other students to ask clarifying questions about the presentations.

5. Following the presentations, hold a large-group discussion about the characteristics, symbols, and meanings the Scriptures use to present the Kingdom of God.

Teacher Note

Explain the deadlines and expectations. Allow at least one class period for the students to work together if you use this learning experience as a group project.

Step 10

Now that the students are closer to the end of the unit, make sure they are all on track with their final performance tasks, if you have assigned them.

If possible, devote 50 to 60 minutes for the students to ask questions about the tasks and to work individually or in their small groups.

1. Remind the students to bring to class any work they have already prepared so that they can work on it during the class period. If necessary, reserve the library or media center so the students can do any book or online research. Download and print the handouts "Final Performance Task Options for Unit 7" (Document #: TX001146) and "Rubric for Final Performance Tasks for Unit 7" (Document #: TX001147). Review the final performance task options, answer questions, and ask the students to choose one if they have not already done so.

2. Provide some class time for the students to work on their performance tasks. This then allows you to work with the students who need additional guidance with the project.

Step 11

Provide the students with a tool to use for reflecting about what they learned in the unit and how they learned.

This learning experience provides the students with an excellent opportunity to reflect on how their understandings of Jesus and messianic prophecies has developed throughout the unit.

1. Prepare by downloading and printing the handout "Learning about Learning" (Document #: TX001159; see Appendix), one for each student.

2. Distribute the copies of the handout and give the students about 15 minutes to answer the questions quietly. Invite them to share any reflections they have about the content they learned as well as their insights into the way they learned.

Final Performance Task Options for Unit 7

The following are the main ideas you are to understand from this unit. They should appear in this final performance task so your teacher can assess whether you learned the most essential content:

- Jesus fulfills both the Covenant and salvation history.
- Knowledge of the communities to whom the Gospels were written can help us to understand the Gospels' similarities and differences.
- The Beatitudes interpret the Ten Commandments and carry the Covenant forward.
- We can encounter Jesus today in the Gospels.

Option 1: A Socratic Seminar

Study the Connections Between the Life of Jesus and the Old Testament

You will take part in a Socratic seminar about how Jesus fulfilled the Covenant. Your teacher will assign you to research one of the following questions about that topic. You will then prepare for the seminar as directed in the next part.

- How has Jesus Christ fulfilled the Covenant made with King David?
- The Gospels make various connections between Jesus and the leaders of the Old Testament. Give examples and explain the purposes of these connections.
- Jesus fulfills the Law presented at Mount Sinai. Give examples to explain how Jesus does this and explain the significance of this new presentation of the Law.
- The Passion of Christ varies according to the Gospel presenting it. Read Matthew 27:1–56, Mark 15:1–4, Luke 23:2–49, and John 18:28–19,42. What does each Passion narrative highlight and (according to your understanding of the Gospels) why?

Prepare for the Socratic Seminar

- Review your class notes and the Gospels to formulate a well-supported answer to your question assigned above.
- Type or neatly write the points you want to make during the seminar. Be sure to cite scriptural passages to support your ideas.
- Bring your written notes and your Bible to class on the day of the seminar. They are required "entrance tickets" to participate.

Document #: TX001146

Option 2: Jesus as the Lamb of God
Study Jesus as the Lamb of God

You will explore Jesus as the Lamb of God by examining art and artists from different periods and artistic schools. You will pick an artistic representation of Jesus, the Lamb of God, and write a reflection about it. You will print out or otherwise recreate a copy of the art to accompany your reflection. Your work will be posted in a gallery for presentation. Take the following steps:

- Read the following passages from John's Gospel for references to Jesus as the "Lamb of God."
  - John 1:29–34 (John the Baptist's testimony to Jesus)
  - John 1:35–42 (the first disciples)
  - John 10:11–18 (the Good Shepherd)

- As background for these passages, read their footnotes in the *New American Bible*. Look up "Lamb" in the *Saint Mary's Press® Essential Bible Dictionary*. Find an online version of this dictionary at the Saint Mary's Press eSource site.

- Choose one artistic representation of Jesus, the Lamb of God. Examples include the apse mosaic "Tent of Heaven" at the San Vitale basilica in Ravenna, Italy; "Adoration of the Lamb," by Jan van Eyck, part of the Ghent altarpiece; and the fresco of Jesus the Good Shepherd from the catacombs of Saint Callixtus. These can be found easily in an Internet search. You may want to try The Web Gallery of Art for European paintings. Check with your teacher if you have trouble with an Internet search for "Lamb of God."

- Check your choice with your teacher. Once your teacher approves the choice, begin by looking carefully at your representation of Jesus, the Lamb of God. Write notes that answer the following questions.
  - What is included in the representation?
  - Who is included in the representation?
  - How are they represented?
  - What is the mood of the representation (happy, sad, triumphant, defeated)?
  - Does the representation do a good job of presenting the meaning of the Lamb of God as found in the passages from John?

- After observing and taking notes on your representation, review the Gospels and your notes from class. Ask yourself the following questions:
  - How does the "Lamb of God" reference to Jesus connect him to salvation history?
  - Why might the "Lamb of God" image have spoken well to the audience John was writing to?
  - Which of the Beatitudes from Matthew's Gospel (5:1–12) match the image of a lamb? How does John's use of this image move beyond the Jewish understanding of the lamb of sacrifice?
  - How does the idea of the "Lamb of God" help you to understand Jesus?

- Continue to take notes and write down the chapters and verses of the passages you find in the Gospels.

- Type or neatly handwrite a two- to three-page reflection on your representation, including proper citations of the Scriptures to support your analysis. Describe specific aspects of the representation, as well as the general presentation of Jesus, the Lamb of God.

- Review your writing for grammar and spelling errors before turning it in.

- Print out or otherwise recreate your depiction of Jesus, the Lamb of God, to hand in with your reflection.

 © 2010 by Saint Mary's Press
Living in Christ Series   Document #: TX001146

Rubric for Final Performance Tasks for Unit 7

Criteria	4	3	2	1
Assignment includes all items requested in the instructions.	Assignment includes not only all items requested but they are completed above expectations.	Assignment includes all items requested.	Assignment includes over half of the items requested.	Assignment includes less than half of the items requested.
Assignment shows understanding of the concept *Jesus fulfills both the Covenant and salvation history.*	Assignment shows unusually insightful understanding of this concept.	Assignment shows good understanding of this concept.	Assignment shows adequate understanding of this concept.	Assignment shows little understanding of this concept.
Assignment shows understanding of the concept *knowledge of the communities to whom the Gospels were written can help us to understand the Gospels' similarities and differences.*	Assignment shows unusually insightful understanding of this concept.	Assignment shows good understanding of this concept.	Assignment shows adequate understanding of this concept.	Assignment shows little understanding of this concept.
Assignment shows understanding of the concept *the Beatitudes interpret the Ten Commandments and carry the Covenant forward.*	Assignment shows unusually insightful understanding of this concept.	Assignment shows good understanding of this concept.	Assignment shows adequate understanding of this concept.	Assignment shows little understanding of this concept.
Assignment shows understanding of the concept *we can encounter Jesus today in the Gospels.*	Assignment shows unusually insightful understanding of this concept.	Assignment shows good understanding of this concept.	Assignment shows adequate understanding of this concept.	Assignment shows little understanding of this concept.
Assignment uses method of communication in a way that clearly conveys what the assignment requests.	Assignment clearly and outstandingly conveys what the assignment requests.	Assignment clearly conveys what the assignment requests.	Assignment at times clearly conveys what the assignment requests.	Assignment does not convey what the assignment requests.
Assignment uses proper grammar and spelling.	Assignment has no grammar or spelling errors.	Assignment has one grammar or spelling error.	Assignment has two grammar or spelling errors.	Assignment has more than two grammar or spelling errors.

Document #: TX001147

Vocabulary for Unit 7

allegory: A literary form in which something is said to be like something else, in an attempt to communicate a hidden or symbolic meaning.

anawim: A Hebrew word for the poor and marginalized.

Essenes: A group of pious, ultraconservative Jews who left the Temple of Jerusalem and began a community by the Dead Sea, known as Qumran.

Evangelists: Based on a word for "good news," in general, anyone who actively works to spread the Gospel of Jesus; more commonly and specifically, the persons traditionally recognized as authors of the four Gospels, Matthew, Mark, Luke, and John.

Gentiles: Non-Jewish people.

Gospels: Translated from a Greek word meaning "good news," referring to the four books attributed to Matthew, Mark, Luke, and John, "the principal source for the life and teaching of the Incarnate Word"[2] (*CCC*, 125), Jesus Christ.

Herodians: A group of Jewish leaders, including the Temple high priests and Jewish royal families, who collaborated with the Roman governors.

Johannine: Related to the author of the fourth Gospel.

Kingdom of God: The reign or rule of God over the hearts of people and, as a consequence, the development of a new social order based on unconditional love. Also called the Reign of God.

Logos: A Greek word meaning "Word." *Logos* is a title of Jesus Christ found in the Gospel of John that illuminates the relationship between the three Persons of the Holy Trinity. (See John 1:1,14.)

Messiah: A Hebrew word meaning "God's anointed one." Translated as "Christ" in Greek.

messianic hope: The Jewish belief and expectation that a messiah would come to protect, unite, and lead Israel to freedom.

messianic secret: A theme in the Gospel of Mark that portrays the disciples and others as recognizing Jesus' identity as the Messiah. However, Jesus directed them not to tell anyone else.

mysticism: A word that comes from the Greek, meaning "to conceal."

parables: Short stories that use everyday images to communicate religious messages.

Paraclete: A name for the Holy Spirit, the Divine Third Person of the Trinity, whom Jesus promised to the disciples as an advocate and counselor.

Pharisees: A Jewish religious group that strictly observed and taught the Law of Moses.

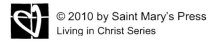

Quelle: Also called the Q Source, a theoretical collection of ancient documents of the teachings of Jesus shared among the early followers of Christianity.

rabbi: An honored teacher in the Jewish tradition.

Sadducees: A group of powerful and often wealthy Jews who were connected to the Temple priests and often disagreed with the Pharisees.

scribes: People associated with the Pharisees or Sadducees who were skilled copyists, professional letter writers, and interpreters and teachers of the Law.

symbol: An object that points to or represents another reality. Sometimes the word *symbol* is used as a synonym of *sign,* and other times it refers to an object that makes present what it signifies.

synoptic Gospels: From the Greek for "seeing the whole together," the name given to the Gospels of Matthew, Mark, and Luke, because they are similar in style and content.

Theophilus: The name given to the audience of the Gospel of Luke and the Acts of the Apostles; it means "lover of God" or "God fearer."

Zealots: People who banded together during the time of Christ to violently resist Roman occupation.

© 2010 by Saint Mary's Press
Living in Christ Series

Document #: TX001148

Biblical Scavenger Hunt for Events in the Life of Jesus

Name: _____

In the time provided, use your biblical navigation skills to locate as many of the following events from the life of Jesus Christ as you can.

Event or teaching from Jesus' life	Matthew	Mark	Luke	John
Angelic Annunciation / wondrous pregnancy				
Signs of Jesus' destiny				
Interventions by Jesus				
Healing the centurion's servant				
Curing Peter's mother-in-law				
Raising the crippled woman up straight				
Cleansing lepers				
Curing the ill and lame				
Healing a woman with a twelve-year hemorrhage				
Making the blind see, the deaf hear, the mute speak				
Calming storms				
Walking on water				
Causing a fig tree to wither				

Document #: TX001149

The Bible: The Living Word of God

Gospel Basics

Name: _____

Fill in the chart below from student book articles 56, 57, 58, and 62, "The Gospel of Matthew," "The Gospel of Mark," "The Gospel of Luke," and "The Gospel of John: God Incarnate."

Gospel Characteristics	Matthew	Mark	Luke	John
Who?				
When?				
Where?				
What?				

Document #: TX001150

Unit 7 Quiz

Name: _____

Part I: Fill in the Blank

Fill in the blanks with the best word to complete each sentence.

1. *Gospel* is translated from a Greek word meaning _____.

2. The Gospels include the birth, life, ministry, teachings, Passion, _____, and Resurrection of Jesus Christ.

3. _____ of the Old Testament provided messianic hope; they foretold the coming of a messiah.

4. Matthew, Mark, and _____ are called the synoptic Gospels.

5. *Synoptic* means "_____," because these three Gospels present Jesus Christ in a similar way.

6. The authors of the Gospels of Matthew and Luke drew from the Gospel of Mark and the Quelle, or the "_____."

7. The Gospel of Matthew emphasizes that Jesus is the _____, or "anointed one," a descendant of King David.

8. Scholars believe _____ was the first Gospel to be written, around AD 65–70.

9. In the Gospel of _____, Jesus presents a new understanding of the Law and can be compared to Moses.

10. In the Gospel of Luke, Jesus shows concern for these three groups of people, among others:

    _____

    _____

    _____

Part II: Short Answer

Write a paragraph to describe the audience to whom one of the Evangelists was writing. How did the audience's circumstances affect the manner in which the Gospel writer portrayed Jesus? Give examples.

© 2010 by Saint Mary's Press
Living in Christ Series

Document #: TX001151

Unit 7 Test

Part 1: Multiple Choice

Write your answers in the blank spaces at the left.

1. _____ The Gospels of Matthew, Mark, and Luke are called the synoptic Gospels because _____.
   - A. they have the same number of chapters
   - B. they use the same images of Jesus
   - C. they are similar in style and content
   - D. the writers had similar backgrounds

2. _____ One way the Gospel of John differs from the synoptic Gospels is that _____.
   - A. it was written much earlier than the others
   - B. it was written by the youngest of the Twelve Apostles
   - C. it presents an image of Jesus as a teacher and prophet
   - D. it uses more symbolic language to express the true identity of Jesus

3. _____ All of the synoptic Gospels emphasize the _____, asserting that Jesus is the Suffering Servant who must die to ransom all humanity.
   - A. Paschal Mystery
   - B. calling of the Twelve
   - C. miracles of Jesus
   - D. role of the Blessed Mother

4. _____ The _____ are the accounts of Jesus' birth and early childhood.
   - A. Acts of the Apostles
   - B. books of the Late Old Testament
   - C. Epistles of James
   - D. infancy narratives

5. _____ The miracles provide credibility to Jesus' words and teachings by concretely demonstrating his power over _____.
   - A. the Pharisees
   - B. the cross
   - C. sin and evil
   - D. atheists

Document #: TX001306

6. _____   The Gospel of John emphasizes the _____.
      A. the parables of Jesus
      B. the divinity of Jesus
      C. the miracles of Jesus
      D. the humanity of Jesus

7. _____   All of the following are true about the part of John's Gospel called the Book of Signs except _____.
      A. it contains seven miraculous cures
      B. it reveals Jesus as the one sent from the Father
      C. it gives special attention to God's presence in the world
      D. it shows Jesus teaching primarily through parables

8. _____   All of the following are true about the Gospels except that _____.
      A. they contradict one another in meaning
      B. they are not identical
      C. they announce that Jesus is the one and only way to the Father
      D. each Gospel presents Jesus' life from a different perspective

9. _____   All of the following prepared the way for the Incarnation except _____.
      A. the Covenants
      B. the Sermon on the Mount
      C. the Law
      D. the prophets of old

10. _____   All of the following are true about the part of John's Gospel called the Book of Glory except _____.
      A. it centers on the Paschal Mystery
      B. it describes Jesus' death on the cross
      C. it describes the Ascension of Jesus
      D. it emphasizes the importance of the Holy Spirit after Jesus' death

11. _____   Which of the following signs or miracles is in the Gospel of John but not in the synoptic Gospels?
      A. Jesus walks on water.
      B. Jesus restores sight to the man born blind.
      C. Jesus restores the health of the official's son.
      D. Jesus feeds the five thousand.

Document #: TX001306

12. _____ The scribes were people associated with the Pharisees and Sadducees, who were all of the following except _____.

    A. skilled copyists
    B. professional letter writers
    C. interpreters and teachers of the Law
    D. judges in Jewish courts

13. _____ The audience of both the Gospel of Luke and the Acts of the Apostles is identified by the title _____, meaning "lover of God."

    A. Theophilus
    B. Marcus
    C. Mephistopheles
    D. Barnabas

14. _____ All of the following are names and titles of Jesus common to all four Gospels except _____.

    A. Christ or Messiah
    B. Lord
    C. Good Shepherd
    D. Son of God

15. _____ Jesus is called the Paschal Lamb because _____.

    A. he was risen from the dead on Easter
    B. he died on a cross to take away the sin of the world
    C. he was born in a stable
    D. he is the Good Shepherd

Document #: TX001306

Part 2: Matching

Match each statement in column 1 with a term from column 2. Write the letter that corresponds to your choice in the space provided. (*Note:* There are two extra terms in column 2.)

Column 1

1. _____ The message of salvation offered to all through Jesus Christ.

2. _____ The place where Jesus was crucified.

3. _____ The one who guided the writers of the Gospels.

4. _____ A Greek word meaning "word," used to refer to the Second Person of the Blessed Trinity, Jesus Christ.

5. _____ A faithful disciple in the Gospel of John, present at critical times in Jesus' ministry.

6. _____ Involves Scripture readings, a homily, and general intercessions.

7. _____ The title given to the authors of the Gospels, Matthew, Mark, Luke, and John.

8. _____ Non-Jewish people.

9. _____ A Greek word that literally means "good news."

10. _____ Persons who travel from place to place explaining the Word of God.

Column 2

A. Liturgy of the Word

B. Covenant

C. itinerant preachers

D. Holy Spirit

E. Golgotha

F. Evangelists

G. *Logos*

H. prophets

I. *kerygma*

J. Gospel

K. Beloved Disciple

L. Gentiles

Document #: TX001306

Part 3: Fill-in-the-Blank

Use the word bank to fill in the blanks in the following sentences. (*Note:* There are two extra terms in the word bank.)

WORD BANK

venerated	signs	rabbi
Liturgy of the Eucharist	Beatitudes	messianic secret
Quelle	Samaritans	miracles
Johannine	Matthean	Magi

1. We use the term _____ to relate to the author of the first Gospel.

2. The _____ are wise men from the East who followed a new star that directed them to the birth of Jesus.

3. The _____ makes present Christ's saving work accomplished through his life, death, and Resurrection.

4. The _____ is an honored teacher in the Jewish tradition.

5. In the Sermon on the Mount, Jesus gave a new interpretation of the Law of Moses through the _____, wisdom teachings in the form of blessings.

6. A theme in the Gospel of Mark is the _____, which portrays the disciples and others as recognizing Jesus' identity as the Messiah, but not telling anyone else.

7. The _____ is a theoretical collection of ancient documents of the teachings of Jesus, shared by his early followers.

8. _____ is a word that means "respected and given devotion."

9. _____ is the Johannine name for the miracles of Jesus.

10. _____ is a word related to the author of the fourth Gospel.

Document #: TX001306

Part 4: Short Answer

Answer each of the following questions in paragraph form on a separate sheet of paper.

1. How does Jesus fulfill the Covenant and salvation history?

2. What were the communities or audiences for the four Evangelists to which they directed the particular focus of the Gospel they wrote?

3. How do the Beatitudes fulfill the Old Law yet provide a clear expression of the New Law?

4. To what do the Gospels invite us in our daily lives?

Document #: TX001306

Unit 7 Test Answer Key

Part 1: Multiple Choice

1. C
2. D
3. A
4. D
5. C
6. B
7. D
8. A
9. B
10. C
11. B
12. D
13. A
14. C
15. B

Part 2: Matching

1. I
2. E
3. D
4. G
5. K
6. A
7. F
8. L
9. J
10. C

Part 3: Fill-in-the-Blank

1. Matthean
2. Magi
3. Liturgy of the Eucharist
4. rabbi
5. Beatitudes
6. messianic secret
7. Quelle
8. venerated
9. signs
10. Johannine

Part 4: Short Answer

1. God came to earth as Jesus Christ and lived among his people; he fulfilled the promises made to our ancestors in faith; Jesus formed a New Covenant with all people and completed salvation history, saving us from sin and death, through his death and Resurrection.

2. Each writer wrote for the community to which he belonged; the writers focused on aspects of Jesus' life and teachings that were most meaningful to their communities and emphasized the religious truth their communities needed. Matthew wrote for a community that wanted to maintain its Jewish roots while believing that Jesus was the Messiah. Matthew, therefore, stresses the fact that Jesus is the fulfillment of the Jewish hopes and prophecies. Mark's audience was non-Jewish Christians facing persecution; he stresses a narrative that seeks to make sense of their suffering and persecution. Luke wrote for Gentiles and Jews as part of God's saving plan. John wrote for both Gentiles and Jews and to strengthen the faith of the local Christian community.

3. The Beatitudes fulfill the Old Law by orienting us toward their true meaning and goal: the establishment of the Kingdom of Heaven. They express the New Law by showing us the end God is calling us to: communion with him in the Kingdom of Heaven where we will see him face-to-face. The Beatitudes reveal that everyone is called to the Kingdom of God.

4. The Gospels invite us to accept Jesus into our hearts and be baptized, becoming members of the Body of Christ, the Church. They call us to participate in the sacramental life of the Church. They challenge us to follow Jesus and to apply his teachings to our everyday lives.

Document #: TX001307

Unit 8 The First Christians: Witnesses to the New Covenant

Overview

This final unit points out Jesus as the fulfillment of salvation history, even as he asked his followers to spread the Good News. The next stage in salvation history, the growth of the Church, emerged in the years following Jesus' death.

Key Understandings and Questions

At the end of this unit, the students will possess a deeper understanding of the following important concepts:

- Jesus charged the Twelve Apostles with the responsibility for spreading the Good News.
- The early Apostles were servant leaders who carried word of the New Covenant in their ministries.
- Paul (originally named Saul) influenced the development of the early Christian Church through his traveling ministry and by the letters he left behind.
- These Pauline letters help us to understand how the Christian community made a transition from Judaism to embrace non-Jewish converts.

At the end of this unit, the students will have answered these questions:

- Who were the Apostles and why are they important?
- Who was Paul (Saul) and what was his influence on early Christianity (also called "The Way")?
- How did the Apostles carry on the legacy of the leaders of Israel in relationship to the Covenant and servant leadership?
- How did the early followers of Jesus expand to include non-Jews as well as Jews?

How Will You Know the Students Understand?

These tools will help you to assess the students' understanding of the main concepts:

- handout "Final Performance Task Options for Unit 8" (Document #: TX001152)
- handout "Rubric for Final Performance Tasks for Unit 8" (Document #: TX001153)
- handout "Unit 8 Test" (Document #: TX001308)

The Suggested Path to Understanding

This teacher guide provides you with one path to take with the students, enabling them to begin their study of the Apostles and the early Church. It is not necessary to use all the learning experiences, but if you substitute other material from this course or your own material for some of the material offered here, check to see that you have covered all relevant facets of understanding and that you have not missed knowledge or skills.

Explain **Step 1:** Preassess what the students already know about the Apostles.

Empathize **Step 2:** Follow this assessment by presenting to the students the handouts "Final Performance Task Options for Unit 8" (Document #: TX001152) and "Rubric for Final Performance Tasks for Unit 8" (Document #: TX001153).

Explain **Step 3:** Fill in gaps in the students' knowledge of the Twelve Apostles.

Empathize **Step 4:** Have the students uncover the importance of the Twelve Apostles.

Empathize **Step 5:** Use art with the Acts of the Apostles.

Explain **Step 6:** Present information about the Acts of the Apostles and about Paul.

Interpret **Step 7:** Present common themes in the Pauline letters.

Apply **Step 8:** Allow the students to discover the classifications and styles of Paul in the Bible.

Empathize **Step 9:** Give a quiz to assess student understanding.

Apply **Step 10:** Explore the role Sacred Scripture plays in the life of the individual and experience prayer with Scripture.

Empathize **Step 11:** Now that the students are closer to the end of the unit, make sure they are all on track with their final performance tasks, if you have assigned them.

Reflect **Step 12:** Provide the students with a tool to use for reflecting about what they learned in the unit and how they learned.

Background for Teaching This Content with These Methods

In addition to finding information about the pedagogical approach used in this manual, you will also find background information on these and other topics at *smp.org/LivinginChrist:*

- "Introduction to the Letters" (Document #: TX001062)
- "The Apostles" (Document #: TX001063)
- "The Acts of the Apostles" (Document #: TX001061)

The Web site also has background information on the following teaching methods:

- "Preassessment Informs Teaching" (Document #: TX001008)
- "Using a Mind Map" (Document #: TX001009)
- "Reading the Bible in Context" (Document #: TX001064)

Student Book Articles

The articles covered in unit 8 are from "Section 4: Revelation in the New Testament" and "Section 5: The Scriptures and the Life of Faith" of the student book. If you believe the students would do the reading more successfully with additional structure, see the handout "Student Notes for Unit 8" (Document #: TX001065) at *smp.org/LivinginChrist.*

- "The Acts of the Apostles" (article 67)
- "The Pauline Letters" (article 68)
- "The Catholic Letters" (article 69)
- "The Book of Revelation" (article 70)
- *"Lectio Divina"* (article 76)
- "The Scriptures and Morality" (article 77)
- "Individual and Communal Prayer with the Scriptures" (article 78)
- "Two Devotional Prayers and Their Scriptural Connections" (article 79)

Scripture Passages

- Acts 1:6–12 (the Ascension of Jesus)
- Acts 2:1–13 (the coming of the Spirit)
- Acts 9:4–6 (Saul's conversion)
- Pauline epistles (selections and main themes)
- Romans 3:9–20 (universal bondage to sin)
- Romans 8:28–39 (God's indomitable love in Christ)
- Romans, chapter 9 (the relationship between Israel and the Gentiles)

- 1 Corinthians 1:11–25 (disorders in the Corinthian community)
- 1 Corinthians, chapter 12 (different spiritual gifts, the Body of Christ)
- 1 Corinthians, chapter 13 (the way of love)
- Galatians, chapter 1 (Paul's greeting, explanation of his call by Christ)
- Galatians, chapter 2 (account of the Council of Jerusalem, discussion of faith and works)
- Ephesians, chapter 1 (the Father's plan of salvation, fulfillment through Christ, inheritance through the Spirit, the Church as Christ's Body)
- Philippians 2:5–11 (description of Christ)
- Colossians, chapter 1 (Paul's prayer, Christ's person and work, Christ in us)
- 1 Thessalonians, chapter 1 (thanksgiving for their faith)

Vocabulary

If you choose to provide a vocabulary list for material covered in both the student book and the teacher guide, download and print the handout "Vocabulary for Unit 8" (Document #: TX001154), one for each student.

Anointing of the Sick	epistle
antichrist	evangelize
Apostle	Gentiles
Ascension	Gnosticism
charism	Holy Spirit
Church	*kerygma*
conversion	martyrdom
Deutero-Pauline	Pauline letters
disciple	Pentecost
ecclesia	the Way

Learning Experiences

Step 1

Preassess what the students already know about the Apostles.

Allow the students to put on paper all their ideas and thoughts in a safe environment and provide you with a preassessment of what they know and associate with the time immediately following Jesus' death and about the work of the Apostles. There are several different options for assessing what your students know and understand before you teach this unit. Note that each option requires preparing different materials.

Option 1: Apostle Association

The students reflect on what they know and how they understand the Apostles, the Acts of the Apostles, and the Pauline letters. You will be able to determine how much you need to present about these topics.

1. Prepare by having Bibles available for each student or reminding the students to bring their own to the next class period.

2. On the day of the learning experience, write the word *Apostle* on the board. Distribute pens or pencils and ask the students to write a definition for Apostles in their notebooks. Allow about 2 minutes for the students to work.

3. When time is up, instruct the students to locate a passage in the Gospels where Jesus calls one or more of the Apostles. Allow about 5 minutes for the students to work.

4. When time is up, ask the students to define the word *Apostle.* Write this group definition on the board. (Example: **Apostle:** From the Greek *apostolos,* meaning "messenger," especially a messenger who is sent on a mission. In the Gospels, Jesus chose the Apostles and sent them on a mission, just as Jesus was sent by the Father to preach the Gospel to the whole world.)

5. Next, write the following questions on the board. Ask the students to write their answers in their notebooks.

   - Who were the Apostles?
   - Where did you find this information?
   - Did you use any resources in your Bible, other than the text itself, to locate this information?

Review the answers with the students. The answers and the material to follow will help the students to understand the role of the Apostles in the covenant relationship with God and to demonstrate how to answer the question "Who were the Apostles and why are they important?"

Option 2: Paul Mind Map

The students will reflect on what they know. The focus questions at the beginning of the unit invite the students to think critically about their understanding of the Apostles and which ones they can identify. This experience will also provide you with a preassessment of what the students know about the Apostles and how much you need to present about their role in salvation history.

1. Prepare by downloading and printing the handout "Mind Map" (Document #: TX001160; see Appendix) one for each student. (Instead of using handouts, you may have the students create their own mind maps in their notebooks: have them draw a large circle in the center of a sheet of paper with a series of smaller connected circles.)

2. Write the word *Apostle* on the board, in a large circle. Distribute pens or pencils and ask the students to write *Apostle* on their copies of the handout. In the smaller circles, have them write words they think of when they hear the word *Apostle.* Allow 5 to 10 minutes for the students to work independently.

3. When time is up, invite the students to share their mind maps with the large group. Write their suggestions on the board.

4. Once a list is created, ask the students what the suggestions have in common. Common perceptions of the Apostles will naturally surface through the students' suggestions.

5. After writing their suggestions on the board, use colored markers to circle words that can be categorized: definition of *Apostle,* names of Apostles, and so on. These categories will help to address God's covenant relationship with the Apostles and answer the question "Who were the Apostles and why are they important?"

Option 3: Basic Letter Writing

Due to the popularity of e-mail and text messaging, many young people are unfamiliar with the process of writing a formal letter. This learning experience provides an opportunity for the students to reflect on what they know and understand about the purpose and process of letter writing. The experience will also help you to determine how much to present about these concepts.

1. Prepare by making available sheets of blank white writing paper and pens or pencils, one of each for each student.

2. Distribute the paper and pens or pencils. Explain that the students will construct letters to their friends. In the letters they will recommend a movie or song. Instruct the students that the letters must include a proper heading, greeting, body, and closing.

> **Teacher Note**
>
> Do not offer more explanation than this. The exercise is meant to determine whether the students know the parts of a letter.

3. To alleviate the students' fears about this assignment, tell them you will not grade their letters, so they need not worry if they do it incorrectly. Allow about 10 to 15 minutes for writing.

4. When time is up, discuss with the large group how to correctly write a letter, modeling a proper letter on the board.

5. As homework, assign the students to correct the format and content of the letters they wrote in class, using the information you just gave them.

6. At the next class period, collect the letters to see the students' progress.

> **Teacher Note**
>
> You will want to assign due dates for the performance tasks.
>
> If you have done these performance tasks, or very similar ones, with students before, place examples of this work in the classroom. During this introduction explain how each is a good example of what you are looking for, for different reasons. This allows the students to concretely understand what you are looking for and to understand that there is not only one way to succeed.

Step 2

Follow this assessment by presenting to the students the handouts "Final Performance Task Options for Unit 8" (Document #: TX001152) and "Rubric for Final Performance Tasks for Unit 8" (Document #: TX001153).

This unit provides you with two ways to assess whether the students have a deep understanding of the most important concepts in the unit: researching one of Paul's epistles or writing a contemporary letter using Paul's style and concerns. Refer to "Using Final Performance Tasks to Assess Understanding" (Document #: TX001011) and "Using Rubrics to Assess Work" (Document #: TX001012) at *smp.org/LivinginChrist* for background information.

1. Prepare by downloading and printing the handouts "Final Performance Task Options for Unit 8" (Document #: TX001152) and "Rubric for Final Performance Tasks for Unit 8" (Document #: TX001153), one for each student.

2. Distribute the handouts. Give the students a choice as to which performance task they select and add additional options if you so choose. Review the directions, expectations, and rubric in class, allowing the students to ask questions.

3. Explain the types of tools and knowledge the students will gain throughout the unit so they can successfully complete the final performance task.

4. Answer questions to clarify the end point toward which the unit is headed. Remind the students as the unit progresses that each learning experience builds the knowledge and skills they will need to show you that they understand who the Apostles were and why they are important in Church history.

Optional Service Project

If you choose to do a service project along with, or instead of, the final performance task options, then use the following directions:

- Find a location where the students can spend an extended amount of time and have a direct experience of helping others in need.

- At the site separate the students into appropriately sized groups to maximize the experience for all. Following the service day, ask the students to write a multiparagraph reflection on their experience. Explain that the paper should focus on the concept of servant leadership and answer the question "What does it mean to be a servant leader and an apostle of Christ today?"

- Finally, have the students connect their concepts of a modern servant leader with one or two of Jesus' teachings (see unit 7).

Explain

Step 3

Fill in gaps in the students' knowledge of the Twelve Apostles.

Review the role of the Twelve Apostles, the way they shared in the Covenant responsibilities with other leaders in the history of Israel, and how Jesus communicated what he wanted the Apostles to do. The PowerPoint "The Apostles" (Document #: TX001082) is available at *smp.org/LivinginChrist* if you would like to use it. A background article called "The Apostles" (Document #: TX001063) is also available on the site.

1. Present the following information to the students. If some students understand the material well enough, you might ask volunteers to share it with the class.

   ➤ Jesus called not only apostles during his lifetime, most notably the Twelve Apostles, but also men and women to be apostles in the early Church. *Apostle* comes from the Greek word *apostolos,* meaning "messenger," especially one sent on a mission.

   Have the students review the names and roles of the Apostles during and after Jesus' lifetime.

- *Simon (Peter)*
- *Andrew*
- *James, the son of Zebedee*
- *Jude Thaddaeus*
- *John*
- *Philip*
- *Bartholomew*
- *Thomas*
- *Matthew*
- *James, the son of Alphaeus*
- *Simon the Zealot*
- *Judas*

➤ Jesus chose people who had the following characteristics. These are the same characteristics the early leaders of Israel—judges, kings, and prophets—possessed.

- They were obedient.
- They understood the need for and purpose of divine justice.
- They were committed to ethical responsibility.
- They were men and women who committed themselves to God and his request for relationship and were willing to be his voice among the people.
- For example, Jesus came to invite men and women to share in his mission by sharing the Good News. This invitation, or calling (see unit 7), can be seen in many Gospel stories.

Teacher Note

Consider reviewing the calling of the Apostles in any of the Gospels to demonstrate their invitation to servant leadership in company with Jesus.

➤ At the time he called these men and women, Jesus offered them unconditional love in exchange for their love and devotion. This two-sided agreement extended the previously existing Covenant. Those men and women who accepted Jesus' invitation to follow him and speak on his behalf became known as his Apostles.

➤ Jesus provided the training necessary for following him and speaking on his behalf through the following actions:

- He spoke to the Apostles in various forms—for example, parables, conversations, speeches, and scriptural interpretations.
- He performed miracles in front of the Apostles to demonstrate the depth of his power, the love of God for his People, and the power of faith to change one's life.

➤ Jesus demonstrated through actions how the Apostles should act and treat one another throughout their lives, even after he was no longer with them.

➤ The Apostles were to take Jesus' teachings, messages, and actions to heart as they attempted to spread the Good News to the world.

Step 4

Have the students uncover the importance of the Twelve Apostles.

The students identify passages in the Gospels that illustrate Jesus teaching the Apostles.

1. Prepare by having enough Bibles available for each student or remind the students to bring their own.

2. To provide context for the students to form opinions, share the following material:

➤ The Twelve Apostles were messengers of the Gospel. The Greek word *apostolos,* meaning "messenger," especially one sent on a mission, was used to describe the twelve men Jesus chose to accompany him on his journey. By spending time with him, listening to him, and witnessing his acts, the Apostles were chosen and sent on a mission by Jesus, just as Jesus was sent by the Father to preach the Gospel to the whole world.

➤ The mission of the Twelve was to spread the Good News to the world.

➤ They were to preach the nature of the Reign of God (also called the Kingdom of God). The Reign was the central message of Jesus' preaching during his earthly ministry: the benefits and advantages of all kinds that flow from his rule to the subjects of this Reign, the Church.

➤ The Apostles were to convert many. The word *conversion* comes from the Greek word *metanoia*, meaning "change of heart."

➤ As a result, the Apostles were in charge of the following tasks:

• **Interpreting Jewish Law.** As founding members of the Way (an early name for followers of Jesus' teachings), the Apostles had the daunting task of interpreting the Jewish Law to help new converts to understand how Jesus fulfills the Abrahamic and Mosaic Covenants.

• **Interpreting Jesus' teachings.** The Apostles had the equally daunting task of interpreting the teachings of Jesus to help new converts and foundling communities to understand how to live out Jesus' teachings in the early first century AD.

3. Next, place the students into four small groups. Assign one Gospel to each small group.

4. Ask the students to locate five passages in their Gospel that portray Jesus teaching a lesson directly or by example. Allow about 10 minutes for the work.

5. When time is up, ask the small groups to identify five passages from the Acts of the Apostles that show the Apostles applying what Jesus taught them. Allow about 10 minutes for the work.

6. When time is up, call the students back to the large group. Instruct the students to write a multiparagraph paper. They will interpret the lessons Jesus taught, interpret how the Apostles applied them, and explain how they themselves could apply the lessons in their own lives. The students will write their papers individually, using the passages their small groups collected. If students need more time, allow them to finish.

7. After collecting the papers, discuss the success of the Apostles in living out Jesus' teachings.

Step 5

Use art with the Acts of the Apostles.

Using the accounts of the Ascension and Pentecost, build on the students' understanding of the Apostles to create a foundation for understanding salvation history.

1. Prepare by having available art materials for the students or ask them to bring their own markers or colored pencils. Download and print the handout "The Ascension of Jesus" (Document #: TX001155), enough for half the students, and the handout "Pentecost" (Document #: TX001156), enough for the other half. Have available enough Bibles for each student and enough sheets of blank writing or drawing paper.

2. On the day of the learning experience, distribute the Bibles or have the students take out their own. Ask half of the students to find Acts 1:6–12, the Ascension of Jesus. Ask the other half of the students to find Acts 2:1–13, the coming of the Spirit.

3. Instruct the students to read their passages silently. Allow about 5 minutes for reading.

4. Evenly distribute the copies of the two handouts so half the students have one and half the other. Provide each student with a blank sheet of paper. Instruct the students to first answer the questions on the handouts. Allow about 5 minutes for the work.

5. When time is up, tell the students they will use their blank sheets of paper to artistically interpret their passage. They may illustrate it, write a

newspaper or magazine article reporting the event, or pick another medium such as poetry, music, and so on. Emphasize that the students must consider the handout questions. Allow the students to use the remaining class time to complete their interpretation, or consider assigning this portion of the learning experience as homework.

6. When the students finish their assignments, ask one student to read aloud the Ascension account from the Acts of the Apostles and one student to read the Pentecost account so all the students hear both stories. Ask the students to display their work in a gallery setting. Ask half the students to display their work and be available to explain it and answer questions while the other half views the depictions. Then have them switch roles.

7. When all the students have viewed the creations, lead a large-group discussion on how the various artistic perspectives help us to more fully understand the Ascension and Pentecost.

Step 6

Present information about the Acts of the Apostles and about Paul.

Acquaint the students with the Acts of the Apostles, Paul, and his letters. Use the PowerPoint "The Acts of the Apostles and Saint Paul" (Document #: TX001083) if you wish. This can be found at *smp.org/LivinginChrist.*

- Assign the students to read the following student book articles before this step:
  - ○ "The Acts of the Apostles" (article 67)
  - ○ "The Pauline Letters" (article 68)
  - ○ "The Catholic Letters" (article 69)

1. Present the following information to the students:

  ➤ What is the book known as the Acts of the Apostles?
  - Written around AD 80 by the Evangelist Luke, the Acts of the Apostles is the second volume in the two-volume work known as Luke-Acts.
  - The Acts of the Apostles picks up where the Gospel of Luke ends.
  - Acts recounts how the early Church grew under the guidance of the Holy Spirit.
  - In the Acts of the Apostles, the Pentecost account tells about the Holy Spirit's coming upon the Apostles and the Church. The Holy Spirit empowered the Apostles to proclaim the Good News. Later in Acts we see the spread of the Church through missionary journeys

made with the goal of taking the Good News of Jesus Christ to the corners of the earth.

➤ What is Pentecost?

- Pentecost is one of the first events in the Book of Acts.
- The Feast of Pentecost celebrates the fulfillment of Jesus' promise to send the Holy Spirit to guide the disciples and their followers as they proclaim the truth of salvation in Jerusalem and beyond.
- We commemorate Pentecost fifty days after Easter—some people call it the birthday of the Church. This is because even though the Church was founded by Christ, it was at Pentecost that the Holy Spirit revealed the Church to the world.
- The Acts of the Apostles recounts how the early Church grew under the guidance of the Holy Spirit.
- Acts begins with a small group of disciples in Jerusalem and ends with a Church spanning the Roman Empire.
- Three people stand out in Acts as models of Christian faith: Saint Peter, Saint Stephen, and Saint Paul.

➤ Who is Saint Paul?

- He lived during the early to middle first century AD.
- He was born into a Jewish community and was initially named Saul.
- He spent the first part of his life persecuting Christians.
- He encounters the Risen Christ on the road to Damascus, in Syria.

Ask volunteers to read aloud Acts, chapters 4–6.

- After his conversion Paul embarks on three missionary journeys to found new Christian communities and spread the Good News of Christ.
- To remain in contact with the communities he helps form, Paul writes letters, offering advice, pastoral encouragement, and teaching.
- These letters are his greatest contribution in founding what became the Christian faith.

➤ What are the Pauline letters?

- They are a series of letters written to various Christian communities in the Mediterranean area covered by modern Greece and Turkey.
- There are twenty-one epistles, depending on the translation of the Bible.
- All the epistles follow a specific pattern.

- Thirteen letters in the New Testament are attributed to Paul or to disciples who wrote in his name. Nine of the letters are addressed to communities and four to individuals. Some, if not all, of the letters Paul wrote are the oldest Christian documents we have, even older than the four Gospels.

- Some of the Pauline letters are grouped into two subcategories: the captivity letters and the pastoral letters. The captivity letters (Ephesians, Philippians, Colossians, and Philemon) are attributed to Paul writing from jail. The pastoral letters (First Timothy, Second Timothy, and Titus) are attributed to Paul and his companions while they were on mission.

- Paul's letters were meant to accomplish two main goals: (1) They were to teach how to address various problems in the different Christian communities. Paul and the other writers taught the members of this new faith how to live out the new law of love taught by Christ. (2) To support and encourage the early Christian communities. By writing to various communities, Paul and the other writers recognized the development of Christian groups throughout the Middle Eastern world. In recognizing these sects, the writers were able to create a loose structure for what would later be termed "Christianity."

➤ What are the catholic letters?

- These seven non-Pauline letters, with the exception of the Letter to the Hebrews, are named after an Apostle or disciple of Jesus. However, biblical scholars believe anonymous authors wrote the letters, using the pseudonym of one of Jesus' Apostles or disciples. The seven letters attributed to the Apostles and disciples (James; First and Second Peter; First, Second, and Third John; and Jude) are known as the catholic letters. The word *catholic* here means "universal" or "general."

- Unlike Paul's letters, which originally were addressed to specific faith communities (although now they are addressed to the universal Church), the catholic letters were originally intended for a general audience or an unnamed individual. Similar to Paul's letters, they offer advice, encouragement, and teaching about community life and faith in Jesus Christ.

- The Letter to the Hebrews is written in the form of a homily and is much longer than the other catholic letters.

- The author of Hebrews supports and enlivens faith in Jesus Christ. Hebrews emphasizes the divinity of Christ, as well as the redeeming power of his death on the Cross. Hebrews heralds the saving plan of God revealed in his Son.

2. At this time you may choose to briefly address the Book of Revelation. This is a book of the Bible that is easily misunderstood and that students are often intrigued with. If you decide to address the Book of Revelation, have your students read the student book article 70, "The Book of Revelation." Share the following points concerning the Book of Revelation:

> ➤ The Book of Revelation is a form of literature known as apocalyptic literature, which uses symbolism and veiled language to communicate its message.

> ➤ It was written by the prophet John during a time of intense persecution of Christians.

> ➤ The author was not intending to predict the future; instead he was writing to the experience of the Christian Churches in Asia Minor at the time.

> ➤ The Book of Revelation was intended to offer hope for a people in crisis. It conveys the message that God is always with us and that in the end God will triumph over evil.

Step 7

Present common themes in the Pauline letters.

As belief in Jesus separated "Christian" Jews from other Jews and then added Gentiles, several issues needed to be sorted through. Share the following major themes that can be found throughout the epistles:

> ➤ **Faith versus Works**

> • Jewish Christians thought they had to follow the Mosaic Law perfectly to reach Heaven, even though they believed in Christ. This was a reasonable misconception because no laws at that point explained how one should live as a Christian.

> • Paul told the communities in Rome and Galatia that it was no longer necessary to follow the Mosaic Law perfectly. Although good works and a just life are necessary for pleasing God, the spirit in which you do them matters more than the execution of them.

> • Therefore, faith in Christ is more important than the execution of the Law without the correct intention.

> ➤ **Unbelievers**

> • Many unbelievers lived in the areas where Christians lived. The Christians were concerned about the persecution they experienced and could not understand how people could not believe in Christ.

- Paul tells the Corinthians that those who do not believe in the Cross are foolish, and God will deal with them appropriately in due time. Christians must learn to live in solidarity with these unbelievers. Jesus would have treated them with respect.
- Therefore, live as Jesus would have lived.

➤ Gentile Christians

- People were confused about whether Gentile Christians needed to live according to the Jewish Law.
- Paul pointed out that this had already been decided at the Council of Jerusalem (see Acts, chapter 15). The Gentile Christians did not have to follow Jewish Law because they were not Jews.
- Therefore, Christianity is something brand new and independent of Judaism.

➤ Preeminence of Christ

- Many Christians still believed in demigods. Although they believed Yahweh was the supreme God and Jesus was the Savior of the world, they still worshipped these smaller gods.
- Paul states that Christians need to reject all demigods. Christians should worship Yahweh alone because he will take care of all their needs.
- Therefore, Yahweh is supreme. Christ dominates all other supposed gods.

➤ Christian Living

- Christians had no idea how to live Christian lives.
- Paul said to look at Jesus' example to know how to live.
- Therefore, do as Jesus would.

Apply

Step 8

Allow the students to discover the classifications and styles of Paul in the Bible.

Instruct the students about the Pauline formula. The students learn about the significance of the letters and discover and use Paul's letter-writing formula to analyze certain epistles.

1. Prepare by downloading and printing the handout "The Format of the Pauline Letters" (Document #: TX001157), one for each student.

2. On the day of the learning experience, distribute the copies of the handout. Review it with the students. Place the students into small groups of three. Assign each group to work with a specific section from an epistle. Tell the students to examine the passage to determine which element of Paul's formula is being used and why. Allow about 10 to 15 minutes for the work.

3. When time is up, call the students back into the large group to share their findings. As one group presents, the other students should take notes to use as review for a quiz.

Step 9

Give a quiz to assess student understanding.

1. In preparation for this assessment, download and print the handout "Unit 8 Quiz" (Document #: TX001158), one for each student. Note that the quiz is fairly comprehensive, in part because both you and the students want to learn what they do not now know in preparation for a test or the final performance tasks.

2. On the day of the quiz, provide 5 to 10 minutes for the students to review their books and notes. Distribute the quiz and provide sufficient time for the students to work on it. If time remains when the students are done, collect the quizzes and then redistribute them so everyone has someone else's. Go through the quiz, allowing the students to correct one another's work and also giving them an opportunity to affirm or change their understanding of concepts. Collect the quizzes and further your analysis about topics that may need more coverage.

Teacher Note

To save paper, use the electronic copy of the quiz from *smp.org/LivinginChrist* and put it up in a visual place via projector, overhead, monitor, and so on. If these options are unavailable, read the quiz to the students slowly. In both cases, have the students record their answers on loose-leaf paper.

Step 10

Explore the role Sacred Scripture plays in the life of the individual and experience prayer with Scripture.

1. In preparation for this step, assign the students to read the following student book articles:

   • *"Lectio Divina"* (article 76)
   • "The Scriptures and Morality" (article 77)

- "Individual and Communal Prayer with the Scriptures" (article 78)
- "Two Devotional Prayers and Their Scriptural Connections" (article 79)

As a part of the reading assignment direct the students to write a one-sentence summary for each of the assigned articles. The sentence should describe the role Scripture plays in the life of the individual in relation to the topic of the article. You will also want to ensure that each student has a *Catholic Youth Bible*® or another Bible for this step.

2. Begin the step by asking the students to share with the class the sentences they wrote. Be sure to explain that just as the early Church learned how to live a Christian life through prayer and the Scriptures, so too can we, through reading and praying with Scripture, grow closer to God and others, better understand the life God calls us to live, and learn to make decisions that are in accord with God's will.

3. Next, explain that as a class you are going to pray using the *lectio divina* method.

4. Have the students turn to page 227 in their student books and find the Pray It! sidebar titled "Practice, Practice, Practice!" Select for the class, or have the class select, one of the readings suggested in the sidebar and ask for a volunteer who would be willing to read the selected passage aloud for the class at the appropriate time.

5. Next, have the students clear their desks of everything except their Bibles and turn to the selected passage in their Bibles.

6. Begin the *lectio divina* experience by calling the class to prayer and providing a few moments of silence.

7. When you feel the class is ready, have the student who volunteered slowly and clearly read the selected passage aloud.

8. Follow the reading by informing the class that the passage will be read aloud a second time, and they are to listen for a word or phrase that speaks to them or intrigues them. Have the volunteer read the passage a second time slowly and clearly.

9. After the Scripture passage has been read aloud a second time, invite the class to take a few moments of silence to reflect on the word or phrase they selected. Then invite the students to silently communicate with God about the phrase or word. Encourage them to not only speak to God, but also pause to hear what God is communicating to them.

10. After several minutes of silence, conclude the prayer experience with the Sign of the Cross.

11. Invite the students to share with the class their responses to the following questions:

   ➤ Was it easy or difficult to quiet your mind for this prayer experience? Why?

> ➤ What word or phrase did you select from the reading?
> ➤ Did you hear or notice something in the passage the second time you heard it that you missed the first time?
> ➤ Was it easy or difficult to communicate with God following your reflection on the passage? Why?
> ➤ What insight or message did you learn or have affirmed through this prayer experience?

12. Conclude this step by stressing that just as the early Church spent time reading and reflecting on the Scriptures, so are we called to spend time with the Word of God. Encourage your students to use the *lectio divina* prayer method for the next three days, using the other passages identified in the sidebar on page 227. You might consider asking your students to write a brief reflection after they have prayed with the other passages, describing their experiences and sharing insights they have gained.

Step 11

Now that the students are closer to the end of the unit, make sure they are all on track with their final performance tasks, if you have assigned them.

If possible, devote 50 to 60 minutes for the students to ask questions about the tasks and to work individually or in their small groups.

1. Remind the students to bring to class any work they have already prepared so they can work on it during the class period. If necessary, reserve the library or media center so the students can do any book or online research. Make extra copies of the handouts "Final Performance Task Options for Unit 8" (Document #: TX001152) and "Rubric for Final Performance Tasks for Unit 8" (Document #: TX001153). Review the final performance task options, answer questions, and ask the students to choose one if they have not already done so.

2. Provide some class time for the students to work on their performance tasks. This then allows you to work with the students who need additional guidance with the project.

Step 12

Reflect

Provide the students with a tool to use for reflecting about what they learned in the unit and how they learned.

This learning experience provides the students with an excellent opportunity to reflect on how their understandings of the Apostles and Paul have developed throughout the unit.

1. To prepare for this learning experience, download and print the handout "Learning about Learning" (Document #: TX001159; see Appendix), one for each student.

2. Distribute the handouts and give the students about 15 minutes to answer the questions quietly. Invite them to share any reflections they have about the content they learned as well as their insights into the way they learned.

The Bible: The Living Word of God

Final Performance Task Options for Unit 8

Important Information for Both Options

The following are the main ideas you are to understand from this unit. They should appear in this final performance task so your teacher can assess whether you learned the most essential content.

- Jesus charged the Twelve Apostles with responsibility for spreading the Good News.
- The early Apostles were servant leaders who carried word of the New Covenant in their ministries.
- Paul (originally named Saul) influenced the development of the early Christian Church through his traveling ministry and by the letters he left behind.
- These Pauline letters help us to understand how the Christian community made a transition from Judaism to embrace non-Jewish converts.

Option 1: Research One of Paul's Epistles to Share

Paul is one of the most—if not *the* most—influential person in early Christianity because of the overwhelming amount of writing he did. It is difficult to fully understand what it means to be a Christian if you do not understand who Paul was and his contributions to Christianity. For this option, you will research one of Paul's letters, write your answers to the questions below, and create a visual way to share your research with your classmates.

Your teacher will assign you an epistle for this performance task. Answer the following questions about that epistle:

1. Which epistle did you research?

2. When was it written?

3. Is your epistle a primary or secondary letter of Paul?

4. If you have a secondary letter, who is the most likely author?

5. Is your letter a Pauline letter or a catholic letter?

Document #: TX001152

6. Does your letter contain all the elements of a traditional Pauline letter?

7. If yes, how can you tell? Cite at least one example from each element.

8. If not, what is missing?

9. What is the message or purpose of your letter?

10. What issues face the readers of the letter, and how does the author attempt to address them?

Present your answers to these questions through some visual means such as a poster, slide show, PowerPoint presentation, multimedia presentation, and so on, as well as in a written report of about two double-spaced pages as a Word document.

Option 2: Writing a Letter to People Today Using Paul's Style and Concerns

Each of Paul's letters addressed or responded to concerns or problems in a particular community. For this option you will identify a specific community's issues and then write a Pauline-like letter to address these concerns or problems.

- Use Paul's letter-writing formula to write a two-page double-spaced "Pauline letter" to a modern community of your choice. (You can use the Letter to the Thessalonians as a model of Paul's style.)
- Identify a concern facing your community, which might be the school, neighborhood, household, city, country, and so on.
- Address this concern and offer advice to solve it.
- Draw from Paul's interpretation of Jesus' teachings.
- After you finish your letter, your teacher will invite you to share your concerns and solutions with the other students.

Document #: TX001152

Rubric for Final Performance Tasks for Unit 8

Criteria	4	3	2	1
Assignment includes all items requested in the instructions.	Assignment includes not only all items requested but they are completed above expectations.	Assignment includes all items requested.	Assignment includes over half of the items requested.	Assignment includes less than half of the items requested.
Assignment shows understanding of the concept *Jesus charged the Twelve Apostles with responsibility for spreading the Good News.*	Assignment shows unusually insightful understanding of this concept.	Assignment shows good understanding of this concept.	Assignment shows adequate understanding of this concept.	Assignment shows little understanding of this concept.
Assignment shows understanding of the concept *the early Apostles were servant leaders who carried word of the New Covenant in their ministries.*	Assignment shows unusually insightful understanding of this concept.	Assignment shows good understanding of this concept.	Assignment shows adequate understanding of this concept.	Assignment shows little understanding of this concept.
Assignment shows understanding of the concept *Paul (originally named Saul) influenced the development of the early Christian Church through his traveling ministry and by the letters he left behind.*	Assignment shows unusually insightful understanding of this concept.	Assignment shows good understanding of this concept.	Assignment shows adequate understanding of this concept.	Assignment shows little understanding of this concept.
Assignment shows understanding of the concept *these Pauline letters help us to understand how the Christian community made a transition from Judaism to embrace non-Jewish converts.*	Assignment shows unusually insightful understanding of this concept.	Assignment shows good understanding of this concept.	Assignment shows adequate understanding of this concept.	Assignment shows little understanding of this concept.
Assignment uses method of communication in a way that clearly conveys what the assignment requests.	Assignment outstandingly conveys what the assignment requests.	Assignment clearly conveys what the assignment requests.	Assignment at times clearly conveys what the assignment requests.	Assignment does not convey what the assignment requests.
Assignment uses proper grammar and spelling.	Assignment has no grammar or spelling errors.	Assignment has one grammar or spelling error.	Assignment has two grammar or spelling errors.	Assignment has more than two grammar or spelling errors.

Vocabulary for Unit 8

Anointing of the Sick: From the Latin *inungere*, meaning "to smear" or "rub on" oil or ointment for medical purposes, referring to an act of applying oil in a religious ceremony or as part of a blessing.

antichrist: A pseudo-Messianism whereby a human being puts himself or herself in the place of God or declares himself or herself to be a new messiah.

Apostle: From the Greek *apostolos*, meaning "messenger," especially a messenger who is sent on a mission. In the Gospels, Jesus chose the Apostles and sent them on a mission, just as Jesus was sent by the Father to preach the Gospel to the whole world.

Ascension: From the Latin *ascendere*, meaning "to climb up," referring to the feast celebrated for forty days after Easter commemorating Christ's being taken up into Heaven to be seated at the right hand of the Father.

charism: A special gift or grace of the Holy Spirit given to an individual Christian or community, commonly for the benefit and building up of the entire Church.

Church: From the Greek *kyriake*, meaning "the Lord's house." *Church* has multiple meanings: (1) the building where Christians gather for worship, (2) a specific Christian denomination, such as Anglicans, Lutherans, Methodists, Presbyterians, and so on, (3) the whole body of Christians, and (4) ecclesiastical authority, in contrast to civil authority, as in the case of Church and State.

conversion: A profound change of heart and a turning away from sin and toward God.

Deutero-Pauline: *Deutero,* from the Greek *deuteros,* meaning "second," and *Pauline,* referring to Paul. Therefore, the term means "secondary writings attributed to Paul."

disciple: From the Greek *discipulus,* meaning "pupil," referring to the original followers of Christ and to all who try to follow Christ's teachings.

ecclesia: A Latin word from the Greek *ekklesia,* meaning "assembly" of all the citizens to consider an issue, referring in Christian usage to the assembly of those called to follow Christ.

epistle: Another name for a New Testament letter.

evangelize: From the Greek *eu,* meaning "good," and *angelos,* meaning "messenger," referring to the spreading of the Gospel (Good News) of Christ.

Gentiles: Non-Jewish people.

Gnosticism: A group of heretical religious movements that claimed salvation comes from secret knowledge available only to the elite initiated in that religion.

 © 2010 by Saint Mary's Press
Living in Christ Series

Document #:TX001154

Holy Spirit: From the Latin *spiritus,* meaning "breath" or "soul," referring to the Third Person of the Trinity, the Paraclete divinely sent to teach and guide the Church to the end of time. The seven Gifts of the Holy Spirit are wisdom, understanding, counsel (right judgment), fortitude (courage), knowledge, piety (reverence), and fear of the Lord (wonder and awe).

kerygma: A Greek word meaning "proclamation" or "preaching," referring to the announcement of the Gospel or the Good News of divine salvation offered to all through Jesus Christ. *Kerygma* has two senses. It is both an event of proclamation and a message proclaimed.

martyrdom: Witness to the saving message of Christ through the sacrifice of one's life.

Pauline letters: Thirteen New Testament letters attributed to Paul or to disciples who wrote in his name. They offer advice, pastoral encouragement, teaching, and community news to early Christian communities.

Pentecost: The fiftieth day following Easter, which commemorates the descent of the Holy Spirit on the early Apostles and disciples.

Way, the: The original name for Christianity during the time of the Apostles.

Document #: TX001154

The Ascension of Jesus

Name: _____

Read the Ascension of Jesus in Acts of the Apostles 1:6–12 and take notes. Then answer the following questions, using complete sentences.

1. How do you think the Apostles felt during and after this event, considering the last time they saw Jesus?

2. What did Jesus ask of them?

3. What might the onlookers have thought and felt?

Document #: TX001155

Pentecost

Name: _____

Read about Pentecost in Acts 2:1–13 (a longer version is found in Acts of the Apostles 2:1–47) and take notes. Then answer the following questions, using complete sentences.

1. How do you think the Apostles felt during and after this event, considering the last time they saw Jesus?

2. What did Jesus ask of them?

3. What might the onlookers have thought and felt?

Document #: TX001156

The Format of the Pauline Letters

- Greeting
  - Comes from sender to receiver.
  - Is highly complimentary.

- Prayer
  - Most often provides a thanksgiving for the efforts and successes of the audience.

- Body
  - Addresses whatever issues the author wants to discuss.
  - Includes general advice about Christian living.
  - Discusses the accomplishments of the community.
  - Pulls from and interprets Jesus' teachings.

- Closing
  - Includes greetings and instructions to specific people.
  - Provides a final blessing.

© 2010 by Saint Mary's Press
Living in Christ Series

Document #: TX001157

The Bible: The Living Word of God

Unit 8 Quiz

Name: _____

Write the letter of the correct answer to each question in the space provided.

_____ 1. Of the letters attributed to Paul, we know that only half of them are actually his work. The rest were written by:

    a. copycats seeking personal fame

    b. people attempting to ruin Paul's reputation

    c. disciples of Paul who mimicked his style

    d. none of the above

_____ 2. If the title of a letter is the name of a place, it was written:

    a. to that place

    b. by an enemy of that place

    c. by someone from that place

    d. by the leader of that place

_____ 3. If the title of a letter is the name of a person, it was written:

    a. to that person

    b. to a friend of that person

    c. by that person

    d. by an enemy of that person

_____ 4. The purpose of an epistle is:

    a. to teach a community about Christ

    b. both to teach a community and to develop it into a well-established Christian group

    c. to help a community understand that Caesar is God

    d. to criticize a community for its lack of faith

_____ 5. When Paul's authority is challenged or he is asked to give an account of himself, he often tells the story of:

    a. the Resurrection

    b. his call by the Risen Christ

    c. his visit to Rome

    d. his tent making

Document #:TX001158

_____ 6. According to one or more letters from Paul, which early Christian community was divided when celebrating the Eucharist and filled with problems due to the contradictions between the cosmopolitan Greek culture and the message and spirit of Jesus Christ?
   a. Corinth
   b. Thessalonica
   c. Rome
   d. Galatia

_____ 7. The typical format of Paul's letters includes all of the following except:
   a. identification of the sender
   b. a thanksgiving
   c. advice pertaining to the specific problems in the community to which he is writing
   d. a thorough telling of Jesus' life and teachings

_____ 8. Those letters definitely written by Paul are known as:
   a. primary
   b. catholic
   c. secondary
   d. pastoral

_____ 9. Those letters most likely written by disciples of Paul are known as:
   a. primary
   b. catholic
   c. secondary
   d. pastoral

_____ 10. Identify the following topics that provided obstacles for the Apostles with the spreading of the Gospel to the Gentiles:
   a. circumcision
   b. Mosaic Law
   c. eating restrictions
   d. all of the above

_____ 11. In his First Letter to the Thessalonians, Paul urges Christians not to grieve for their loved ones who have died as do those without hope, because Christians who have died should be considered to have:
   a. fallen asleep in Christ
   b. been saved from persecution
   c. received a second chance at Heaven
   d. received no chance of Heaven

Document #: TX001158

_____12. The epistles that contain a universal message for all Christians regardless of community, culture, or geographical location are known as:

    a. primary

    b. Christian

    c. secondary

    d. catholic

_____13. Central to all the epistles are the following three main concepts that describe a life that mirrors Christ's:

    a. faith, love, and the pursuit of happiness

    b. way, truth, and life

    c. faith, love, and charity

    d. faith, hope, and love

_____14. Regarding unbelievers, Paul urges his friends in Corinth and Philippi to live in solidarity with those who believe differently from them. He argues this is the best way to live a Christian life because:

    a. Jesus preached the equality of all, and God will deal with unbelievers in his own time.

    b. The fate of unbelievers is entirely up to human beings.

    c. God does not like unbelievers and will like Christians less if they associate with unbelievers.

    d. God is indifferent to this situation.

_____15. Throughout his two most famous works, Paul argues that to gain salvation, one needs:

    a. faith in Jesus alone

    b. good works in either small or large amounts

    c. both faith in Christ and good works in some amount

    d. neither faith nor good works; we have no control over our destiny

Document #: TX001158

Unit 8 Test

Part 1: Multiple Choice

Write your answers in the blank spaces at the left.

1. _____ Paul presents Jesus as the _____, because he models obedience accepting death on the cross.
   A. Lamb of God
   B. New Moses
   C. Light of the World
   D. New Adam

2. _____ On the Feast of Pentecost, the house where the disciples gather is filled with the Holy Spirit in the form of a "strong driving wind" that rests as _____.
   A. "doves that fly over them"
   B. "smoke rising from the ashes"
   C. "tongues as of fire"
   D. "angels sent from God"

3. _____ The letters of Paul provide all of the following except _____ to the new Christian communities.
   A. warnings
   B. advice
   C. pastoral encouragement
   D. support

4. _____ In the books following the Gospels, we see all of the following except _____.
   A. an insight into the spread of Christianity
   B. an insight into the challenges faced by the first Christians
   C. the spread of the Church through missionary journeys
   D. miracles performed by the followers of Jesus

5. _____ Two recurring themes in Paul's letters are Jesus is the path to salvation and _____.
   A. Jesus came to call only Gentiles
   B. the Church is the Body of Christ
   C. the road to salvation is an easy one
   D. martyrdom should be a wish for all true Christians

Document #: TX001308

6. _____ Beginning with the _____, the Acts of the Apostles recounts how the early Church grew under the guidance of the Holy Spirit.

   A. Sermon on the Mount
   B. changing of Saul's name to Paul
   C. promise of the Spirit and the Ascension of Jesus
   D. Last Supper at Passover

7. _____ First Peter does all of the following except _____.

   A. encourage Christians not to lose faith
   B. remind readers to remain true to the teachings of Jesus
   C. warn against false teachers who claim that Jesus will not come again
   D. curse those who would deny Jesus

8. _____ Some of the Pauline letters are grouped into two subcategories: the captivity letters and the _____.

   A. pastoral letters
   B. friendly letters
   C. missionary letters
   D. business letters

9. _____ The author of the Book of Hebrews uses typical Jewish argumentation to show that _____ and the perfect sacrifice, thus embodying the New Law.

   A. Jesus is the doer of many miracles
   B. Jesus is the new and perfect High Priest
   C. Jesus made Mary the greatest of human beings
   D. Jesus' miracles were directed at Gentiles in foreign lands

10. _____ The Letter of James stresses all of the following except _____.

   A. the importance of both faith and good works for salvation
   B. that true faith leads to good works
   C. that self-pride should be the basis of good works
   D. that good works are the fruit of faith in Jesus Christ

Part 2: Matching

Match each statement in column 1 with a term from column 2. Write the letter that corresponds to your choice in the space provided. (*Note:* There are two extra terms in column 2.)

Column 1

1. _____ Positive virtues that are produced through the Gifts of the Holy Spirit.

2. _____ Missionary in nature, risking all for the greater glory of God.

3. _____ The fiftieth day following Easter, which commemorates the descent of the Holy Spirit on the early Apostles and disciples.

4. _____ A pseudo-messianism whereby a human being puts himself in the place of God.

5. _____ Special graces and tools that support spiritual growth, happiness, and wisdom.

6. _____ Another name for a New Testament letter.

7. _____ A group of heretical religious movements that claimed salvation comes from secret knowledge available only to the elite.

8. _____ Letters in the New Testament intended for a general audience or unnamed individual.

9. _____ Witnessing to the saving message of Christ through the sacrifice of one's life.

10. _____ This Sacrament brings a special grace to those who suffer from serious illness or who are in danger of death.

Column 2

A. Gifts of the Holy Spirit

B. catholic letters

C. Baptism

D. fruits of the Holy Spirit

E. Anointing of the Sick

F. Pentecost

G. martyrdom

H. atheism

I. epistle

J. Gnosticism

K. true discipleship

L. antichrist

Part 3: Short Answer

Answer each of the following questions in paragraph form on a separate sheet of paper.

1. How did Jesus charge the Apostles with the responsibility to spread the Good News?

2. How did Saint Peter, Saint Stephen, and Saint Paul promote the evangelical and missionary efforts of the early Church?

3. How did Saint Paul influence the development of the early Christian Church?

4. What were some of the key points in the Pauline letters that sought to embrace non-Jewish converts?

Document #: TX001308

Unit 8 Test Answer Key

Part 1: Multiple Choice

1. D
2. C
3. A
4. D
5. B

6. C
7. D
8. A
9. B
10. C

Part 2: Matching

1. D
2. K
3. F
4. L
5. A

6. I
7. J
8. B
9. G
10. E

Part 3: Short Answer

1. First, God sent the Holy Spirit on Pentecost to empower the Apostles to spread the Good News. Later, in the Acts of the Apostles, we see the spread of the Church through missionary journeys made with the goal of spreading the Gospel to the corners of the earth. Thus all people are invited into the Body of Christ. The Church is the goal of God's plan. Through her all participate in the joy of communion with God, leading to complete glory in Heaven.

2. Saint Peter, Saint Stephen, and Saint Paul stand out as embodying the evangelization and missionary efforts of the early Church. Saint Peter preaches a message of repentance and forgiveness. He calls disbelieving Israelites to a conversion of heart so the risen Messiah may wipe away their sins. Saint Stephen prophesies about how Jesus' life, especially his death and Resurrection, fulfills the Torah. For this preaching he becomes the first martyr. Saint Paul embarks on three missionary journeys to bring the Light of Christ to all.

3. First, Paul would go on missionary journeys and establish Christian communities. To remain in contact with these communities, he wrote letters offering advice, pastoral encouragement, and, most important, teaching. Two of the recurring themes of his letters are that Jesus Christ is the path to salvation and that the Church is the Body of Christ. In the first area, Paul portrays Jesus as the New Adam, perfecting the role of our first parent by his obedience to God and dying on the cross. Using terms like *Son, the Christ,* and *Lord,* Paul emphasizes Jesus' connection to his Father and his divinity. In the second area, Paul emphasizes the importance of each person's contribution to the Body of Christ, the Church.

4. Paul emphasizes the divinity of Jesus Christ, as well as pointing out that while Jesus was the fulfillment of the promises of the Old Testament, his life and words were so unique as to be open to all, regardless of their background.

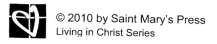 © 2010 by Saint Mary's Press
Living in Christ Series

Appendix
Additional Resources

"Mind Map" (Document #: TX001160)
"Jigsaw Process" (Document #: TX001161)
"The Socratic Seminar" (Document #: TX001015)
"Socratic Seminar Symbol Codes" (Document #: TX001014)
"Student Evaluation for the Socratic Seminar" (Document #: TX001013)
"Rubric for an Oral Presentation" (Document #: TX001174)
"Learning about Learning" (Document #: TX001159)

Mind Map

First, write the class prompt word or phrase in the center circle. Then in the other circles, write a word or phrase you associate with the center word or phrase. Extend even more circles from the center and from the other circles for brainstorming.

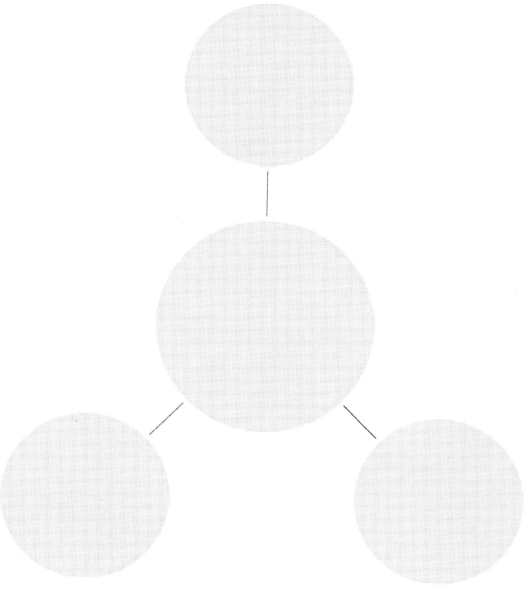

Document #: TX001160

Jigsaw Process

1. What topics does each of the four documents address?

   Document 1:

   Document 2:

   Document 3:

   Document 4:

2. What do the four documents have in common?

   a.

   b.

   c.

   d.

3. How are the four documents different?

   a.

   b.

   c.

   d.

4. If you had to create a title to unify these four documents, what would you choose? Why?

   a. Title:

   b. Reason:

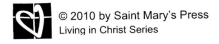
Document #: TX001161

The Socratic Seminar

This class seminar will give you the opportunity to test your analytical and discussion skills through oral debate. This seminar is carried on in a very structured way, so it is important to learn the process and the rules.

The Process

1. Before the seminar, the teacher will form the class into two or more groups. Your group will be assigned a question for you to consider and craft an individual response to before class. You will need at least a two-paragraph response to the question, well thought out and citing appropriate sources.

2. The teacher will arrange the classroom chairs into an inner circle and an outer circle. There will be one extra chair in the inner circle, so the inner circle will have one more chair than the outer circle.

3. Half of the class or will sit in the inner circle. The other half of the class will sit in the outer circle. When you are in the outer circle, you will observe one inner-circle student during the conversation.

4. The extra chair in the inner circle is called the "hot seat." If, as an outer-circle student, you would like to enter into the conversation of the students in the inner circle, you may choose to sit in the hot seat and wait to be invited to speak by a classmate in the inner circle. When called on, you may speak to one of the following or similar issues:

   - Ask an inner-circle student to clarify a statement.
   - Ask an inner-circle student to support a statement.
   - Respectfully correct an incorrect statement.
   - Draw attention to a point that has not yet been addressed.
   - Help redirect the seminar back to the original topic.

Remarks from the hot seat should be brief and respectful.

5. Your teacher will not be an active participant in the discussion. She or he will be noting the behavior of the inner-circle students as they converse.

6. An inner-circle student will state the topic and begin the discussion. Then the outer-circle students will complete their observation handouts. They will then share general observations (without naming names) about both positive areas of discussion and areas that need improvement.

7. You will then switch circles and repeat the process. A volunteer states the question or topic.

© 2010 by Saint Mary's Press
Living in Christ Series   Document #: TX001015

Expectations for Participation

Both the handout "Student Evaluation for the Socratic Seminar" (Document #: TX001013) and the following lists of positive and negative contributions will describe what type of behavior your teacher expects.

Positive Contributions to the Seminar

You will contribute to the Socratic seminar in a positive way if you do the following:

- participate in conversation
- analyze the background text, if relevant, with excellence
- make an outstanding point
- make a good connection to earlier class material
- pose a good question
- allow another speaker to speak before you
- focus the group back on topic
- invite someone to participate
- provide primary support for your argument from literature or the Scriptures

Negative Contributions to the Seminar

You will negatively contribute to the Socratic seminar if you do the following:

- interrupt another student
- ridicule another student's statements rather than disagree
- repeat points without adding new ideas or material
- do not respond when called on to participate
- derail the conversation (get it off track)
- dominate the discussion

Socratic Seminar Symbol Codes

Positive Contributions

√ = participates in conversation

! = excellent analysis of literature

* = outstanding point or connection to earlier material

? = poses a question

A = allows another speaker to speak first

F = focuses group on topic

@ = invites someone to participate

S = support position using a primary source (Scripture or literature)

Negative Contributions

I = interrupts another student

R = repeats points without adding new ideas or material

U = unresponsive when called on to participate

D = derails the conversation

Dom = dominates the discussion, does not allow others to participate

© 2010 by Saint Mary's Press
Living in Christ Series

Document #: TX001014

Student Evaluation for the Socratic Seminar

Participant Name _____

Evaluator Name_____

Write your comments in the center column for either positives or negatives.

Positives		Negatives
Uses text directly, if relevant		Makes irrelevant comment
Makes a relevant statement		Monopolizes conversation
Asks a relevant question		Is distracted or distracting
Pays attention		Moves focus away from purpose

Document #: TX001013

Naturally invites someone to participate		Does not speak
Makes a connection to self, text, world		
Asks a question that elicits a response		

Rubric for an Oral Presentation

Criteria	4	3	2	1	0
Pitch, Pauses, and Clarity	Used perfect pitch, correct number of pauses, and clear and distinct speaking at all times with no mispronunciations.	Used correct pitch, paused occasionally, and spoke distinctly and clearly at all times. Mispronounced one word.	Rarely worried about pitch or pauses, yet spoke clearly and distinctly most of the time.	Did not worry about pitch or pauses and did not speak clearly most of the time.	Did not worry about pitch, pause, or clarity and did not speak clearly.
Eye Contact	Maintained excellent eye contact with audience.	Showed balance of eye contact between the audience and materials.	Eye contact shifted between the audience and materials in a way that distracted from the effectiveness of the oral presentation.	Minimal eye contact. Long periods of time when student did not look at audience.	Never established eye contact with audience and focused more on note cards and other materials.
Use of Auxiliary Materials (Note Cards, Technology, Visuals)	Exceptionally incorporated all auxiliary materials into presentation.	Incorporated auxiliary materials into presentation.	Attempted to incorporate auxiliary materials into presentation but not effectively.	Auxiliary materials distracted from effectiveness of presentation.	No auxiliary materials were used.

Learning about Learning

We can understand ourselves better by taking the time to review the process of learning the material in a unit.

Respond by using the scale below. Put a mark where you think your understanding falls. Then write your answers to the other questions below.

Unit Number and Name _____

Knew none of this material before   **Knew everything already**

What was your favorite learning experience in this unit and why? Do you usually enjoy this type of learning experience?

What was your least favorite learning experience and why? Do you usually find this type of learning experience challenging?

How did your understanding of the unit's subject matter change throughout the unit?

Was anything you learned particularly interesting? Why?

Write any other observations you have.

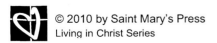

Acknowledgments

The scriptural quotations in this book are from the New American Bible with Revised New Testament and Revised Psalms. Copyright © 1991, 1986, and 1970 by the Confraternity of Christian Doctrine, Washington, D.C. Used by the permission of the copyright owner. All rights reserved. No part of the New American Bible may be reproduced in any form without permission in writing from the copyright owner.

The excerpts on pages 31, 32, 33, 33, 51, 51, 53, 54, 54, 55, 75, 79, 79, 81, 81, 82, handout "Reading Notes and Questions for Student Book Articles 9–12" (Document #: TX001105), 104–105, 159, and handout "Vocabulary for Unit 7" (Document #: TX001148) are from the English translation of the *Catechism of the Catholic Church* for use in the United States of America, second edition, numbers 115, 117, 110, 111, 45, 229, 31, 46, 68, 68, 96, 316, 317, 404, 70, 71, 230, 96, page 496–497, and numbers 125 and 125, respectively. Copyright © 1994 by the United States Catholic Conference, Inc.—Libreria Editrice Vaticana. English translation of the *Catechism of the Catholic Church: Modifications from the Editio Typica* copyright © 1997 by the United States Catholic Conference, Inc.—Libreria Editrice Vaticana.

Unless otherwise noted, the definitions in this book are adapted from *The Catholic Faith Handbook for Youth*, Second Edition (Winona, MN: Saint Mary's Press, 2008), copyright © 2008 by Saint Mary's Press; *Saint Mary's Press® College Study Bible* (Winona, MN: Saint Mary's Press, 2007), copyright © 2007 by Saint Mary's Press; and *Saint Mary's Press® Essential Bible Dictionary*, by Sheila O'Connell-Roussell (Winona, MN: Saint Mary's Press, 2005), copyright © 2005 by Saint Mary's Press. All rights reserved.

The list of what makes up a mature understanding on pages 9–10 is from *Understanding by Design*, expanded second edition, by Grant Wiggins and Jay McTighe (Alexandria, VA: Association for Supervision and Curriculum Development [ASCD], 2005), page 84. Copyright © 2005 by the ASCD. Used with permission of ASCD.

The excerpts on pages 28 and 31–32 are from *I'm Glad You Asked: 60 Common Questions Catholics Have About the Bible,* by Mark R. Pierce (Winona, MN: Saint Mary's Press, 2008), page 26. Copyright © 2008 by Mark R. Pierce.

The information on how to find a scriptural reference on the handout "How to Find a Scriptural Reference" (Document #: TX001088) is adapted from *Teaching Manual for "Written on Our Hearts: The Old Testament Story of God's Love,"* Third Edition, by Mary Reed Newland (Winona, MN: Saint Mary's Press, 2009), pages 43–44. Copyright © 2009 by Saint Mary's Press. All rights reserved.

The charts on the handouts "Biblical Exegesis Chart" (Document #: TX001090), "Biblical Exegesis Worksheet" (Document #: TX001096), and "The Ten Commandments" (Document #: TX001115), the cycle of redemption bullet

To view copyright terms and conditions for Internet materials cited here, log on to the home pages for the referenced Web sites.

During this book's preparation, all citations, facts, figures, names, addresses, telephone numbers, Internet URLs, and other pieces of information cited within were verified for accuracy. The authors and Saint Mary's Press staff have made every attempt to reference current and valid sources, but we cannot guarantee the content of any source, and we are not responsible for any changes that may have occurred since our verification. If you find an error in, or have a question or concern about, any of the information or sources listed within, please contact Saint Mary's Press.

Endnotes Cited in Quotations from the *Catechism of the Catholic Church*, Second Edition

Unit 1
  1. *Dei Verbum* 12 § 3.

Unit 3
  1. Cf. Council of Trent: Denzinger-Schönmetzer, *Enchiridion Symbolorum, definitonum et declarationum de rebus fidei et morum* (1965) 1511–1512.

Unit 7
  1. *Dei Verbum* 18.
  2. *Dei Verbum* 18.